LECTURES ON THE ETHICS

OF

T. H. GREEN, MR. HERBERT SPENCER, AND J. MARTINEAU

LECTURES
ON THE ETHICS

OF

T. H. GREEN
MR. HERBERT SPENCER, AND
J. MARTINEAU

BY

HENRY SIDGWICK

SOMETIME KNIGHTBRIDGE PROFESSOR OF MORAL PHILOSOPHY IN THE
UNIVERSITY OF CAMBRIDGE, AND AUTHOR OF 'THE METHODS OF
ETHICS' AND OF 'OUTLINES OF THE HISTORY OF ETHICS
FOR ENGLISH READERS'

London
MACMILLAN AND CO., LIMITED
NEW YORK: THE MACMILLAN COMPANY
1902

PREFACE

THE Lectures which this volume contains were not prepared for publication by Professor Sidgwick, and are therefore unhappily without the modifications and improvements which they might have received at his hands. Indeed he did not give any directions with reference to their publication, but left them, with other ethical papers, in my care, to be dealt with as might seem most advisable. With regard to the Lectures on the late Professor Green and on Mr. Herbert Spencer, they are an examination, expository and critical, of the views of Transcendental or 'Idealist,' and Evolutional Ethics, as put forth by their most distinguished exponents. Before the publication in 1874 of *The Methods of Ethics*—the great constructive achievement of which was unification of Intuitionism and Benthamite Utilitarianism — the prominent doctrines in English ethical thought were the intuitional and utilitarian views, and these were currently regarded as being in thorough - going antagonism to each other. Later, Professor Sidgwick came to regard the Transcendentalist and Evolutionist schools as the principal rivals in contemporary English Ethics of his own system. This he most often calls

v

by the name *Utilitarianism,* but it might be described as *Utilitarianism on an intuitional basis,* by which phrase he has occasionally referred to it. Readers of *The Methods of Ethics* have sometimes complained that it does not contain a more detailed consideration of Green's ethical theory. Green's *Prolegomena to Ethics,* however, did not appear until after the publication of the early editions of Professor Sidgwick's book. The same is true of Mr. Herbert Spencer's *Principles of Ethics,* and of Dr. Martineau's *Types of Ethical Theory,* which latter is probably the most influential recent work on Ethics from an entirely 'intuitional' standpoint. The following Lectures are thus to some extent supplementary to *The Methods of Ethics.* For the above reasons it has been decided, with Mrs. Sidgwick's concurrence, to publish them without delay. They are printed substantially as they were delivered ; but in preparing them for the press I have frequently had in mind the following passage from Professor Sidgwick's editorial Preface to Sir John Seeley's *Introduction to Political Science :*—

I have here and there omitted repetitions more suitable to an oral lecture than to a book, and once or twice altered the position of sentences ; and, generally speaking, have made such corrections as I thought it probable the author would have made before publishing the lectures. In the books prepared by himself for publication, Seeley was, as I know, unsparing of pains in rewriting such portions as did not come up to his ideal. I have felt, therefore, that it was unjust to his memory to let this posthumous book go forth without such correction of inadvertencies as I was able to make. No reader can feel more strongly than I do how inadequate a substitute this is for his own revision.

In the present case, indeed, I think no reader could

feel so strongly as I do how utterly inadequate a substitute for the Author's own revision any such 'correction of inadvertencies' as it has been possible to make must be.   But even without his revision, these Lectures, which Professor Sidgwick's pupils listened to with delight, seem to me to have extraordinary interest and value.—Besides the emendations above indicated, I have supplied (or completed) references, and have quoted the passages indicated in the manuscript.   It was Professor Sidgwick's custom in his oral lectures to read passages from the book on which he was lecturing, and occasionally commentaries or expositions from his own published works—though in the latter case the quotation was more often a restatement.   It should be mentioned that portions of his articles in *Mind* on Green's and Martineau's Ethics (*Mind*, 1884, 1885, 1887), and on Mr. Herbert Spencer's *Data of Ethics* and *Justice* (*Mind*, 1880 and 1892), were used by Professor Sidgwick in the composition of his lectures on those writers—though for the most part not without many verbal alterations.

As regards the omitting of repetitions occurring in the manuscript, this has been done to some extent, but in several cases to have made such omission would have entailed more alteration than seemed justifiable.   And, moreover, in most instances the repetitions are not mere repetitions, but to a large extent restatements.

I must add that I am responsible for the Analytical Summary prefixed to the Lectures.   And in conclusion, I desire gratefully to acknowledge the invaluable help received from Mrs. Sidgwick, both in advice on points of difficulty and in reading the proofs throughout.

E. E. CONSTANCE JONES.

GIRTON COLLEGE, CAMBRIDGE,
    July 1902.

ANALYTICAL SUMMARY

LECTURES ON GREEN'S ETHICS

LECTURE I

GREEN'S METAPHYSICAL BASIS

WHILE Mr. H. Spencer proposes to establish Ethics on a 'scientific' basis, Green considers that what is moral is essentially distinct from what is 'natural,' and is incapable of explanation by history or evolution
Pp. 1–2

Green holds that the ultimate end of rational conduct is a self-realisation of the one Divine Mind which gradually reproduces itself in the human soul. This ethical view is connected with his view of cognition in general. He maintains that to explain the knowledge we have of that all-inclusive unalterable system of relations which we find in nature, the supposition of some combining agency is necessary ; that such an agency in each man's experience is his intelligent self, which unites the objects of his experience while distinguishing itself from them ; and that hence, as the condition of nature being real otherwise than merely as for us, we must recognise the action of some unifying principle analogous to that of our understanding. Indeed Green, by a transition of which the cogency is not apparent, passes from the affirmation of analogous action to the affirmation of identical quality, and says that nature in its reality implies not merely an all-uniting agency which is not natural, but a thinking self-distinguishing consciousness like our own . Pp. 2–10

And the agency is further regarded as eternal and complete, our own empirical knowledge being an imperfect reproduction or limitation in us of this eternally complete consciousness. To this we may object that it is difficult to see how the unity of the individual's consciousness can be maintained when thus divided between the Divine Eternal Mind out of time, and the function of an animal organism in time, which the Eternal Mind somehow uses as its vehicle. But putting aside this difficulty, and assuming the necessary existence of a Divine, eternally complete, combining, self-distinguishing, and self-objectifying agency, and the relation of man to it to have been established in Book I. (*Metaphysics of Knowledge*), it still remains to ask Green : What bearing has this metaphysical doctrine on ethical problems ? How are we to obtain from it an ideal of holiness, or of an infinitely and perfectly good will ? . . . . . . Pp. 10–14

ix

LECTURE II

GREEN'S VIEW OF FREEDOM, AND OF DESIRE, INTELLECT, AND VOLITION

LECTURE III

GREEN'S VIEW OF MORAL (INCLUDING IMMORAL) ACTION

LECTURE IV

GREEN'S VIEW OF THE GOOD WILL, AND TRUE GOOD

LECTURE V

GREEN'S ACCOUNT OF THE MORAL IDEAL

LECTURE VI

GREEN'S VIEW OF GREEK ETHICS

In chapter v. of Book III., in which Green turns to a historical account of his Moral Ideal with special reference to Greek Ethics, he fails in his aim of showing that the *popular* conception in Greece of Virtue or Human

Excellence either sprang from the demand for an abiding self-satisfaction, or recognised a state of will or character of human beings as the ultimate object in which this satisfaction was to be found   .   .   Pp. 80–81

He says that in the ideal of Virtue of the Greek philosophers, we find the first clear expression of the conviction that every form of real goodness must rest on a will to be good which has no object but its own fulfilment. But this view ignores the special and prominent characteristic of the teaching of Socrates and his followers, that the difference between Virtue and Vice depends primarily on the state of a man's intellect or knowledge. In the qualified Socratic doctrine maintained by Plato, it is still not Will to be good but Knowledge of Good that is highest and most essential .   .   .   .   .   .   Pp. 82–84

Aristotle recognises more fully than Plato the inadequacy of mere knowledge to produce practical virtue, and the unity of Virtue is for him merely a generic unity, including Speculative Wisdom (which is concerned about eternal truth, objects higher than human good and evil) and Practical Wisdom (in which the moral Virtues are involved). And in trying to form a consistent notion of Practical Wisdom, Aristotle is embarrassed between (1) the view that good conduct should contain its end in itself, and (2) the common-sense tendency to regard Practical Wisdom as chiefly exercised in providing those inferior goods which contribute to human wellbeing .   .   .   .   .   .   Pp. 84–86

The chief schools of philosophy sprung from Socrates did indeed hold that Virtue or Human Excellence is the whole (or the main part) of the true good of individuals, and that Virtue to be truly Virtue must be chosen for its own sake. But here their agreement ended, and it misrepresents the relation of Knowledge to Virtue as conceived by the ancient thinkers to lay the stress that Green does on Will .   .   .   Pp. 86–87

In the case of Aristotle, it is misleading to describe his moral excellences merely as excellences of Practical Thought, because he recognises a semi-rational element of the soul, capable indeed of obeying reason, but also capable of conflicting with it. And confining attention to the thought-element, the view that for Aristotle morality was determined by interest in wellbeing interpreted as realisation of the soul's faculties, is open to the objection of not affording definite guidance in any particular case of conduct. Green's answer to the difficulty —that in order practically to determine Ultimate Good we may turn for enlightenment to the established rules of arts and sciences, and families and states—could not have been adopted by Aristotle, who regarded it as the function of Ethics to regulate all other arts.

Pp. 87–88

Aristotle in his *Ethics* gives us not merely the moral estimate of the philosopher, but also the social estimate of his age and country ; but he does not suggest that Wisdom, Courage, Temperance, and Justice were valued by Common Sense as conducive to the unfolding of the capacities of the rational man in full harmonious activity. In his Theoretical Excellence it is not the *will to know what is true* that is important, but the *exercised faculty* of knowing what is true. Similarly of the *will to make what is beautiful*. And of Courage, on the one hand Aristotle simply conceives the brave man as realising moral beauty in his act ; and Green's view that he held the essence of the virtue to be endurance of pain and fear in the service of the State, is wide of the mark. On the other hand, there is less agreement among the Greek philosophers in the definition of ἀνδρεία than Green suggests. And of Temperance, Aristotle says that the aim of the temperate man is (as in the case of

LECTURE VII

GREEN'S TREATMENT OF HEDONISM

It is sometimes supposed that Green's attack on Hedonism is effective if we grant his metaphysical doctrine that the self, which is non-natural and therefore free, is not in time.   He does, however, both in the metaphysical and ethical parts of his reasoning, apply terms with a temporal meaning to self-conscious subjects, and time-determinations seem essential to his conception of the Universe and of the self so far as ethical.   A similar difficulty occurs in Kantian Ethics   . Pp. 100–101

In considering Green's relation to Utilitarianism we are forced to abstract (as he himself does) from the conception of the subject out of time.   The first part of Green's polemic against Hedonism is aimed at *Psychological Hedonism*—the doctrine that the object of man's conscious desire and voluntary aim is nothing but pleasure (and avoidance of pain).   In his rejection of this doctrine and his explanation of its prevalence we may concur.   But the analysis which leads him to reject Psychological Hedonism seems equally effective as against his own doctrine that the self-conscious agent always aims at self-satisfaction.

On the whole, Green's view of the relation of self-satisfaction to the satisfaction or extinction of desire seems to be that the attainment of *any* particular object of desire brings at least a partial and transient Self-satisfaction, though complete and permanent satisfaction cannot be found in vicious self-seeking. — But it is difficult to distinguish Satisfaction from Pleasure : if by *Satisfaction* Green means the cognitive element of the consciousness of attaining a desired end, this seems (1) not in accordance with the common usage of terms (2) not rightly regarded as in itself desired or ultimately desirable.   And in some cases of attainment and consequent extinction of desire, there seems to be no *satisfaction*, if satisfaction implies pleasurable consciousness.

Partly owing to imperfect acquaintance with the course of English Ethical
thought, Green persistently mixes up his polemic against Psychological
Hedonism with his polemic against *Ethical Hedonism*—that is, the
doctrine that Happiness is the right end of action .   . Pp. 102–105
Confining attention to Ethical Hedonism, we find that the argument against
it is directed chiefly to four points : (1) Duality of Rational Self-Love
and Rational Benevolence ; (2) Uncertainty of Hedonistic calculation
as a source of practical weakness ; (3) Essential transitoriness of
pleasure ; (4) The notion of a Sum of Pleasures.   As to (1), it was the
main aim of *The Methods of Ethics* to exhibit this dualism and the need
of reconciling the divergent ends, and Green's own notion of Perfection
(in the wider sense) does not avoid a similar duality.   Again, as regards (2), *The Methods of Ethics* aims at bringing out clearly the uncertainties of hedonistic calculation, and however great these may be,
the difficulties of Green's view seem indefinitely greater.   What
criterion does he offer for preferring one sort of realisation of capabilities
to another ?   (3) If reflection on Virtue, and even on Green's account of
Virtue (*e.g.* Justice), shows that it contains implicit reference to further
good, and if to the reflective mind nothing but happiness appears to be
good in itself, without reference to an ulterior end—is any answer
needed to the man who is dissatisfied with happiness merely because it
is subject to the conditions of Time ?   Time is a condition of human
consciousness, and therefore of every good of consciousness.   (4) Green's
objection to Sum of Pleasures simply, seems to resolve itself into (3)
objection to transitoriness of pleasure, since he admits all that Ethical
Hedonism requires here, namely, that desire for a sum or contemplated
series of pleasures is possible.   Green further argues here that Ethical
Hedonism is inconsistent with Psychological Hedonism, since *Sum of
Pleasures* (which Ethical Hedonism takes as End) is not *Pleasure*.   To
this it may be replied that pleasures can be summed in thought, and it
is as so summed that they attract a man *qua* rational being.   *Desire of
pleasure* is no doubt different from *desire of greatest amount of pleasure*,
but the latter is the form which desire of pleasure takes in a reflective
mind   .   .   .   . Pp. 105–110
Passing to the objections to taking *greatest possible sum of pleasures* as end,
Green says that this is as unmeaning as *greatest possible quantity of time
or space*, being an end which admits of indefinite increase and which
for ever recedes, and hence cannot serve the purposes of a criterion.
But we can and do speak of the greatest possible quantity of time and
space obtainable for given purposes under given conditions.   And for a
Utilitarian aiming at greatest possible happiness under given conditions,
the fact that his aim is limited by his foresight makes irrelevant Green's
objection on account of indefinite increase, while even a possibly infinite
series may be capable of being made greater or less, and may so furnish
a criterion.   Further, an end which we aim at realising must be in the
future.   And if an end be an object of rational aim, sought for itself,
whether attained in successive parts or not, Maximum Happiness will
provide a serviceable criterion of conduct as long as any one's prospective balance of pleasure over pain admits of being made greater or
less by immediate action in one way or the other   .   . Pp. 110–113
To Green's objection that moral approval is impossible without reference to
an ideal of a perfect state of existence, it may be replied that such
approval can be and is given to the preference of *more* good to *less* good.
Green fails to see that the Utilitarian's Ultimate Good is not a Utopia
which we may come nearer to or imitate, but a kind of existence which

b

LECTURE VIII

GREEN'S TREATMENT OF HEDONISM (*continued*)

LECTURES ON MR. SPENCER'S ETHICS

LECTURE I

CHAPTERS I. AND II. OF DATA OF ETHICS (PART I. OF THE PRINCIPLES OF ETHICS)

MR. SPENCER aims at establishing rules of right conduct on a scientific basis, and at thus filling the gap left by the disappearance of Supernatural Ethics and avoiding the defects of morality as it is. Evolutionist and

Associationist Moralists often mean by *a scientific treatment of morality* merely an investigation of the laws according to which ethical beliefs and sentiments have come into existence.   We may note that such psychological or sociological investigation has not necessarily any tendency to establish the authority of the current morality of which it traces the history.   Indeed it is not morality as it is (which Mr. Spencer regards as defective) that he attempts so to establish, but morality as it ought to be.   Such ideal morality can, he holds, be established by Science (Biology, Psychology, Sociology).   In his view scientific consideration of conduct in general shows us (1) a supreme or ultimate end to the realisation of which human actions are universally or normally directed, and (2) enables us to determine the kind of conduct by which this end may be best attained   .   . Pp. 135–138

The establishment of the end is the main subject of Mr. Spencer's first three chapters.   He considers it important to regard the portion of human conduct to which ethics relates as part of the larger whole of universal conduct, and this is defined as an *adjustment of acts to ends*, which becomes more complex and elaborate as animals become more developed, and the main distinction of the conduct of the lower animals as compared with the higher is a relatively simple and relatively incomplete adjustment of acts to ends.   According to Mr. Spencer, the ultimate end throughout the scale of the adjustments which constitute life, is the continuance and further development of those adjustments themselves. And though the actions of any individual may be partly adjusted to the initiation, prolongation, and enlargement of other lives besides its own, still *Quantity of Life* is the supreme end of universal conduct.   The view is thus doubly teleological.

In his *Replies to Criticisms on 'The Data of Ethics'* Mr. Spencer misapprehends the intention of the Author's remark that, while the point of view of *The Data of Ethics* is frankly teleological, in *The Principles of Biology* pains are taken to avoid teleological implications Pp. 138–142

LECTURE II

DATA OF ETHICS—CHAPTERS III. IV. AND X.

The conclusion to which Mr. Spencer has led us is that the end to which life in general is more and more adjusted as it becomes more and more evolved, is *Quantity of Life, taking Width in as well as Length,* and that conduct is *good* which tends to preservation of life so understood.   We have thus an Ultimate End or Good defined non-hedonistically.   But an ethical end cannot be proved by Biology.   And in fact Mr. Spencer does not really maintain his non-hedonistic biological end, but asserts in § 9 that the good is universally the pleasurable, and that *pleasurable* and *painful* are the primary meanings of *good* and *bad*.   Substantially he gives the most decided preference to Pleasure over Life as Ultimate End, and is thus not a pure Evolutionist in Ethics, but an Evolutionistic Hedonist.   At the same time he assumes an optimistic view as to the coincidence of Life and Pleasure, which needs more argument.   The Utilitarian moralist, indeed, is not bound to confute Pessimism, but Mr. Spencer is bound to do this and more.   If Quantity of Life is the end, and also Pleasure is the end, he is bound to prove that coincidence of Life and Pleasure which he takes for granted.   To meet this difficulty he refers to his chapter on *The Relativity of Pains and Pleasures*, and affirms that the problem is solved by the process of adaptation of life to its environment which is continually going on.   But all which experience gives us reason for inferring is, that actions preservative of the individual or the race will be, generally speaking, less painful than those that have an opposite tendency, and that the pains normally endured will not be sufficiently intense to destroy life   .   . Pp. 143–153

This leaves open the possibility that the stimulus to organic actions should be painful, the actions themselves indifferent, and the result merely relief from pain.   And on the one hand, in as far as actions become instinctive or mechanical, they tend to be less accompanied with feeling, while, on the other hand, it seems quite possible that ever new adjustments will be required, and the equilibrium between individuals and their environment remain but partial and incomplete.   And further, even supposing it to be true that pleasure will eventually accompany every mode of action demanded by social conditions, it still does not follow that maximum quantity of pleasure will always accompany maximum quantity of life.   And whatever we may hope as to the future, it remains true that at present there is a wide divergence between the two ends.   Mr. Spencer's view here appears to be that complete coincidence of life-sustaining and pleasure-giving activities, though it may be assumed in Absolute Ethics, cannot be similarly assumed in Relative Ethics, which is concerned with the guidance of humanity here and now.   This distinction, however, is not directly explained until the close of the treatise   .   .   . Pp. 153–156

The main drift of chapter iv., on *Ways of Judging Conduct*, is that in Mr. Spencer's view the various ethical theories—theological, political, intuitional, or utilitarian—are characterised either by entire absence of the idea of causation or by inadequate presence of it.   He instances (1) the opinion that there is no other rule of conduct than the alleged will of God ; (2) Plato, Aristotle, and Hobbes, who are said to find in State enactments the sources of right and wrong ; (3) Intuitionists, who are said to believe in innate moral perception ; and (4) the Utilitarian school, which is charged with adopting an empirical and inductive method instead of deductions to necessary conclusions.   What is said of Plato and Aristotle involves historical misrepresentation.   The element of truth in Hobbes's view is not done justice to, the Intuitionist view is caricatured, and the reconciliation of Intuitionism by means of Evolution, given in chapter ix., is here left out of account.   Utilitarians do, no doubt, adopt a method which is largely empirical, but this is not because they refuse to recognise causation, or the general importance of scientific deduction   .   .   . Pp. 156–160

LECTURE III

DATA OF ETHICS—CHAPTERS V. TO VIII.

A main cause of difficulty in dealing with chapters v. to viii. is that Mr. Spencer takes as established the as yet unproved coincidence between Life and Happiness, and holds that if the Utilitarian will trace the characteristics of evolution in Life, he will be enabled to substitute the truly scientific method for ordinary empirical Utilitarianism.   But if the two ends diverge, the method is illegitimate.

The question placed before us at the end of chapter iv. is : Assuming that the ultimate end is happiness, by what method should we determine

the means to this end ? Mr. Spencer thinks that a deductive method
should be substituted for the mainly inductive one used by the older
Utilitarians, and implies that the four scientific 'views' of chapters v.
to viii. will show how the transformation is to be effected Pp. 161–162

Taking first chapter v. on the Physical View, we learn that 'moral' conduct
has in the highest degree the characteristics of definiteness, coherence,
and heterogeneity to which all physical progress moves. As regards
the definiteness and coherence of good conduct, Mr. Spencer appeals confidently to Common Sense. (But surely conduct may be coherently and
definitely selfish, and in some cases an indeterminateness which leaves
room for spontaneity is valued.) Mr. Spencer argues, and with force,
that with regard to heterogeneity Common Morality does not support
his view ; but he overlooks a difficulty from the double point of view
of the individual and the social organism. We may imagine a condition in which the individual develops *pari passu* with his society, but
we have no adequate evidence that history is conducting us to such a
Utopia. Hence we cannot say broadly that conduct here and now
tends to general happiness in proportion as it exhibits the characteristics of definiteness, coherence, and heterogeneity. It may be maintained that perfect conduct must be perfectly definite and coherent, but
as regards the physical world, we can only conceive it to be indefinite
or incoherent relatively to an imperfect intellect ; and relatively to
human intellect, the indefinite in certain parts of conduct is judged to
be better . . . . . . Pp. 162–165

Passing to the Biological View, Mr. Spencer tells us that according to this,
the ideally moral man is one in whom all functions are fulfilled in
normal proportion. But since in our actual transitional state moral
obligations of a supreme kind often necessitate conduct which is
physically injurious, the only practical precept which we reach is
the undisputed maxim that it is our duty *cœteris paribus* to preserve
our health in the highest degree. If it be said that the principle of
performing every function is at least useful as pointing out an ideal, we
must answer that the ideal humanity to which it would completely
apply is so remote that we cannot obtain even an ideal that could be
useful to us here and now . . . . Pp. 165–168

And the case is somewhat similar with the argument to show that pleasure-
giving acts are life-sustaining, and that painful acts are injurious to
life. Hence here again we see that the guidance afforded by Mr.
Spencer's biological law cannot supersede the empirical method of
ascertaining effects of action on happiness. And chapter vii. on the
Psychological View furnishes further evidence of the vagueness and
inadequacy of the guidance afforded by Mr. Spencer's biological data.
For while in chapter vi. he reprimands men and moralists for their
neglect of *immediate* pleasures and pains, in chapter vii. he is inclined
to allow that the moral progress of man has largely consisted in his
increased tendency to regard remote pleasures and pains and overrule
the force of the more proximate, and is ready to explain the fact
scientifically.

Thus, finally, all that Mr. Spencer enables us to say seems merely to amount
to this, that immediate pleasure is to be sought and immediate pain
avoided when there is no reason to suppose that such pursuit or avoidance will bring with it a loss of balance of pleasure hereafter—and this
no Utilitarian denies . . . . . Pp. 168–170

In chapter vii. Mr. Spencer gives an account of the origin and development
of our moral sentiments. He describes the notion of Moral Obligation

as originally evolved in savages from the vague dread of the anger of other men, living and dead—dread of the actual chieftain, which gradually grows into distinctness, becomes the political sanction, dread of the former chieftain's ghost promoted to a deity becomes the religious sanction, regard for the praise and blame of fellow-men becomes the social sanction—these generally harmonise with and support each other. The strictly moral feelings and restraints to which these are preparatory, and which grow out of these, consist in the representation not of extrinsic and factitious but of intrinsic and necessary natural effects. The moral feelings and restraints having originated from these political, religious, and social authorities, and under conditions made possible by them, come to be in conscious experience quite independent of the earlier restraints. The special feeling of obligation is referred to (1) consciousness of higher authority as guiding to welfare, (2) coerciveness imported into moral restraint from the associated political, religious, and social restraints.—The latter, Mr. Spencer holds, will fade as the moral motive becomes distinct and predominant.—But there is some want of clearness, since the feeling of coerciveness seems to be identified with the feeling of obligation itself, and so Mr. Spencer reaches the conclusion that the sense of duty or moral obligation is transitory. But we do not see why the element of authoritativeness should disappear along with the element of coerciveness.

The above account of the gradual growth into independence of truly moral restraint does not seem to furnish any help towards making Utilitarian Ethics deductive . . . . . Pp. 170–175

In the chapter on the Sociological View, Mr. Spencer observes that the modifications of conduct necessitated by the social state have come to constitute the chief part of the moral code, and he lays down fundamental rules of action which will be considered in the next Lecture. But we are faced here by the fundamentally important question, left open at the conclusion of chapter iii. : Why, and how far, should I concern myself about evil to others, when the sympathetic pain which their evil causes me is not so great as to outweigh the loss of pleasure involved in my taking trouble to remove their pain ?

The difference between the strictly moral restraint on the one hand, and the political, religious, and social restraints on the other hand, are not to be found, as Mr. Spencer suggests, in a difference as to directness and proximity, nor can we treat as fundamental his distinction between *artificial* or *factitious*, and *necessary natural* consequences. The essential difference is that in truly moral feeling, in the main, it is evil to others, sympathetically apprehended, that is influential.

Pp. 175–177

LECTURE IV

DATA OF ETHICS—CHAPTERS XI. TO XIV. AND CHAPTER VIII.

In answering the question : *Whose* happiness ought the individual agent to seek ? Mr. Spencer points out that both pure Egoism and pure Altruism must be rejected. We may hope, he thinks, that ultimately *Each will find his own in all men's good*, but at present general happiness is to be achieved mainly through the adequate pursuit of their own happiness by individuals ; while, reciprocally, the happinesses of the individuals are to be achieved in part by their pursuit of the general happiness. But this formula does not recognise the possibility there is that one's

ANALYTICAL SUMMARY OF CONTENTS xxiii

own happiness and the general happiness may be presented as alternatives.

Mr. Spencer does not directly face this problem, for the reason, as it would seem, that he does not clearly distinguish the question of Ultimate End from that of Proximate End. For while his arguments against undue altruism assume universal happiness as the ultimate end and criterion of right conduct, he blames Bentham and his followers for accepting the same end and standard, and seems to treat this position as identical with the theory which makes general happiness the sole *immediate* object of pursuit. But this latter theory is remote from Bentham's, while at the same time it is only against it that Mr. Spencer's arguments are effective. To the Hedonist's question : *Whose* happiness is to be considered by the individual agent? Bentham does not give a very clear answer, but his proposition :—Every one to count for one, and no one for more than one—if understood with the obvious qualification, seems incontrovertible and implied in the adoption of general happiness as end. On the whole, it seems that Mr. Spencer's polemic against the Utilitarianism of Bentham and Mill is directed against the doctrine that conduciveness to general happiness should be taken as the *immediate* end. But Mill and still more Bentham are far from advocating an altruism which inculcates self-sacrifice and self-suppression without limit or reserve, while the practical claims of Egoism are clearly recognised in *The Methods of Ethics*—thus the doctrine against which Mr. Spencer is arguing in chapter xiii. appears to be an incongruous mixture of English Utilitarianism and Comtist Altruism, and even for Comte there is a better case than Mr. Spencer admits . . . . Pp. 178–187

While accepting Mr. Spencer's view of the necessity, for general happiness, of some practical compromise between Egoism and Altruism, we may urge that the fact that there must be 'a compromise' does not determine whether it shall be that in which the individual pursues the happiness of others so far as it is consistent with his own, or that in which he pursues his own so far as it is consistent with maximum happiness generally. Mr. Spencer does not affirm that the two always coincide, hence he has still to answer the question : Which of the two alternative compromises ought I to take?—The Author's answer here is, that unless we assume or prove the moral order of the world, there is a conflict between rational convictions ; and he holds that the assumption of moral order is normal to reflective man and a postulate of Common Sense. If we conclude that Mr. Spencer would say that an individual ought to choose the compromise framed on the universalistic principle, we still have to face the question : Can this compromise be determined by the deductive method which he advocates? . . Pp. 187–189

Turning back to chapter viii. on the Sociological View, we ask : Does this show us how Utilitarianism can be made deductive? Here Mr. Spencer infers that because war is a cause of the sacrifice of individuals to the community, therefore when wars cease, all such sacrifice will cease.— But there seems no reason why the sacrifice of some individuals to others should not go on in a community, even when it is not menaced from outside by antagonistic societies. *E.g.* there may be industrial antagonisms within the society. Mr. Spencer's fallacious inference here seems to prejudge the whole dispute between his Individualism and Modern Socialism.

There is, he tells us, a final permanent code which voluntary co-operation implies, and which alone admits of being definitely formulated, and so constituting *ethics as a science* in contrast with *empirical ethics*. Passing over the difficulty due to our not knowing *how* ideal the state is to which Mr. Spencer's ethics relate, and deferring consideration of the utility of the final permanent code for men here and now, we turn to its chief rules as given in chapter viii. These are (1) Injure no one in person, estate, or reputation ; (2) Observe contracts ; (3) Make spontaneous efforts to further the welfare of others.—We may admit that these rules belong to a final permanent code and will be observed in an ideal community ; but it does not appear that Mr. Spencer by means of sociological considerations enables us to know it with a scientific certainty unlike that which the Utilitarian can attain who forms his view of the *media axiomata* of Ethics from experience . Pp. 189–194

LECTURE V

DATA OF ETHICS—CHAPTERS XV. XVI. AND VIII.

In considering chapter xv. we should keep distinct three questions, which Mr. Spencer does not always keep distinct, owing partly to his disposition to reduce paradoxically the possibility of giving a definite answer to (2), viz. : (1) What would be right for an individual to do in an ideal society ? (2) What is right for an individual to do here and now ? (3) What is commonly thought to be right, either in the particular community of which I am a member, or any other ?
Pp. 195–196

The Author does not (as Mr. Spencer suggests) exclude either indifferent acts, or acts of which the moral character is not definitely cognisable. He holds (*a*) that what Mr. Spencer calls the *least wrong* action, is that which *ought* to be done, and therefore *right* ; (*b*) that indifferent acts are less frequent than Mr. Spencer implies, and that in doubtful cases conservative considerations would turn the scale in favour of ordinary morality more often than Mr. Spencer allows. The main issue between him and Mr. Spencer is as to the value of Absolute Ethics. In *Data of Ethics* Mr. Spencer recognises that Relative Ethics is important, but he regards this as imperfect, as only relatively right, because it produces some pain. In chapters xv. and xvi. Mr. Spencer's whole effort is directed to show that this Relative Ethics ought to be preceded by Absolute Ethics, and he parallels Ethics with Mechanics and Astronomy. It is against the more extreme view of Absolute Ethics given in Mr. Spencer's *Social Statics*—the view that Absolute Ethics is the only kind of Ethics with which a philosophical moralist can possibly concern himself—that the first part of the argument in *Methods of Ethics*, Book I. chap. ii. § 2, is directed. Only the second part of that argument is directed against the view given in *Data of Ethics*, but Mr. Spencer has not noticed the following objections which are there brought against this more moderate view :—(1) Granting that Mr. Spencer's ideal society (in which the voluntary actions of all the members cause pleasure unalloyed by pain anywhere) is one which we can conceive as possible, it seems quite impossible to ascertain *a priori* the nature of the human beings composing such a society with sufficient definiteness and certainty to enable us to determine their code of conduct. Mr. Spencer does not profess here to offer more than a few scanty indications of such a code, but among those that he gives (of which the most important is the formula of Absolute Justice as the fundamental prin-

ciple for regulating social co-operation) there seems to be nothing
of consequence which is not also highly disputable . Pp. 197–205

And Mr. Spencer's two analogies—Geometry and Physiology—seem well
adapted to illustrate what is *not* to be found in his Ideal or Absolute
Ethics : *e.g.* in Geometry we have definite conceptions of ideal or
abstract geometrical forms, and there is close approximation between
these and the boundaries of the actual spaces with which we deal. So
again of Physiology ; for we have important social factors with
functions punitive and militant, which are actually organised with the
view of producing pain. Even if we could construct scientifically Mr.
Spencer's ideal morality, such a construction would not help us much
in solving the practical problems of actual humanity, since a society in
which, *e.g.*, there is no such thing as punishment, is so unlike our own
that it would be idle for us to attempt any close imitation of its rules
of behaviour. And which of the rules of the ideal code it would be
desirable to conform to, and how far, could only be known by careful
employment of the empirical method.

Taking a sociological illustration from the notion of Justice, on which Mr.
Spencer in *Data of Ethics* lays so much stress, it may be asked whether
we can get by means of Sociology a clearer, better established, more
precise view of Justice ? § 52 teaches that co-operation can only be
maintained by a just apportionment of benefit to achievement (or effort),
and that this is to be brought about by fulfilment of voluntary agreements.—But experience shows that equal efforts do not always produce
equal results ; is it just to apportion benefit to result or to effort ? And
(as has been pointed out) just apportionment is not attained by fulfilment of contract. Shall we then (with the Socialist) restrict freedom
in order to obtain juster apportionment ? Or will such restriction do
more harm than good (as the Individualist contends) ? Mr. Spencer's
Sociology ignores the difficulty which confronts us here, and he does
not observe that the principle of payment for services gives a very
different result from the principle of free contract.

Again, we get no answer from Sociology in chapter viii. to the question
whether we may hope in the future for a great extension or a great
reduction of the sphere of Positive Beneficence.

Mr. Spencer points out that his conception of an ideal Ethics really lies
latent in the beliefs of the moralists ; and no doubt the conception of
an ideal man is always present in a latent form, but the whole point of
the delineation of the ideal man (or sage) by the Stoics, who made
most of the conception, was that an ideal man can live in an un-ideal
society . . . . . . Pp. 205–213

LECTURE VI

THE INDUCTIONS OF ETHICS (PART II. OF THE PRINCIPLES OF ETHICS)

The Data of Ethics (Part I. of *Principles of Ethics*) gives a general survey of
the subject, and shows the reader what kind of premises are available
for answering the practical question, What am I to do ? It gives the
relation of Ethics to other sciences, especially Biology and Sociology,
determines the ultimate end of human conduct, and defines the method
to be adopted in a scientific investigation of the right rules of human
action. This investigation, it is explained, includes two great divisions,
personal and social, the first comprehending actions which are primarily

judged as affecting the agent himself, the chief rules of which are worked out in Part III. on *Ethics of the Individual Life*. The second division (*The Ethics of Social Life*) comprehends actions judged as good or bad mainly by their results to others. These actions fall into two groups: (1) those which achieve ends in ways that do or do not unduly interfere with the pursuit of ends by others, and are considered in Part IV. (*Justice*), and (2) those which influence the states of others without directly interfering with the relation between labour and results, and are considered in Parts V. and VI. (*Negative Beneficence* and *Positive Beneficence*). And under each of these heads we have the double problem presented by Absolute and Relative Ethics respectively. Further complication is introduced by the recognition of two different aspects of the ultimate end and criterion of right action (since Life and Happiness do not always coincide), and by the question which arises in case the agent has to choose between his own Life or Happiness and that of others. On the whole, we must take Mr. Spencer to hold that it is Happiness, and the General Happiness, which is the right end and standard, though the question, *Why* am I to seek the General Happiness? is not definitely answered by him . . Pp. 214–218

Mr. Spencer's establishment of the end is not definitely distinguished from that of ordinary Utilitarianism. As regards the ascertainment of means to the End, he explains that ordinary Empirical Utilitarianism does not sufficiently recognise causation, and he aims at determining deductively what actions tend to happiness or its opposite.—But if Absolute Ethics is distinguished from Relative Ethics, it becomes clear that as regards the latter Mr. Spencer does not really offer us any other general system than Empirical Utilitarianism. So that his contention here seems to become again a question as to the value of Absolute Ethics. And what he aims at reaching inductively by help of Part II. is Absolute Ethics and an ideal society to which it primarily relates. The inductions are designed to show that this ideal society to which Absolute Ethics belongs is the ultimate result to which the evolution of human society and morality is tending, through a series of stages in which Relative Ethics is required . . . . . . Pp. 218–220

In Part II. Mr. Spencer seeks (1) to disprove the current intuitional morality, and (2) to show that the leading cause which retards the development of morality is the influence of War, and the habits and sentiments which War normally brings with it. He distinguishes between the terms *ethical* and *pro-ethical*, and in a wider sense is disposed to call any idea and sentiment of obligation *ethical;* but in a narrower and more proper sense would restrict the term to ideas and sentiments which refer to the intrinsic results of conduct, and not to ideas and sentiments derived from external authorities, and coercions and approbations—religious, political, or social—which he would prefer to call *pro-ethical*. The details of his induction in Part II. are (he says with some exaggeration) concerned almost exclusively with what is pro-ethical . . . . . . Pp. 220–223

In considering the relation between Law and Morality, we are led to note that Mr. Spencer overlooks the distinction drawn in ordinary consciousness between the ethico-political judgment on actual law as good or bad, and the ethical judgment on the duty of Order or Law-observance. Modern Common Sense certainly holds that it is generally the duty of a private person as such to obey a law judged to be bad, and this view is clearly sustained by utilitarian considerations. And when he says that it comes to be felt more and more that legal coercion is warranted only in as far as law is an enforcer of justice, if he means that it is a mark of political progress when men judge the laws they obey, and aim at the removal by constitutional means of those which they judge to be unjust, we may agree with him. But if he means that the habit of disobeying laws judged to be unjust has been growing and may be expected to grow, then his view of history seems superficial and his political outlook gloomy   .   .   . Pp. 223–225

Returning to Mr. Spencer's negative thesis, we may pass briefly over this, partly because it is less original than the other, partly because he does not seem to have a clear idea of what ought to be proved in order to refute his intuitional opponents. We may indeed agree with him that any appeal to Common Sense cannot be final. But he seems in his treatment here to be attacking an indefensible form of the view to which he is opposed, and as his real attitude towards the Intuitional theory is less hostile than would appear from Part II. taken alone, further consideration may be deferred till we come to the fuller exposition in Part IV.

In Mr. Spencer's view the sentiments and ideas current in any society become adjusted to the kinds of activity predominant in it, so that while a life of constant external enmity generates a code in which aggression, conquest, and revenge are inculcated, a life of settled internal unity generates a code inculcating justice, honesty, and veracity, and, moreover, a moral sense adapted to the moral requirements ; so that nothing is needed but a continuance of absolute peace externally, and a rigorous insistence on non-aggression internally to ensure the moulding of men into a form naturally characterised by all the virtues. But he gives no reason for his optimistic conclusion here, that the hiatus which has hitherto existed between the current moral *code* of a society and the ordinary moral *conduct* of its members will cease when war ceases. And even if it were proved by his selection of facts, that morality between man and man is *affected* by war between society and society, those facts have no tendency whatever to prove that such morality is thereby *adapted* or *adjusted* to the needs of a society in this condition of external enmity. Indeed Mr. Spencer's historic instances strikingly show that a society becomes worse fitted for the struggle for existence with other societies by the prevalence of homicide, robbery, and thieving within it. Increase in the cohesion of a tribe or nation, obtained by putting down internal strife, tends to make it stronger for external warfare, and external war tends to develop the superior cohesion which strengthens a society for such war. And reference to historical instances goes to show that private aggression and robbery connected with militancy are largely due to the disorder and partial inhibition of ordinary governmental functions produced by war, and that the moral ideal, in respect of justice, honesty, veracity, etc., as between man and man, is not materially higher in countries where militancy has least predominance. It may be said in Mr. Spencer's behalf, that we have not anywhere seen freedom from war tried completely and for a long enough time, but the point is that the thesis is not supported even by the method of Concomitant Variations.

Further, impartial reflection on the morality of our own age and country seems to show that though English morality as regards external aggression may be open to criticism, yet we may recognise here, and also in the case of other modern nations, that it is not fighting simply, but *fighting for rights* that is approved and admired   . Pp. 226–235

Mr. Spencer in his general view of the conflict of the *Ethics of Enmity* and

the *Ethics of Amity* overlooks the distinction between (1) the conception
of War as right and good, and the qualities leading to success in war
as the highest virtues, when duty to the State is paramount and duty
to humanity not recognised, and (2) the conception of War as right in
our actual society.   The latter difficult ethico-political question he does
not help us to solve, and indeed in the main his point of view is
sociological rather than ethical.   But if he takes the position that it is
not his primary business to work out the rough empirical compromise
between the Ethics of Enmity and the Ethics of Amity, which is all that
we can hope to attain at the present stage of our development, he ought
to have maintained a greater impartiality of tone.   And his Sociology is
one-sided as well as his Ethics, for he almost entirely ignores the
whole attempt of the moral consciousness of civilised man to *moralise*
war and its effects.

To sum up very briefly Mr. Spencer's contentions in Part II. : he is mainly
concerned with proving (1) that men have not in common any *innate* or
intuitive sense of right and wrong ; (2) that the influence of War, and
the habits and sentiments which War normally brings with it, have
continually confused and perverted the ethical ideal of mankind
through the strange mingling of the Ethics of Enmity with the Ethics
of Amity.   A life of peaceful industrial co-operation relieved from
militancy would render general and predominant the reign of Justice,
Honesty, Veracity, and Good Faith, and the ideal code would become
approximately applicable and accepted   .   .   . Pp. 235–239

LECTURE VII

In Part III. Mr. Spencer passes to consider Morality as it ought to be.   He
thinks that in order to free ourselves from the misleading influences of
the code we have been brought up under, we must ignore established
doctrines and even accepted meanings of fundamental words, and go
direct to facts.   He would, *e.g.*, eliminate from *Duty* and *Obligation* the
notion of subjection to authority ; but he is not consistent about
authority, because his own recognition of the authority of Reason is
fitful and incomplete, and he does not see that the authority implied
in Common Sense Morality is that of Reason.

He begins by an attack on moralists and Common Sense for ignoring in
ethical judgments acts conducive to the life, health, vigour, and
pleasure of the agent, and gives reasons for regarding this one-sided
conduct as mischievous.—It may be said in reply that no doubt
Common Sense and leading moralists do not inculcate the promotion of
the agent's health and vigour in proportion to its utilitarian importance,
and do not encourage the pursuit of pleasure for self.   And Mr.
Spencer's arguments have force, but his attack is exaggerated, and he
does not deal with the practical argument for the one-sidedness of
moralists, namely, that it is important to lay stress on the duties that
men are most inclined to neglect, and that the pursuit of private
pleasure is not, on the average, among these.   He forgets in his polemic
that current morality with all its limitations is a fundamentally important part of the complex adjustment of a human society to its
environment, and that the moralist ought to study this adjustment,

not assuming that it cannot be improved (for the moralist and his criticism are also a part of the adjustment), but in order that his criticism may be thoroughly instructed and circumspect . Pp. 240–244

Passing to the detail of Mr. Spencer's discussion, we find that the practical precepts and counsels which he gives under the heads of activity, rest, nutrition, stimulation, culture, and amusement, are not only disappointingly familiar, but are also counsels in trying to apply which we have had to refer to our own personal experience and the experience of others. Indeed, Mr. Spencer does not suggest any other course, as far as Relative Ethics is concerned.—What then is the value here of the deductive method insisted on ? The only definite deduction that we find is (§ 215) to the effect that from the point of view of Absolute Ethics, stimulants of every kind—or at any rate the daily use of them— must be reprobated. But in this deduction, the question seems to be begged in the premises. Of course if the life of Utopian man is perfectly adjusted without stimulants, it will follow that stimulants are superfluous ; but what right have we to make this assumption ? And again, why is it that a considerable space in the individual's life in the ideal state should be filled by amusements ? Why should they—any more than tea, alcohol, tobacco, and a sense of moral obligation —have a place in that perfect adjustment by which every activity of a human being is attended by pleasure unalloyed with pain ? .   . Pp. 244–248

We may note that in Mr. Spencer's chapters on Amusements there are novelties deserving of attention. But in respect of the methodical and scientific treatment of the questions discussed, he still fails to satisfy us. The important question here is the question of method. Mr. Spencer is indeed consistent in using empirical reasoning when giving practical advice in detail in this Part III. But he seems to use the method rather hastily and rashly.

Finally, it may be observed with reference to the relation between *The Ethics of Individual Life* (Part III.) and *The Ethics of Social Life* (Parts IV. V. VI.), that though the *life* is individual, the *ethics* are inevitably only partially so. No one who accepts General Happiness as the end should treat duty to others as of secondary importance.

Pp. 248–252

LECTURE VIII

THE ETHICS OF SOCIAL LIFE—JUSTICE (PART IV. OF THE PRINCIPLES OF ETHICS) CHAPTERS I. TO VIII.

The assumption which Mr. Spencer too easily made in Part I.—that actions conducive to Maximum Life would also be conducive to Maximum Happiness—is maintained in Part IV. ; and this duality in the conception of the End, and the liberty he reserves to himself of passing from Life to Happiness and back to Life, are sources of serious confusion.

In chapter i. on *Animal Ethics* acts are said to be good which are conducive to maximum life, and we get the following principles : (1) Within the family group—during early life—most must be given where least is deserved ; (2) after maturity is reached benefit must vary directly as worth—*worth* being measured by fitness for the conditions of existence. (2) is limited by (1) and also by the consideration (3) that if the constitution of the species, and also its conditions of existence, are such that sacrifices of some of its individuals so subserve the welfare of the species as that the numbers are better maintained than they would otherwise be, then there results a justification for such sacrifice. —Here we note two difficulties:—(*a*) Why the limitation to maintenance of *numbers ?* (*b*) Does *justification* mean *shown to be in harmony with justice ?*—However, Mr. Spencer does not consider (3) to be so essential as (1) and (2), and holds that in considering (2)—the principle of Justice—we are concerned only with the *social* (not the *family*) sphere. This limitation of the range of Justice seems mistaken, and is not maintained throughout Part IV.   .   .   . Pp. 253–256

Of the law of the species as composed of adults only, Mr. Spencer says that though, in a sense, this law holds without qualification in sub-human life, yet in another sense this sub-human justice is extremely imperfect both in general and in detail, since there are species the sustentation of which depends on the destruction of other species, this implying that the species preyed upon have the relations between conduct and consequences habitually broken. — Surely, however, the existence of a predatory species is part of the conditions of existence of the species which is its prey, and if the latter is devoured, its unfitness to the conditions of its existence seems to be demonstrated.   If it be answered that enemies are causes of death which so operate that superior as well as inferior are sacrificed, it must be pointed out that the term *superior* as here used is exposed to a threefold ambiguity.   Adaptation of species in accordance with biological laws must be adaptation to an actual environment, and if worth is measured by fitness to conditions of existence, that which manages to live is more worthy than that which dies—hence *sub-human justice* cannot be said ever to be imperfect. This principle of sub-human justice—that which is qualified to live under its conditions of existence deserves to live—is very unlike anything that has ever been current as a principle of justice in human relations.   Taking into account the further qualification of the individualistic law of sub-human justice by the conditions of gregariousness, Mr. Spencer considers that conditions such that by the occasional sacrifices of some members of a species, the species as a whole prospers, are relative to the existence of living enemies outside the species.   But this seems an arbitrary assumption.   He goes on to lay down as absolute for gregarious animals the condition that each member of the group while carrying on self-sustentation and sustentation of offspring shall not seriously impede the like pursuits of others   . Pp. 256–260

Human Justice Mr. Spencer states to be a further development of sub-human justice—the law by which the human species is preserved being that, among adults, the individuals best adapted to the conditions of their existence shall prosper most, and individuals least adapted shall prosper least.   Thus each individual ought to receive the benefits and the evils of his own nature and consequent conduct.   Here we may note (*a*) *prosper* ought to mean *shall be preserved and shall produce offspring ;* (*b*) it is too strong to say *the* law ; (*c*) we do not on reflection think it just that a man should suffer for what is not due to wilful wrong-doing.— Comparing §§ 257 and 269 it is not clear whether Mr. Spencer considers desert to depend on intention and moral effort or on achievement.

An important modification—peculiar to the human species—of the individualistic law of adult life is introduced, we are told, by the fact that this highest gregarious creature is distinguished by the characteristic of fighting his own kind ; and the sacrifices entailed by wars between groups of human beings have been far greater than the sacrifices made in defence of groups against inferior animals.   But when the stage of human evolution is reached at which ethical considerations come to be entertained, offensive war, in Mr. Spencer's view, ceases to be justifiable. And even defensive war must ultimately disappear ; so that the qualifications of the principle of justice introduced by war are seen to belong only to Relative Ethics . . . . Pp. 260–264

On the above it may be observed that the effects of gregariousness as it appears in man seem to be not quite adequately conceived, and the supposed effects of evolution to be somewhat arbitrarily assumed. Again, Sociology and Ethics seem too much mixed up, and it is too hastily assumed that the necessity of subordinating the welfare of the individual to that of the species arises solely from war. For granting that it would be advantageous that war should cease, it does not follow that it will cease. Granting that industrialism will put an end to militancy, it does not follow that industrial conflicts will cease. Granting, finally, that industrial conflicts will cease, it does not follow that Mr. Spencer's individualistic principles of justice will then reign unchecked ; for the cessation of conflict may be brought about by such an implication of interests and development of sympathy as will render all men members one of another to an extent hitherto unknown . . Pp. 264–265

Turning to Mr. Spencer's account of the psychological development of the Sentiment and Idea of Justice, we find he begins with what he calls the *egoistic sentiment of Justice.* But this, which seems to be irritation at interference with the pursuit of egoistic ends, is rather a condition of the sentiment than the sentiment itself. Mr. Spencer goes on to explain how the altruistic sentiment of justice comes into existence by the aid of a pro-altruistic sentiment compounded of dread of social dislike, dread of legal punishment, dread of divine vengeance, and fear of retaliation. Then, society being held together by this pro-altruistic sentiment, the development of sympathy through gregariousness thus maintained produces the genuine altruistic sentiment of justice. This account, though to a great extent true, does not seem to give quite a large enough or early enough place to the influence of sympathy.

In Mr. Spencer's view, granting the elements which he enumerates, there gradually emerges and becomes definite the idea of a limit to each kind of activity up to which there is freedom to act. This is the *Idea of Justice,* and it contains two elements : (1) Inequality, as regards merit and reward, since men differ in their powers, and hence unequal amounts of benefit are implied ; (2) Equality, as regards the mutual limitations of men's actions, since experience shows that these bounds are on the average the same for all. The appreciation of these two factors in human justice has long remained unbalanced, but Mr. Spencer by co-ordinating, as he says, the antagonistic wrong views reaches the following formula of Justice :—Each man is free to do that which he wills, provided he infringe not the equal freedom of another man.—It may be noted that Mr. Spencer seems to overlook here the distinction between Ideal and Conservative Justice, and also that in the development of the idea of justice he gives too little prominence to equality. And the inequality which is indeed an element in the Greek view of Justice is not the inequality that results from non-interference, but the inequality that belongs to distribution according to desert. In Aristotle's conception of Justice, and in Greek Common Sense as interpreted by him, Equality is prominent . . . . Pp. 265–269

In an Appendix Mr. Spencer discusses the relation between his own view and Kant's, and points out that while Kant prescribes Freedom absolutely, he himself only prescribes it as a means to general happiness. Thus the difference between the older Utilitarians and Kant is one of principle, while the difference between them and Mr. Spencer is one of method. Mr. Spencer goes on to say that in Kant's view of Freedom the negative element, or obligation to respect limits, is the dominant idea, whereas, in his own case, the positive element—the right to freedom of action— is primary. But Kant in the passage referred to is giving the formula of right legal coercion—prevention of interference with the actions which constitute the life of each and conduce to the subsequent main- tenance of his life—and this Mr. Spencer accepts . . Pp. 269–272

To prove the formula three lines of argument are adopted: (1) The evolutional argument from general biology—this argument has been already answered. (2) It is attempted to be shown that History exhibits a gradual growth of the conception of Justice into distinctness. —This does not seem to be proved by the evidence adduced. (3) Mr. Spencer seems disposed to affirm the Law of Equal Freedom to be self- evident *a priori*, though relatively vague and requiring methodical criticism.—To this the Author has to say that it is not self-evident to him. And it does not appear how the appeal to Evolution could settle a controversy of this kind. Indeed, Mr. Spencer does not contend this, and anticipates only scorn for his doctrine from the reigning school of politics and morals. And he complains equally of prevalent Common Sense. If his doctrine is said to be accepted as ideal, it may be said that it is likewise accepted as ideally just that a man should not suffer for no fault of his own, and that it is not clear why experience of past human life should have produced a trustworthy intuition as to ideal relations.

In Mr. Spencer's application of the formula of justice there seems some danger of confusion between legal and moral rights, and between legal rights as actually established and those which ought to be established. And his assertion that instead of rights deriving their warrant from law, it is law that derives its warrant from them, seems dangerously ambiguous.

In examining in particular cases how far there is such correspondence as Mr. Spencer implies between legal enactments and his corollaries from the law of equal freedom, we shall need to keep carefully in view the distinctions between (1) the ideal rights of an ideal society, (2) legal rights as they ought to be here and now, (3) actual legal rights.
Pp. 272–277

LECTURE IX

Mr. Spencer and the Author agree in holding that the greatest happiness of the aggregate of persons affected by actions is the ultimate end, and that in the main the service that any one sane adult should be legally compelled to render to others should be merely the negative service of non-interference—except as regards fulfilment of contract. The differ- ence arises when Mr. Spencer declares that his formula for Justice may be treated as an absolute ethical principle, that the rights which ought to be legally established in an actual state may be ascertained by deductions from this principle, and that law derives its warrant from them. Mr. Spencer's principle of Justice is, we know, the Law of Equal Freedom.—Now Freedom is opposed not merely to physical restraint, but also to the moral restraint caused by fear of pain due to

hand, as selfish as now.—The case of Incorporeal Property brings out further the difficulty of explaining and justifying, on Mr. Spencer's view, the differences in the treatment of different kinds of property—a difficulty which is easily overcome on the Utilitarian view. The distinction between the case of Patents and other incorporeal property is rightly drawn. As regards Gift and Bequest, even if we grant to Mr. Spencer that such right of property as is justifiable by the Law of Equal Freedom involves right of gift, it does not therefore involve right of bequest. And further difficulties arise, which show that here again the law of equal freedom is inadequate for the required deduction.

The right of Exchange is a corollary from the right of Gift, and is deducible from the law of equal freedom ; but this is not so with the contract to render future services, in discussing which Mr. Spencer seems not to clearly distinguish between *making* and *enforcing* a contract. He seems not to notice the general limitation of the enforcement of contract in actual law, but discusses as exceptional the case of a man contracting himself into slavery, and holds that such a contract traverses the ultimate biological principle of justice from which Social morality grows, that the judgment of the contracting parties ought to be overruled here though not elsewhere, and that the Exchange in this case is so monstrously unequal that its terms may be called incommensurable. But all these contentions are highly disputable.

It may be observed, by way of criticism, that modern protectionism can hardly be due to militancy, and that there are difficulties similar to those already pointed out, in the deduction from the formula of Justice, of the rights of Free Belief and Worship, of Free Speech and Printing.

Pp. 286–295

In chapters xx. and xxi., relating to the rights of women and children, Mr. Spencer speaks as though those who would restrict the freedom of women, wish to do this on a principle of *rights proportionate to faculties*. But we may observe that it is intended to provide artificial *protection* as well as artificial *limitation*, though there is perhaps a practical justification for Mr. Spencer's view.

In considering the case of married women, Mr. Spencer passes too lightly over the question, Why, and how far, ought freedom of contract to be limited ? From the individualistic point of view we must note that restraints on free contract in marriage can only be justified in the interests of children.

In considering the mutual rights and duties of children and parents, it becomes evident that we need to use a formula different from Mr. Spencer's formula of justice. To settle the claim of children we have to go to Utilitarianism ; to settle that of parents, perhaps to some law of fair exchange. And ought the Parent or the State to determine what aids and opportunities are due to children ?

Turning again to the relations of husbands and wives, we are told that Justice appears to dictate a certain kind of compromise in the division of responsibility and power. But the principle of Justice here can certainly not be the Law of Equal Freedom, and this is the more surprising because the relative powers and duties of the married *might* be settled by free contract.

As regards political rights of men and women, though it is a sound principle that political rights should be connected with political burdens, it can hardly be concluded that political rights should be confined to those who are prepared personally to fight. But at any rate the principle has nothing to do with the Law of Equal Freedom, and it certainly does not

LECTURE X

NEGATIVE BENEFICENCE AND POSITIVE BENEFICENCE (PARTS V. AND VI. OF THE PRINCIPLES OF ETHICS)

With regard to Parts V. and VI. Mr. Spencer explains that the Doctrine of
Evolution has not furnished as much guidance as he had expected, and
in chapters iv. to vii. of *Negative Beneficence* and in *Positive Beneficence*
he falls back, for the most part, on somewhat familiar and trivial appli-
cations of empirical Utilitarianism. His suggestion that Poor-Relief,
whether State-paid or organised by charitable associations, should be
replaced by the old method of private relief, is more original but
highly unpractical, and he does not sufficiently recognise the difficulty
and complication introduced by taking the double point of view—
that of the Society and that of the Individual—in referring here to the
evolutional formula and the survival of the fittest   .   Pp. 309–312

LECTURES ON MARTINEAU'S ETHICS

LECTURE I

INTRODUCTION

MARTINEAU'S *Types of Ethical Theory* includes a critical account of the doctrines
of certain other writers on Ethics, along with an exposition and defence
of his own. He does not, however, give his own system either at the
beginning or at the end, but has placed first a critical exposition of
certain leading thinkers—chiefly Plato, Spinoza, Comte—who belong to
European but not to English thought. Then comes his own system ;
and lastly, a discussion of the leading English modes of ethical thought,
under three heads   .   .   .   .   Pp. 315–316
The explanation of this arrangement is, that Martineau regards Ethics as
properly psychological, and holds that some methods or systems are
erroneous because they do not (as he does in his *Idiopsychological* system)
accept the story that the moral consciousness tells of itself, but are either
on the one hand *Unpsychological* or on the other *Heteropsychological*.
And the Unpsychological systems he regards as either (1) *Metaphysical*
or (2) *Physical*, both excluding any proper notion of responsibility.
Again (1) may be either *Transcendental* (*e.g.* Plato's) or *Immanental*
(as *e.g.* Spinoza's). Of (2) Martineau takes Comte as a type, and he
holds that the Metaphysical type (1) survives in the school of Hegel.
Martineau has probably been led to treat first in his book the systems which
he classes as unpsychological, by his view that the development of psychological ethics is altogether peculiar to Christendom. But this view is
disputable, though no doubt the prominence of the notion of the Ego
and of the question of Free Will is characteristic of modern thought.
Comte may, indeed, fairly be called Unpsychological, but the general
description which Martineau gives of the systems which he calls Physical
is quite compatible with acceptance of the introspective method—as in
the case of Spencer. And this fact—awkward for his classification—
Martineau sees in the Introduction to his second volume, though he does
not recognise it in the Introduction to the first volume. It may,
however, be admitted that clear recognition of Introspective Psychology
as a distinct study, and the attempt to base ethics on it as so recognised,
does belong to modern thought, and so far may justify his putting the
Unpsychological systems first.
Martineau justifies the priority of the Idiopsychological over Heteropsycho-

logical systems in his arrangement, by the consideration that it is best first to define the inner facts of conscience itself with the best precision we can attain, and then to compare with the Idiopsychological Ethics so obtained the several attempts to find the phenomena under other categories by advocates of any scheme of Heteropsychological Ethics. We may agree with his doctrine that we must have a clear and full view of the existing moral consciousness before we can estimate any Psychological theory that professes to explain it, and also with what he says of the psychogony of evolutionists ; but it must be noticed that the unwarranted assumption *that the story which the moral consciousness tells of itself is one and the same in all cases,* underlies his whole procedure.

Pp. 316–322

As regards the first postulate which Martineau lays down, this assumption does not hold ; for while the Author agrees with him that the broad fact of the moral consciousness is that we have an irresistible tendency to pass judgments of right and wrong, and that when I pass such judgments on my own conduct I speak of *my Duty,* he holds (against Martineau) that it is even inconceivable that the authoritativeness or bindingness of moral rules should depend essentially on the fact that they emanate from another Person. The authoritativeness or obligatoriness of the rule of right is not, he holds, necessarily connected with the view that Truth implies a Thinker who thinks what is true. This may be further cleared up by reference to the analogy which Martineau draws between mathematical and moral truth. The Author, however, wishes here to point out that in his view the Authority of Conscience is just the Authority of Reason in its application to practice.—Martineau lays down that we ought to accept as veracious the immediate depositions of our own *Faculties* (by which, he explains, he does not mean *separate agents*). The Author would accept intuitions as veracious so far as they can be freed from inconsistency and conflict, and also propositions logically implied in such intuitions—but not as quite equally certain, since the process of educing the implication is one liable to error.—As regards the postulates of different faculties, the Author agrees with Martineau that so far as the spheres of the faculties are really distinct, the postulates of one need not harmonise with those of another ; but so far as two lines of thought lead to conclusions that contradict each other, the division of spheres seem only acceptable as a provisional practical solution.

Pp. 322–328

LECTURE II

FUNDAMENTAL ETHICAL FACT

The Fundamental Ethical Fact, Martineau says, is that distinctively as men we have an irresistible tendency to pass judgments of right and wrong, of merit and demerit. And the objects on which our moral judgment is directed are *persons exclusively,* and not *things,* and thus what we judge is always the Inner Spring of an action as distinguished from its outward operation, and the principle of moral judgment is directly opposed to the maxim that the only value of good affections is for the production of good actions . . . . Pp. 329–330

The difference thus indicated between Utilitarianism and Martineau appears on examination to be at any rate less than appears at first sight. This may be brought out by considering the two forms of moral judgment—the Jural, in which Ought, Right, or Duty are used ; and the Æsthetic, in which Goodness and Badness are predicated. The former when used ethically are applicable only to volitions—*i.e.* to actions viewed on their psychical side. Martineau uses the two pairs of terms, but he appears to regard the judgment of good and ill (or evil) as non-ethical. The true view, however, seems to be, that though there are many things called good and ill which it is not in our power to produce or hinder, yet in calling such things *good* and *evil* it is none the less implied that they are the kind of things which we ought, as rational and sentient beings, to desire and aim at, or try to avoid, for ourselves and others. Hence all judgment of *good* and *ill* is directly or indirectly ethical. And the difference between Common Sense and Utilitarianism, as regards the outward act, is that the former regards Prudence and Benevolence as merely two rules among others, while Utilitarianism holds that the rule of promoting the greatest good is supreme, and interprets the highest good as happiness. It seems, therefore, not to be inconsistent with Utilitarianism to hold that specifically moral judgments and sentiments are applicable to human volitions only, and at the same time that the ultimate criterion of right volitions is that they should tend to promote the general happiness.

LECTURE III

THEORY OF PRUDENCE, MERIT AND DEMERIT, NATURE OF MORAL AUTHORITY

The Author agrees with Martineau in accepting the distinction between Moral and Prudential, but does not accept as important his antithesis between Springs and Effects, nor agree with his extrusion of End from moral judgment.   Martineau has cut himself off from the view that it is the *intention to produce certain results* which we judge, by his assertion that it is the characteristic of impulse to send us *blindly* forward.

We may agree with Martineau that moral judgment or volition is conceivable apart from pleasure and pain, but not with his paradoxical definition of Prudence as *self-surrender to the strongest impulse*, with suppression of the *ulterior considerations* which it is the very essence of Prudence to take into account in the control of impulse.   And even when he does, later, take ulterior consequences into account, he still maintains that the prudential scale arranges motives in order of strength.—But if prudence arranges motives in any scale, it must be in accordance with an estimate of the whole foreseen consequences to the agent's happiness of the acts to which they prompt.

In Martineau's view that the corrective consequences of precipitate action are creations direct or indirect of our moral constitution, though this may be allowed as regards compunction of the agent and indignation of fellow-men, it surely cannot be so as regards the suffering in fortune and health due to rashness and inexperience   .   .   Pp. 339–342

Martineau seems not to speak quite clearly in answer to the question : Do Interest and Duty always coincide ?   In the Author's view, Merit and Worth mean the quality of action and character that it is right to praise, and he holds that as regards the agent it is rather *worth* than *merit* that he should aim at in himself.   What Martineau gives is rather a theory of Demerit than of Merit, and we may agree with him in holding that a bad act is judged to be worse in proportion to the slightness of the inducement, but not in the reason which he gives for this.   We may further agree that the terms *merit, meritorious,* apply to conduct rather than to character, and that we do not attribute merit to God.

Pp. 342–345

As regards Authority, the Author holds (1) that it attaches to the judgment of rightness ; (2) that the judgment, unless erroneous, is valid for all minds ; (3) that though it may be passed in one particular case, it is valid for all similar cases ; but that this judgment implies *another person* only in the sense that it implies a universal reason which the judging individual shares so far as he judges truly.   The Author thinks that the conception of one's self as a part of a larger whole inevitably comes in when the individual takes the point of view of Universal Reason, and he agrees with Martineau that the notion of authority in the rule, *Seek the good of the larger whole,* cannot be extracted from the conception of the relative bulk of the larger whole.   He holds that the individual arrives at it by the conception of the similarity of the other parts of the whole to himself.   Their similarity in other ways being apprehended, the conclusion is inevitable that each has an ultimate good similar to his own, and equally valuable from the point of view of universal reason   .   .   .   .   .   Pp. 345–347

Martineau holds that what I ought to do includes more than what others may reasonably censure me for not doing ; and he considers that what Reason imposes is the obligation of conforming to the type of perfect humanity—this latter view is argued against in *Methods of Ethics,* Book III. chapter xiv.

As regards the authority of Prudence, Martineau admits that we commonly condemn imprudence even where no interests are visibly affected except the offender's own.   The Author's disagreement with Martineau here, consists merely in recognising the axiom that *Hereafter is to be regarded as much as Now, apart from any relation to others.*

In chapter v. Martineau seems to mix up two distinctions : (1) that between
instinctive and purposive impulses ; (2) that between disinterested
impulses and impulses which aim at pleasure.   His distinction between
Primary and Secondary impulses seems true and important.   But the
primary impulses are not normally blind in the mature human being,
and they do not cease to be extra-regarding when a clear foresight of
their immediate end is added to them.   And in any case it would seem
that such impulses are not morally judged as blind   . Pp. 347–350

LECTURE IV

SPRINGS OF ACTION

The Author—approaching the examination of Common Sense from a point
of view fundamentally different from Martineau's—holds that the
verdict of Common Sense, even when clearly pronounced, is not final,
and that if it is found to conflict with clear deductions from self-evident
principles, it has to be dissented from.   This view is, he holds, confirmed by a study of the history of morality, which shows not only
change, but also progress through wider experience, fuller knowledge,
more extended and refined sympathies.

He holds that the elimination from current and accepted morality of any
elements of error, confusion, and uncertainty which may be found to
lurk in it, is the fundamental problem of Ethics, which can only be
solved by the construction of an ethical system—and that for this two
things are necessary : (1) to reach a clear conception of the Ultimate
End or Good ; (2) to penetrate to fundamental universal intuitions
determining the individual's duty of promoting general good.—It does
not appear, however, that this true moral system is to be found where
Martineau looks for it, since it would seem (1) that the judgments of
Common Sense on particular volitions have not the final decisiveness
which he apparently credits them with ; and (2) that judgment on
motives is secondary to judgment on intentions—though, no doubt, we
have to take account of the distinction between *good* and *bad*, *higher*
and *lower* motives   .   .   .   .   . Pp. 351–354

Martineau gives the details of his classification of the Springs of Action from
the Psychological as well as from the Ethical point of view.   The
Author does not propose to criticise in detail the psychological classification, but points out certain defects in it.

He then goes on to indicate his general and fundamental disagreement with
the plan on which the ethical scale is constructed, noting that, in his
view, there is no such *universal* relation of higher and lower as
Martineau affirms between any pair of impulses, but that it is rather
the case that in all or most cases, a natural impulse has its proper
sphere, within which it should be normally operative, and that in any
given case the answer to the question which of two conflicting motives
should prevail, must depend upon the particular conditions and circumstances.   Also it has to be remembered that as the character of a moral
agent becomes better, the motives that we rank as higher tend to
enlarge their normal sphere of operation.   And the aim in moral regulation and culture, as far as relates to motives, is (1) to keep the lower
motive within due limits as long as we cannot substitute for it the
equally effective operation of a higher ; (2) to effect gradually the
substitution of higher for lower up to a limit which falls short of com-

plete exclusion of the lower motive.   Thus we may agree with Butler that though it is to be wished that men would act from a higher motive than passionate resentment, yet, as things are, this motive is often a salutary balance to the weakness of pity.   Similar considerations apply to the *Love of Ease and Sensual Pleasure* which comes lowest in Martineau's scale.

In cases where the conflict begins as a duel between two or more such motives, it is probable that higher motives would come in, and that it would be the intervention of these that would decide the struggle so far as it was decided rightly.   And supposing the conflict serious and the decision deliberate, the case ought, in the Author's view, to be carried up for decision into the court of the motive which he regards as supreme, *i.e.* the desire to promote universal good understood as the happiness of sentient beings generally.   So he holds that such a scale as Martineau has drawn up of motives arranged according to their moral rank, can never have more than a very subordinate ethical importance—the final appeal should be to the effects of action on happiness   . Pp. 354–361

In answer to the above, Martineau sets forth that he does not admit a special class of motives, distinguished from the rest as *virtuous motives ;* that he admits no absolute and constant *highest motive*, the question of *higher* and *lower* being relative ; and that he does not admit Reason to be a spring of action at all.   He thus furnishes a striking illustration of the differences in the moral experiences of different minds.

Martineau's denial of any constant and absolute highest motive is surprising, especially when we consider what he says, in speaking of altruistic affections—that sometimes the election between several possible actions must be made by reference to the balance of pleasurable and painful effects.   And it is even more surprising when we examine the particulars of chapter vi. and note the important place which he there assigns to the Canon of Consequences and to 'virtuous' motives,— *e.g.* in the case of Love of Gain, Fear, Resentment, the Primary Affections, Generosity (with which Gratitude is somewhat oddly connected), Justice and Veracity, and the conflict between Friendship and Pity.

The question of the estimation of *Mixed Incentives* presents a special difficulty, which Martineau does not satisfactorily get over, and in his discussion of Justice (inaccurately defined as *treatment of persons according to their deserts*) and Veracity, Love of Justice and Love of Truth stand out clearly as distinct though derivative impulses.

In discussing the question how far a life must be chosen among the springs of action which he enumerates, Martineau seems to hold that higher motives should be substituted for lower as far as possible, thus himself making the highest motive supreme, and the judgment between any particular lower motives merely subsidiary.

And, finally, he admits that computation of pleasurable and painful consequences is already involved in the preference of any given spring of action   .   .   .   .   .   . Pp. 361–374

ON T. H. GREEN'S

PROLEGOMENA TO ETHICS

LECTURE I

GREEN'S METAPHYSICAL BASIS

I MAY conveniently commence the discussion of Green's view by contrasting it with that of Mr. Herbert Spencer, which I propose to consider side by side with it. Spencer and Green represent two lines of thought divergent from my own in opposite directions, but agreeing in that they do not treat Ethics as a subject that can stand alone. Spencer bases it on Science, Green on Metaphysics.

In discussing Spencer we shall be dealing with an attempt to 'establish Ethics on a scientific basis.' Now this, I hold, cannot be done to the extent and in the manner in which Mr. Spencer tries to do it. 'Science' relates to what is, has been and will be, Ethics to what ought to be : therefore the fundamental principles of the latter must be independent of the former, however important and even indispensable Science—especially Biology and Sociology—may be in the working out of the system of rules And Science—in particular Psychology and Sociology—may trace the origin of moral sentiments and ideas, but it cannot itself supply a criterion of the validity of moral principles, or authority of moral sentiments.

B

In fact, we see in chap. iv. of Mr. Spencer's *Data of Ethics*, that his real ethical end,—Happiness,—is not determined by any appeal to positive science, but dialectically by consideration of the common moral judgments of mankind; and the question, fundamentally important for the individual : *Whose* happiness, if mine and others' lead to divergent courses? receives no satisfactory discussion from him at all.

In Green, on the other hand, we have an attempt to establish Ethics on a basis which is avowedly not scientific but Transcendental. His whole argument depends on an 'antithesis between the natural and the moral'; on the demonstration that there is a 'subject-matter of inquiry which does not consist of matters of fact, ascertainable by experiment and observation,' in which subject-matter a place is assigned to morals. I agree in this—except that I should not say 'antithesis'—but I agree as to knowledge of what ought to be being irreducible to knowledge of what is, has been and will be, and I agree in regarding it as fundamentally important to establish the right relation between the two. But I cannot agree in Green's view of that relation.

His central doctrine is that there is an 'originative function of the reason,' a 'determining agent in the inner life of man,' of which no 'natural history can be given.' Here my view would be that 'a natural history' of the development of the Practical Reason, so far as it is exhibited in the morality of different ages and countries, is just what can be

given ; what physical science cannot now give —
and what there is no reason for supposing that it
ever will give—is a complete explanation of this
development.

But Green is not concerned with the Practical
Reason alone. His Ethical view is based upon a
metaphysical view. Or—to use the Kantian terms,
as Green is a Kantian—his Metaphysic of Ethics is
connected with his Metaphysics proper. The question
which in Book I. he is trying to answer is, ' Whether
the experience of connected matters of fact, which in
its methodical expression we call science, does not
presuppose a principle which is not itself any one or
number of such matters of fact, or their result '
(*Prolegomena to Ethics*, § 8, p. 11). In short, in
order to exclude a naturalistic explanation of the
Practical or Moral Reason, he begins by trying to
show that the cognitive faculty or intellect in its
scientific exercise is not a part of the Nature that it
knows.

Now I quite agree that no attempt to give a
physical explanation of Cognition, or even to analyse
it completely into more elementary psychical facts,
has succeeded : or in my opinion is likely to succeed.
I am not, however, able to follow Green in the
connexion which he tries to establish between Ethics
and Metaphysics. I shall presently try to show that
— even granting the soundness of Green's Metaphysical reasoning — it cannot really give to his
Ethical view the support that he hopes to obtain
from it.

4 ON GREEN'S ETHICS

But the intimate connexion of Green's Ethics with his Metaphysics—in his own view—renders it necessary to deal briefly with the latter, which is given in Book I. of the *Prolegomena to Ethics*. In the *Introduction*, in which his point of departure is indicated, there is also a criticism of 'Naturalistic' Ethics, on which it may be worth while to dwell for a moment as giving an opportunity of showing clearly the relation between Spencer and Green. For Naturalistic Ethics, as viewed by Green, is something like Spencerian Ethics—a species of the same genus; though Green's account of its 'explanation' of morality is less elaborate and ingenious than Spencer's own.

If a man 'has persuaded himself that the human consciousness, as it is, can be physically accounted for,' he will not, says Green, 'find any further difficulty in thus explaining that language of moral injunction which forms so large an element in its expression. He will probably trace this language to the joint action of two factors—to the habit of submission to the commands of a physical or political superior, surviving the commands themselves and the memory of them, combined with that constant though ineffectual wish for a condition of life other than his own, which is natural to a being who looks before and after over perpetual alternations of pleasure and pain' (§ 7, p. 10).[1]

This explanation has two parts—one of which we

---

[1] Unless otherwise stated, references in the text are to Green's *Prolegomena to Ethics*.

may call the ideal of Duty or Virtue, the other the ideal of Self-interest. Let us confine ourselves to the former, as that with which the moralist is primarily concerned, and for Green's brief phrases substitute Spencer, as our representative of Naturalistic Ethics.[1]

According to Spencer the notion of 'ought' or 'moral obligation' represents the collision of a later evolved or more representative 'higher' feeling, with a lower, earlier or less representative, feeling. So far as the sense of obligation is truly moral, what the more representative feeling represents is the natural and necessary pain or loss of pleasure—to himself or to other sentient beings—resulting from action; but in the sense of obligation which at present exists in man the coercive element as distinct from the authoritative element is due to the survival of associations with the moral sentiment of fear of evil, or annoyance, to the agent from political, religious or social sources (chief, ghost promoted to god, his fellows who disapprove).

Can we, then, apply to Spencer Green's remark when (§ 8, p. 10) he says—

'The discovery, however, that our assertions of moral obligation are merely the expression of an ineffectual wish to be better off than we are, or are due to the survival of habits originally enforced by physical fear, but of which the origin is forgotten, is of a kind to give us pause. It logically carries with

---

[1] Cf. chap. vii. of Spencer's *Data of Ethics* (Part I. of *Principles of Ethics*).

it the conclusion, however the conclusion may be disguised, that, in inciting ourselves or others to do anything because it ought to be done, we are at best making use of a serviceable illusion.'

Does this explanation of Spencer explain away moral obligation so that, as Browning's Blougram suggests, 'law so analysed' does not 'coerce you much'? I think it does, as regards the Ultimate End, so far as this is General Happiness unreconciled with Private Happiness. But a distinction is required. To say that a man 'ought' to sacrifice his own happiness to the happiness of others seems to me—as to Green—unmeaning on Spencer's view. So far as a man's motive for sacrifice is truly moral according to Spencer, it can only mean that he will suffer certain sympathetic pains if he does not sacrifice himself; but by hypothesis less than if he does, as he is supposed to make a sacrifice on the whole. And if a man judges that he 'ought' to do anything not on the whole conducive to his own happiness, through a survival of association with the fears of chief, ghost, etc., he is—as Green says—under the sway of illusion, according to Spencer's own view—at any rate he is under the sway of feelings that have no correspondence with any present reality. For the danger of legal penalty he is accustomed to separate and estimate by itself; and as for religious fear—that belongs in Spencer's view to decaying 'supernatural Ethics.'

The case is otherwise if we suppose the Happiness of Self and of Others to be reconciled through sym-

pathy, or so far as we suppose this; in this case the
'ought' merely expresses the effect on the agent's will
of sympathetic apprehension of pain to others.   This
is no illusion, but a fact of his developed nature;
and if through sympathy he—in moments of reflection and deliberation—desires and prefers the
general happiness, this sense of obligation may be
consistently regarded by him as authoritative—just
as the sentiments representative of remote pain
to one's self, when they restrain the appetites. 'I
ought to be just,' will mean to the Spencerian
philosopher 'I foresee and feel sympathetic aversion
to the diffused social evil caused by injustice'; just
as 'I ought not to drink port after dinner' will often
mean 'I foresee and feel an egoistic aversion to the
organic pains of gout.'

It may be said that in either case the motive that
presents itself as authoritative—regard for the general
happiness in the one case, regard for private happiness in the other—may be held to be authoritative
because it springs from a deeper, more permanent,
more comprehensive sentiment than the impulse
opposed to it.   But I agree with Green in regarding this as an inadequate basis for morality for ordinary
men.   It cannot deal effectively with the empirical
conflict between private and general happiness: it
cannot satisfactorily (*i.e.* completely) answer the
question: Why should I try to be more sympathetic
than nature has made me?

How does Green, then, supply the deficiency which
he finds in 'naturalistic' ethics?   In order to answer

this question we must, as I have said, introduce his metaphysical views to some extent, but, as I shall try to show, it is not necessary to introduce them to more than a very limited extent: because even if we grant his metaphysical conclusions, they really carry us but a very little way towards his ethical view.

Green's doctrine as to the basis of morality, in the most comprehensive account which he gives of it, is stated to be a *Theory of the Good as Human Perfection* (§ 352). The Perfection which is thus taken to be the ultimate end of rational conduct is otherwise described as the 'realisation,' 'development,' or 'completion' of human 'faculties' or 'capabilities.' If we ask further to what part of man's apparently composite nature these 'faculties' or 'capabilities' belong, we are told that they are 'capabilities of the spirit which is in man' to which, again, a 'divine' or 'heaven-born' nature is attributed. The realisation of these capabilities is, in fact, a 'self-realisation of the divine principle in man'; that is, of the 'one divine mind' which 'gradually reproduces itself in the human soul.' 'God,' we are elsewhere told, 'is a Being with whom the human spirit is identical, in the sense that He *is* all which the human spirit is capable of becoming' (§ 187, p. 198). Hence the conception of the Divine Spirit presents to the man who is morally aspiring an 'ideal of personal holiness' with which he contrasts his own personal unworthiness.

Now this view is, I conceive, in harmony with the prevalent religious sentiment of the present age. It would not, probably, be accepted by all orthodox theologians : some would find the conception of God here suggested too anthropomorphic : but the prevalent view, I conceive, would regard it as a legitimate inference from the statements of Scripture : while others would hold that it is knowable by direct intuition. In what I am about to say I wish it to be clear that I am not concerned with this theological doctrine regarded as attained in either of these ways, or obtained in the Kantian way by starting with the Practical Reason and postulating God and Immortality : or by recurrence to the 'physico-theological argument from design.' I am not concerned with any of them, for none of them is Green's way. According to Green this conclusion is attainable by philosophical reasoning on ordinary knowledge and facts of ordinary experience. We have to ask, therefore, how this relation of man to God is philosophically known, and what definite and reasoned content can be given to this notion of a Divine Spirit. It would appear from the order of Green's treatise, and the proportions of its parts, that an answer to these questions was intended to be given in Book I. on the *Metaphysics of Knowledge*. Here we are certainly introduced to a 'spiritual principle in nature' corresponding to the spiritual principle implied in all human knowledge or experience. It is argued (§§ 27, 28) that to constitute the 'all-inclusive system of relations,' 'single and unalterable,' which we find in nature, properly understood, something beyond nature is

needed : ' something which renders all relations
possible,' and supplies the ' unity of the manifold '
which is involved in the existence of these relations. ' A plurality of things cannot of themselves
unite in one relation, nor can a single thing of itself
bring itself into a multitude of relations . . . there
must therefore be something other than the manifold
things themselves which combines them.'   Such a
' combining agency ' in each one's experience is his
own intelligence, his intelligent self, which unites the
objects of his experience while distinguishing itself
from them.   Hence if we suppose nature to be real
' otherwise than merely as for us,' we must ' recognise
as the condition of this reality the action of some
unifying principle analogous to that of our understanding ' (§ 29).   Indeed, Green passes from the
affirmation of *analogous action* to the affirmation of
identical quality, and says that nature in its reality
implies not only an all-uniting agency which is not
natural, but a thinking self-distinguishing consciousness like our own.

I do not precisely understand where the cogency of
this transition comes in : I should have thought that—
so far as Green's argument goes—we might suppose
that the unifying principle in the world was possibly
not self-conscious ; but I do not propose to dwell on
this point.   His conclusion seems at any rate clear,
that the world is inconceivable without a self-distinguishing thinker.   We further find that this principle
of synthesis or unity is ' eternal,' in the sense that it
is not in time, and ' complete,' in the sense that its

combining agency extends to all conceivable objects;
and that our own empirical knowledge can only be explained as an imperfect reproduction or limitation in us
of this eternally complete consciousness.   What becomes of the unity of the individual's consciousness
when it is thus split up between an eternally complete
consciousness out of time, and a function of an animal
organism which this eternal mind, limiting itself
somehow, makes its vehicle, I do not now ask.   Let
us assume that its indivisible reality is maintained.
Here I only wish to point out that the above meagre
statement gives substantially all the characteristics
which Green explicitly attributes to the 'spiritual
principle' disclosed to us in Book I.—and all, I
submit, that can possibly be known about it by the
lines of reasoning there developed.   And I am confirmed in this view by the passage in Book III. chap.
ii. (§ 180, p. 189), in which the 'conclusions so far
arrived at' are summarised ; since there also the 'one
divine mind' which 'gradually reproduces itself in
the human soul' is not represented with any other
'constant characteristics' beyond those of being a
unifying, self-distinguishing, self-objectifying consciousness.   'If,' says the author expressly, 'we
mean by personality anything else than the quality
in a subject of being consciously an object to itself,
we are not justified in saying that it necessarily
belongs to God' (§ 182, p. 191).   Supposing, then,
that the argument in Book I. is completely cogent,
it still remains for Green to explain the bearing of
it on the problems of Ethics : to explain how we

are to get an 'ideal of holiness,' of an 'infinitely
and perfectly good will,' out of this conception of a
combining, self-distinguishing, and self-objectifying
agency : to explain what perfection the human spirit
can aim at, so far as it is merely conceived as the
reproduction of such an agency, except the increase
of knowledge, extensively or intensively—the presence
to the combining intelligence of a more extensive
manifold of combined objects, or the presence of
them as more effectively combined. As we shall
find, nothing can be more unlike this conception
than Green's moral ideal ; in which, indeed, as I
shall hereafter argue, knowledge rather occupies a too
subordinate place ; but, assuming his metaphysical
arguments valid, and his ethical view sound, there
seems to me a great logical gap to be filled up in
passing from the one to the other.

It may be said perhaps that though the Divine
Mind cannot be *known* to us as more than a combining intelligence, the source of the systematic unity of
nature, we may and ought to *believe* it to be more ;
and that Green must be supposed to mean this when
he describes the 'attitude of man towards an infinite
spirit' as 'not the attitude of knowledge' but only of
'awe and aspiration' (§ 302). But the reason he
gives for excluding the attitude of knowledge is a
reason which, so far as it is valid at all, applies
precisely to that conception of the spiritual principle
which is given in Book I. : 'Knowledge,' he says, ' is
of matters of fact or relations, and the infinite spirit
is neither fact nor relation.' Now since the net

result of the *Metaphysics of Knowledge* is at any rate to establish the necessary existence of an eternally complete thinking consciousness which is 'neither fact nor relation,' but yet 'needed to constitute' facts and relations, it seems to me merely an eccentric subtlety of metaphysical terminology to say that we have no 'knowledge' of such an eternal mind : as we have at any rate, if we have followed assentingly a hundred pages of close argument, a reasoned conviction with regard to it. However this may be—whether this conviction be knowledge or not—I cannot perceive that Green ever seems aware of the barrenness of this conviction for his ethical purposes; and he certainly nowhere offers us a suggestion of any other reasoning by which his philosophical conception of the Divine Mind might be turned into one capable of furnishing us with an adequate ethical ideal. I, at least, can find no grounds in the argument of Book I. for attributing to Green's spiritual principle any such characteristic as the term 'holiness' expresses : I cannot even find adequate reasons for attributing to it anything analogous to Will. It is merely, so far as I understand, an eternal intellect out of time, to which all time and its contents are eternally and (we may say) indifferently present : being equally implied in the conception of *any* succession, it is not shown to carry with it the conception of progress towards an end in the series of motions or changes of which the process of the world in time consists. The series might be altogether purposeless—a meaningless round of change—and still the 'unification' which appears to be the sole function of Green's eternal mind would be none the less completely performed.   And even if we grant that such a progress is implied in the development of the eternal consciousness in *us*, it is, as I have already said, still a purely intellectual progress, a growth of that which knows in knowledge alone.   At least I do not see how Green's metaphysical argument bestows on it any other characteristic.   With this remark I leave the Metaphysics of Book I. for future consideration, observing however that a similar discrepancy between the conclusion which Green seems desirous of maintaining and the conclusion for which he really supplies grounds, appears to me discoverable in his chapter on *Freedom of the Will*, which forms a transition from the purely Metaphysical to the properly Ethical part of his treatise.

LECTURE II

I HAVE dwelt on the gap between Green's metaphysical basis and his ethical structure, partly because
herein lies the justification for separating the two as
they are separated in our study: partly because the
tendency which I find in Green to overrate the
Ethical importance of his metaphysical spiritualism—
if I may use the word—appears strikingly in his
discussion of Freedom. In criticising this I shall
confine myself to the meaning which the term appears
to have in the *Prolegomena*.

I refer to this point because Green is—avowedly
—a disciple of Kant; and in Kant there is a confusion, to which I have elsewhere[1] drawn attention,
between what I have called (1) 'neutral' freedom,
realised equally in good and bad choice, on which
moral imputation is commonly held to depend; (2)
'rational' freedom, realised in choice determined by
reason, good or virtuous volition.

Now whatever else may be said of Green's Free-

---

[1] *Methods of Ethics*, Book I. chap. v. § 1, and Appendix on the Kantian
Conception of Free Will (6th ed. referred to, unless otherwise stated).

dom, at any rate it may be said that it is equall realised in virtuous and vicious action, since both the virtuous and the vicious man are equally unlike a mere animal in having a self-distinguishing consciousness, which is the essential point of Green's Freedom. It seems to me therefore different from the kind of Freedom which is only realised when the Will is in accordance with Reason.

But in an *Essay on Freedom* (*Works*, ii. p. 308) Green uses the term in this other (Kantian) sense, saying that the 'determination of the Will by reason constitutes moral freedom or autonomy.' Comparing the footnote to § 99 of the *Prolegomena*, however, I think we may infer—with the editor—that Green in the *Prolegomena* deliberately determined to omit any reference to Freedom in this other sense—*rational freedom* as I have called it. It appears to me reasonable to suppose that he thought it well to avoid the confusion which the double use of the term would be likely to cause.

I regard Green's view — in spite of the eager advocacy of 'Freedom' in a sense—as being, for all practical purposes, pure Determinism. 'Freedom of Will' in Book II. corresponds so far to 'Freedom of Intelligence' in Book I. that Freedom only means the non-naturalness of a self-distinguishing consciousness, —only means that the motive in a human volition is what it is through the operation of a self-distinguishing consciousness, which, as he has already told us, is not a part of nature. It is in this sense and this alone that man's will is said to be 'free' in the *Prolegomena*.

I submit that this kind of 'freedom' is not sufficient really to justify moral imputation : because if we ask why the particular self-distinguishing consciousness called John makes a virtuous choice, and the particular self-distinguishing consciousness called Thomas makes a vicious choice, the explanation, according to Green, must be entirely sought in the particularity of the chain of natural causation in each case. I wish to make this quite clear : because my complaint against the school to which Green belongs is that, on this fundamentally important question of Freedom they tend to confuse the reader's mind by trying 'to run with the hare and hunt with the hounds,' and to get the moral satisfaction of a Libertarian view, together with the scientific satisfaction of a Determinist view.

Let us see how this peculiar view of Freedom is arrived at by Green. We find that he states the question as follows in § 87, p. 93 :—

Now, *prima facie*, as will be admitted on all hands, this causality of motives effectually distinguishes the world which moral action has brought, and continues to bring, into being, from the series of natural events. In the latter the occurrence of an event does not depend on an idea of the event, as a desired object, being previously presented. If then moral action is to be brought within the series of natural phenomena, it must be on the supposition that the motives which determine it, having natural antecedents, are themselves but links in the chain of natural phenomena; and that thus moral action, though distinguished from other kinds of natural events by its dependence on prior ideas, is not denaturalised, since the ideas on which it depends are themselves of natural origin.

The question whether this is so is the point really at issue in regard to the possibility and indispensableness of a Moral Philosophy which shall not be a branch of natural science; or, if

we like to put it so, in regard to the freedom of moral agents.   It is
not the question commonly debated, with much ambiguity of terms,
between ' determinists' and 'indeterminists'; not the question
whether there is, or is not, a possibility of unmotived willing ;
but the question whether motives, of that kind by which it is
the characteristic of moral or human action to be determined,
are of properly natural origin or can be rightly regarded as
natural phenomena.

This statement shows clearly a Determinist bias :
since it is not the ' possibility of unmotived willing '
which is the Libertarian's conception, but power of
acting in accordance with the higher motive given by
Reason or Moral Judgment, instead of in accordance
with a non-rational motive.—However, Green's point
is that a merely animal want is *not* a motive to human
action, this being the action of a self-conscious being.
It only becomes a motive, so far as upon the want
there supervenes the presentation of the want by
a self-conscious subject to himself, and with it the
idea of a self-satisfaction to be attained in the filling
of the want.   ' To every action,' he says, ' morally
imputable, or of which a man can recognise himself
as the author, the motive is always some idea of the
man's personal good — an idea absolutely different
from animal want, even in cases where it is from
anticipation of the satisfaction of some animal want
that the idea of personal good is derived ' (§ 95,
p. 98).

Here we get—what by the way we did not get in
the case of the ' indivisible self' in Book I.—a definite
tertium quid produced by the action of a self-
conscious subject on the processes of the animal
organism with which it is mysteriously united,—an

'idea of personal good' or 'self-satisfaction.' The
motive of an action morally imputable 'is constituted by an act of self-consciousness which is not a
natural event; an act in which the agent presents
to himself a certain idea of himself doing or enjoying
—as an idea of which the realisation forms for the
time his good . . . the moral quality of this act . . .
depends on the character of the agent . . . this has had
. . . a history. . . . But,' Green says, it has been 'a
history in which an eternal self-distinguishing consciousness . . . has throughout been operative upon
wants of animal origin' (§ 95, p. 99). For instance,
Esau's act is morally imputable, since it is determined
by 'his own conception of himself as finding for the
time his greatest good in the satisfaction of hunger'
(§ 96, p. 100). Man is 'free or self-determined in
his motive' because of this presence of self-consciousness. The self 'is so far a . . . reproduction of the
one supreme subject . . . that the product carries
with it . . . the characteristic of being an object to
itself' (p. 102). That is, Green admits that 'the
kind of good which at any point in his life a person
presents to himself as greatest depends . . . on his
past experience—his past passion and action, and on
circumstances,' but he thinks it maintains the human
agent's freedom to say that 'throughout the past experience he has been an object to himself,' and the
circumstances presuppose self-consciousness similarly
(§ 99, p. 102).[1]

It seems to me, then, that determinism wins on the

---

[1] Cf. *Prolegomena*, §§ 101, 102, p. 105.

substantial issue ; for if we ask why a particular self
is determined to present to itself a given idea rather
than any other, as its greatest good, we cannot find
the answer in the universal element of the self which
is common to all particular selves—saints and sinners
alike—we must therefore find it in the particular element.   How far Green sees this, I never quite know.
He seems so satisfied with having proved that the
desires of any human being are not merely animal
wants, and that, therefore, any man is ' free ' or
' self-determined ' in the motive from which, as a
self-conscious human agent, he acts, that he hardly
seems to see that his account of the making of the
human motive under this double operation — presentation of animal wants, and self-distinction of the
self-conscious subject from them—removes responsibility altogether from the individual, and makes
imputation illusory.

   That the motive ' lies in the man himself, that he
makes it '—*i.e.* that it is what it is in consequence of
the activity of a self-conscious intelligence—' and is
aware of doing so ' (§ 102, p. 106), does not really
make any difference, if that in his character which
causes him to make his motive good or bad is due to
its past history : and this would seem to be the case on
Green's view, as there is nothing in the mere presence
of self-consciousness—in the ' reproduction of itself
on the part of the eternal self - conscious subject
of the world '—the ' self-distinguishing and self-
seeking subject ' (§ 106),—to determine its goodness
or badness.

As I have observed, the view attributed to the
'champions of free will' in § 103, pp. 106, 107, does
not appear to me one that there is the least occasion
for them to hold.   There is not the least reason for
Libertarians to affirm that choice is without motive :[1]
only that the 'identification of the man's self with
a particular desire or aversion,' which on Green's
view is 'the act of will,' cannot be regarded as
determined by motives.   Now, according to Green it
would seem to be so determined : the desire of self-
satisfaction to be gained in a particular way is, he
holds, the volition (§ 104, p. 108) : and this seems
clearly not 'free' in any important sense : since it is
determined by the agent's 'character'—i.e. by his
'habitual' or 'steady' direction of himself, by a con-
centration of his faculties towards the fulfilment of
certain purposes; and the particularity of his character must be attributed, as we have seen, to its past
history.   (This view is not affected by what is said
in §§ 110, 111.)

Nor do I understand how Green considers it
important to assert (§ 108) that 'an action which
expresses character has no *must* in the physical sense
about it,' if it be admitted that this action is 'as
necessarily related to character and circumstances
as any event to the sum of its conditions' (§ 109),
if 'what a man now is and does is the result . . . of
what he has been and done' (§ 110), if whether

[1] Cf. *Prolegomena*, §110, 'arbitrary freak of some unaccountable power
of unmotived willing,'—a bizarre description of the power of acting in
accordance with reason in spite of any previous concessions to passion.—Cf.
also Reid, *Works*, Hamilton's edition (1863), ii. 607.

or no in any case the wish to be better shall prevail depends upon 'the social influences brought to bear upon the man' (§ 110, p. 114).[1]

It thus seems to me that Green's use of the terms 'freedom' (cf. 'free effort to better himself,' § 112) and 'self - determination' is misleading : since any particular man's effort to better himself, as its force depends at any moment on his particular past, is not 'free' or 'self-determined' in the only important sense.

I pass to discuss some peculiarities of Green's view of the relations of Desire, Intellect, and Volition, with which—so far as the question is more than merely verbal—I am unable to agree, but which it will be instructive to examine carefully, in order, as far as possible, to make clear the exact points of difference. Taking first Desire and Reason, we find him saying (in § 116) of the opposition between Desire, Reason, and Will, that it has sometimes ' been represented as lying rather between different desires, of which reason however (according to the supposition) supplies the object to the one, while some irrational appetite is the source of the other ; the will being the arbiter which determines the action according to the rational or irrational desire.' He thus states my view, as in opposition to his own ; but I do not see that my view is opposed to the statement in § 117, where he says we shall find reason to hold that

---

[1] Of course this 'dependence of an individual's present on his past' is not incompatible with his 'seeking or being able to become better than he is' (*Prolegomena*, § 110)—as Mill long ago pointed out.

there is one subject or spirit, which desires in all a man's experiences of desire, understands in all operations of his intelligence, wills in all his acts of willing; and that the essential character of his desires depends on their all being desires of one and the same subject which also understands, the essential character of his intelligence on its being an activity of one and the same subject which also desires, the essential character of his acts of will on their proceeding from one and the same subject which also desires and understands.

The conscious unity of the self appears to me to co-exist with a consciousness of conflict of desires, and of conflict of non-rational impulses with rational judgment. But (§ 129) Green says that when we speak of Desire conflicting with Reason, *Desire* 'is a logical abstraction which we are mistaking for reality.' Here there seems to me to be a misapprehension. What he is concerned to maintain is that Desire is in our experience inseparable from self-consciousness and from the operation of intellect. But this no one denies. In speaking of 'irrational Desire' as 'conflicting with Reason,' I do not mean a desire divorced from thought, but a desire directed to an action which we at the same time judge to be bad or incompatible with our highest good : *e.g.* desire of the pain of another human being, in the case of malevolent impulse—of escape from a post of duty and danger, in the case of a cowardly impulse: 'Revenge' or 'Fear' in such cases may obviously be in a sense rational, *i.e.* accompanied with much activity of thought, though the object of either impulse may be at the same time judged to be bad.

Now I ask myself why Green fails to recognise this obvious truth. As we shall see, it would not be true to say that he fails altogether : but it is obscured for him partly by the misapprehension above mentioned, partly by the fact that he (1) is inclined to refuse the term 'desire' to any 'solicitation' as he calls it, except one with which a man identifies himself, while (2) desires with which a man identifies himself he conceives as a desire for personal good. Compare the following passages in chapter ii. of Book II. :—

> It is clear that the important real distinction is between the direction of the self-conscious self to the realisation of an object, its identification of itself with that object, on the one side . . . and, on the other side, the mere solicitations of which a man is conscious, but with none of which he so identifies himself as to make the soliciting object his object—the object of his self-seeking—or to direct himself to its realisation (§ 143).
>
> In the act of will the man does not cease to desire. Rather he, the man, for the first time desires, having not done so while divided between the conflicting influences (§ 146).[1]

Green would, in the cases above suggested, say : Either you do not yield to the impulse of revenge or fear—then it is merely a *solicitation;* or you do —then you identify yourself with the impulse and —mistakenly no doubt—regard the object as your personal good. In fact Green ignores wilful choice of evil. This is involved in his account of motive given in the previous chapter; compare §§ 91, 92, and (most explicitly) § 99, where he says that 'It is the particular human self . . . that in every moral action, virtuous or vicious, presents to itself some

---

[1] § 152, however, is more doubtful :—"The true distinction lies between passions as influences affecting a man—among which we may include 'mere desires' if we please—and the man as desiring, or putting himself forth in desire for the realisation of some object present to him in idea, which is the same thing as willing."

possible state or achievement of its own as for the time its greatest good, and acts for the sake of that good.'

In a passage in chapter i. of Book III., indeed, Green does seem to recognise wilful choice of evil. There is, he says, 'essentially or in principle an identity between reason and will; and widely as they become divergent in the actual history of men (in the sense that the objects where good is actually sought are often not those where reason, even as in the person seeking them, pronounces that it is to be found), still the true development of man, the only development in which the capabilities of his 'heaven-born' nature can be actualised, lies in the direction of union between the developed will and the developed reason' (§ 177, p. 185 [1]). On the whole, however, he is so far under the influence of ancient Greek and especially Aristotelian modes of thought as to ignore usually, and expressly exclude sometimes, that wilful choice of wrong known to be wrong which is so essential an element in the modern Christian moral consciousness of ' sin.'

As to Desire and Will, the truth is, the question Green is discussing from § 138 onwards appears to me partly a verbal one. Green does not deny what I call 'conflict of desires' (only he prefers to call them 'solicitations'), nor, I suppose, the opposition of such solicitations to a moral judgment or resolution —and I agree that the desire which is 'a motive in

---

[1] Cf. the Author's *Unreasonable Action* (published in *Mind*, for 1893, N.S. vol. ii. No. 6, and reprinted in the volume entitled *Practical Ethics*).

an imputable human action' is a desire which *prevails* and causes volition.   But there seems to me no doubt that I can recognise a distinction in kind between (*a*) the psychical fact of desire as an impulse to which I do not necessarily yield (compare §§ 143, 144), and (*b*) the psychical fact of volition, resolution, determination, making up one's mind to aim at something (compare § 140), and the distinction does not lie in the definiteness of the object.   Green calls (*b*) 'identification of self with (1) object to be realised,' or (2) with impulse.   I do not recognise the correctness of this description — at least with regard to (1).   And it seems to me more convenient and more in accordance with usage to restrict 'desire' to (*a*).   Hence to say (*e.g.*) that '*every* desire implies an *effort* on the part of the desiring subject' seems to me misleading—when a desire is checked the 'effort' is the other way.   This does not imply (compare § 142) that when we have resolved or willed to aim at an object, desire *ceases* and gives place to volition; to say that the 'final preference is not desire' is not to say that it excludes desire; rather, in my view, desire as distinct from volition is stronger after the preference than before. Green's argument to show that 'the principle of action is a will which is not desire' seems to me therefore to be vitiated by a false opposition of alternatives.

But there is a psychological question whether the initiation of action takes place under the influence of desire without the psychical fact of resolve : certainly I think that in some cases this latter is at any rate

evanescent, and that in such cases—in opposition to
Green's view (§ 147)—actions are *less* imputed.   It
certainly seems to be the common-sense view that
in bad actions which have not been preceded by
deliberation there is *less* guilt.   This is my first
more than verbal disagreement with Green as to
Desire and Will.   The second is, that in my view
what is personally, or deliberately, chosen, is to be distinguished from what is chosen as 'right,' 'good' or
'reasonable'—the latter terms being used as equivalent (compare § 146).   I hold, as before said,
that in 'wilful sin' I have chosen evil known as
such ; on the other hand, in deliberate self-sacrifice
I have preferred the 'good' of others to mine—not
consciously identified it with mine.

The view that in the case of what I call will—and
what Green calls desire and the identification of self
with impulse or object—I 'take the object for my
good,' is connected with the account of the 'recognised opposition between Will and Intellect' in § 148,
which is briefly given as follows in the editor's analytical summary, p. xviii. :—' In spite of the involution
of intellect and desire or will (§ 134 foll.) there is a
clear distinction between the speculative and practical
employments of the mind ; and therefore, if the former
be called thought and the latter will, these may be distinguished and even opposed.'   On this I should say,
first, that speculative activity is a department of practice or conduct ;—*e.g.* the discovery of a sought relation between existing things (§ 149) is an 'imagined
object' which the researcher desires to bring into real

existence—and as such exhibits the phenomena of
desire and volition of which we have previously been
speaking. No doubt the desires and volitions in this
case may have no relation to a 'moral ideal,' but this
may be true of the desires and volitions of the most
purely practical man, in business or pleasure. I think
that Green has not sufficiently thought out the relation of 'moral action' spoken of in §§ 150, 151, to
'action for realisation of a moral ideal' (§ 148). He
can hardly mean that the mere adoption of an end
of action as one's good (even if non-hedonistic)—*e.g.*
getting into Parliament or becoming a millionaire—
is always equivalent to the adoption of a moral ideal,
or always involves desire for realisation of a moral
ideal.

Secondly, as regards 'practical thought,' certainly I
do not hold that thought and desire are separate
elements that together make up will (§ 152, p. 157);
but in one sense I hold that willing is more than
thinking, since it involves thought, but the thought
may occur without it. Taking Green's own statement that willing is 'the direction of a self-conscious subject to the realisation of an idea' (§ 151,
p. 157), I should say that it involved the mere presence of the idea and something more. Green would
say: Yes, the thought of its realisation as the agent's
good. No, I reply; something more still—Compare
Ovid's *Video meliora proboque, deteriora sequor.*

In Green's treatment Desire, Intellect, and Will,
doubtless difficult to separate in expression, are too
much fused in *conception.*

LECTURE III

GREEN'S VIEW OF MORAL (INCLUDING IMMORAL) ACTION

In the last Lecture I was examining Green's view of the relations of Desire, Reason, and Will, and trying to make clear the points of agreement and disagreement between his view and mine.

Green seems to me to be in the main arguing against a view of the division of the Ego into separate and separately operating faculties, which I certainly do not hold; nor did I ever know anybody who did hold it, though some thinkers may have expressed themselves unguardedly. For example, in speaking of Desire as conflicting with Reason or Judgment I do not mean that the conflicting or irrational desire operates divorced from thought or intellect, but merely that I am conscious of—call them 'solicitations' if you like—impelling me to seek intermediate ends perhaps, or ends which I judge to be bad, or to do actions which I judge to be wrong.

So again, as regards Desire and Will. When I distinguish the state of desiring an object and choosing to aim at it, I do not mean—as Green seems to think—that desire ceases when volition

29

begins. To say that the final preference is not desire is not—as Green seems to think—to say that it excludes desire; rather, in my experience the desire is usually intensified by that act of voluntary choice which Green calls identification of myself with the desire.

On the other hand, to say that every desire implies effort on the part of the desiring subject seems to me to mix up things so diverse as *feeling an impulse to do a thing* and *trying to do it.*

A more important disagreement relates to the relation of Reason and Will (compare § 99). It seems to me fundamentally important to distinguish between *choice* (even deliberate choice) and *judgment as to choice-worthiness*, since they may diverge. I hold, as before said, that what a man chooses is not always chosen as his good, since (*a*) in wilful sin he chooses what he judges bad on the whole, and (*b*) in conscious self-sacrifice he prefers the good of others to his own. Green's view as to self-sacrifice I will consider later.

For convenience, I will here give briefly my distinctions between the different kinds of human action, apart from the consideration of what particular ends are in question.

I distinguish actions which are done :—

(1) Unconsciously.

(2) Instinctively—that is, without an antecedent idea of the result to be obtained by the action—actions that are without even rudimentary 'intention.'

(3) With intention but without clear self-consciousness (in which self-consciousness is
   evanescent)—therefore without reference to
   self as cause.

(4) With *personal* choice, implicit consciousness
   that one could have determined otherwise,
   but without *rational* choice—*i.e.* not *as good.*
   (Observe the necessity of distinguishing
   rational from *personal*, and even from
   deliberate, choice.)

(5) Against rational judgment, moral or prudential.
   We may have wilful choice of what is known
   to be evil—'wilful sin'—also deliberate
   sacrifice of my own good to another's.

(6) In accordance with rational judgment, moral
   or prudential, which may of course be mistaken.

A further disagreement is, that the idea which ante-
cedes volition is *not* in my view, as it *is* in Green's (§ 95,
p. 99), the idea of one's self doing or enjoying : even if
the idea of one's self doing be granted to be a necessary
antecedent of volition (I do not think it is always
or normally present consciously), it is not this idea
which represents the object desired, sought, or chosen ;
for instance in the case of posthumous fame.

One more point : I do not even think that the
emergence of clear self-consciousness necessarily
involves the conscious adoption of an end. When I
am under the influence of desire, the Ego is sometimes present as a mere spectator, letting desire
operate ; but there is usually a consciousness that it

could check it, except when the transition from
feeling to action is very rapid—when we act, as is
said, 'involuntarily.'

As to the question—of fundamental importance in
ethical psychology—whether the vicious man makes
his vicious choice knowingly, I think Green's identification or fusion of Reason, Desire, and Will seems to
interfere with his raising the question clearly. But
in most passages he seems not to contemplate any
divergence between 'choice' and 'judgment of choice-
worthiness.'

I pass now to examine more particularly how a
character is determined to be virtuous and vicious.
For this we must look more closely at the characteristics of 'moral' action, in Green's wide sense, in
which 'moral' means 'properly human'—*i.e.* the
action of a self-conscious subject. According to
Green, what a self-conscious subject aims at in every
volition is always 'self-satisfaction.' In Book II.
chapter i. first we distinguish 'moral' or 'properly
human' action, from action in which it is animal
wants that are impulses: whereas in properly human
actions it is 'consciousness of wanted objects.'
Then at a further stage we have 'the idea of a satisfaction on the whole' (§ 85, p. 91). It is the first
antithesis which Green for some time is concerned
to press. 'A consciousness of wanted objects . . .
yields . . . the conception of something that *should
be* as distinct from that which *is* . . . [objects] to
which real existence has yet to be given' (§ 86, p. 92).

Further, we find that 'the idea of an object in

which self-satisfaction is to be sought ' is essential to
properly human volition (§§ 88, 89, pp. 93, 94).   Or,
in different phrase, ' the motive in every imputable
act . . . is a desire for personal good . . . the idea
of what the personal good for the time is may be
affected by the pressure of animal want,' but this
want is not ' a component of the desire ' (§ 91, p. 96).
' It is superfluous to add good *to himself* ' (§ 92)—
human choice, according to Green, is necessarily
egoistic in form.   A moral action is an action
determined by a conception of personal good (compare
§ 95).

Observe that what Green calls a moral action in
this sense is not necessarily an action done under the
influence of the Moral Ideal, or the desire for the
True Good.   *Moral* is here and elsewhere used in a
wider sense, including *immoral*—*moral* meaning *acts
of a being capable of virtue and therefore also of
vice.*   So there are two questions :—

(1) Whether the normal motive in moral actions
in this wide sense, including what are ordinarily
conceived as non-moral (possibly immoral) actions—
of human beings as such, is desire of Personal Good
or Self-satisfaction.

(2) Whether the motive in right action is desire
for one's own True Good, or True Self-satisfaction,
and if so what this is.   The latter question we may
conveniently defer for the present.

As regards the first question, we have to ask,
What is the meaning of Self-satisfaction ?   This
involves the question, What is self in its *appetitive*

D

aspect, regarded as a desiring, wanting entity ?   For,
observe, as so viewed, it is no longer merely the
knowing, combining, self-distinguishing, self-objectifying consciousness ¹ which Book I. shows us, and
which, according to Green, an analysis of our empirical knowledge requires us to regard as a reproduction
of a similar universal consciousness.

We can hardly conceive such a consciousness as
having in its own nature—if I may be allowed to use
the word nature with regard to it—any desires or
wants, except a desire or striving for increase of
knowledge, which would render it a fuller reproduction of the eternal consciousness.   But the self we
know is very unlike this.   Green will not, indeed,
allow us to think that it has merely animal wants or
appetites, or even merely desires that are in part
animal wants : but he recognises that it has desires
which ' originate in animal want or susceptibility to
animal pleasure, in the sense that without such want
or susceptibility they would not be ' (§ 125, p. 129).
He affirms that

those desired objects which are of most concern in the moral
life of the civilised and educated man who has outgrown mere
sensuality are not directly dependent on animal susceptibilities
at all.   It is not merely their character as objects which the
man makes his good that they owe to self-consciousness.   The
susceptibilities in which the desires themselves originate, unlike
the susceptibilities to the pain of hunger or pleasure of eating,
do not arise out of the animal system, but out of a state of
things which only self-conscious agents can bring about (§ 126).
    . . . [Thus our loves,] envies, jealousies, and ambitions—
whatever the resemblance between their outward signs and
certain expressions of emotions in animals—are all in their proper
nature distinctively human because all founded on interests
possible only to self-conscious beings.   We cannot separate such

passions from their exciting causes. Take away those occasions of them which arise out of our intercourse as persons with persons, and the passions themselves as we know them disappear (§ 126, p. 131).

It must be admitted that Green leaves obscure how these other desires originate : and he seems to me to treat too lightly their obvious resemblances, so far as we can judge from outward signs and expressions, to the emotions of animals. It is paradoxical to deny that they may be traced ultimately to animal feelings, as modified by the supervention of self-consciousness carrying with it a consciousness of the individuality of other persons. Certainly animals feel love, envy, jealousy; and no reason is suggested why a reproduction of the eternal consciousness should have these emotions, independently of the conditions of the animal organism to which it is subject. Admitting Green's account of the manner in which the self - conscious self reacts upon the desires thus originated, so that they become something different from what they would be in a merely animal soul : admitting that it presents to itself objects of desire, distinct from itself and from each other, and that in seeking the realisation of any particular object it is always seeking its own satisfaction; I should still have inferred that it is only because it has 'supervened upon the appetitive life' of an animal organism that the self-conscious self has such desires for the realisation of objects at all. Grant that they are desires that only a person can have : grant that they depend largely on the distinction between self and other persons—the question

remains : How does a person come to have them ?
And to this question Green seems to exclude the
obvious answer, while giving no other.

However, let us leave this question of origin : let
us take—as Green takes—as an essential characteristic
of moral action, as explained in Book II., the presence
of this self-distinguishing and self-seeking consciousness, identifying itself with different particular desires
—or rather usually with a complex resultant of
several distinguishable desires, none of which are
merely animal, though some of them originate in
animal wants : what, in Green's view, is the self-satisfaction of this self-distinguishing, but multifariously
desiring entity ? It is not quite easy to say, but
I think we may affirm the following two things
of it :—

(1) It is a state of a self-conscious person that
accompanies the consciousness of attainment of a
desired end ;

(2) It is distinguishable from pleasure ;—though
pleasure may accompany it, and we may expect to
find it in pleasure.   (This is the vicious man's mistake.)

The question then is : Should it be identified with
the ' satisfaction or extinction of the desire ' which
occurs when the desired object is attained ?

A man desires, let us suppose, to taste a bottle of fine wine,
to hear a certain piece of music, to see Athens, to do a service
to a friend, to finish a book that he has in hand.   In each case
the desired object, as such, exists only in his consciousness, and
the desire for it involves the consciousness of the difference
between such existence of the desired object and that realisation
of it towards which the desire strives, and which, when attained,

is the satisfaction or extinction of the desire (§ 131, pp. 135, 136).

Green here seems to say that satisfaction of desire is extinction of desire, but self-satisfaction certainly does not mean self-extinction. What then is it? I do not think Green is quite clear on this point. Some passages certainly *suggest*—but they do not positively affirm—that a partial or particular self-satisfaction is always gained in the attainment of a desired object, though not satisfaction on the whole (see § 104, top of p. 108). Other passages seem to imply that though 'self-satisfaction is sought in all enacted desire' (§ 158) it is not necessarily gained when the desired object is attained. We are told that though self-satisfaction is continually sought by moral agents in the realisation of the objects of particular desires, — due to the conditions under which the self-conscious subject exists in the human organism,—it cannot be really found there. 'The conditions of the animal soul, . . . no sooner sated than wanting, are such that the self - determining subject cannot be conscious of them as conditions to which it is subject . . . without seeking some satisfaction of itself that shall be independent of these conditions' (§ 175). Accordingly, though Good is defined as 'that which satisfies some desire' (§ 171), Moral good or the True good is defined as 'an end in which the effort of a moral agent may really find rest' (§ 171)—or, as Green elsewhere expresses it, 'an abiding satisfaction of an abiding self' (§ 234).

If we might distinguish (*a*) partial, (*b*) complete

self - satisfaction, we might perhaps express Green's view by saying that in any 'enacted desire' (*a*) is gained but (*b*) not. If so, in the passages in which Green says that 'self-satisfaction is not to be found' in vicious self - seeking, he must be understood to mean complete and permanent, not partial and transitory, self-satisfaction.

It is clearly characteristic of wrong or vicious choice in Green's view, that 'permanent' or 'abiding' self-satisfaction—'rest'—is not gained; whether any self-satisfaction is transiently gained is not so clear. If this is so, then in moral action, whether virtuous or vicious we may say that according to Green what is sought is complete self-satisfaction, and we may take as the characteristic of wrong action, that the vicious man seeks the self-satisfaction where it cannot be found, in the gratification of sensual appetites, etc.

But now, why does he? As we saw, Green makes it quite clear that it is 'because he is now so made,' though he seems to think that it maintains Freedom to insist on the fact that his self-consciousness has been present in the process of making himself so. But does his previous history make him do it? And does he do it against knowledge?—To the latter question, as I before said, Green seems to give in-consistent answers. But it is very important to know whether the vicious, no less than the virtuous, man seeks self - satisfaction where he *thinks* it will be found. Is it from an intellectual error that he goes wrong? As I have said, passages may be quoted on

both sides. Though Green says that every moral
agent, the voluptuary no less than the saint, is
' seeking self - satisfaction,' or more explicitly,
' presents to himself some possible state or achievement of his own as for the time his greatest good,'
which seems to imply that he thinks the pursuit of
pleasure is the best way of reaching it : he also says
(§ 177, p. 185) that ' the objects where good is
actually sought are often not those where reason,
even as in the person seeking them, pronounces that
it is to be found,' and that his ' will does not answer
to his reason '; but I do not perceive that he offers
any adequate reconciliation of the two classes of
statement.[1]

The passages which suggest that in Green's view
vicious choice is always made under an illusory
belief that the end chosen is the chooser's greatest
good, are the more numerous. There is, however, an
uncertainty arising from a want of distinction in
certain passages of Green's between good *as attained*
or *realised*, and good *as sought*. Ordinarily, if we
say that every one, in any act, seeks what he regards
as, or believes to be, his greatest good, we mean that
he seeks to bring about some result which (as he
believes) when brought about will have more of the
quality of good than some other result compared
with it. When adopted as end, what is adopted is
good in anticipation or idea : when realised, it is good in
reality. Hence the illusion—when there is illusion—

[1] I should say that certainly his will does not answer to his reason : and
in this lies the importance of the distinction between will and intellect just
mentioned. ' Willing the best' is not the same thing as conceiving it.

lies in the want of correspondence between the present idea and the future fact of attainment.

Still there are passages in Green in which he seems to regard a result aimed at as acquiring completely the quality of 'good' not when it is realised but when we determine to seek it. Compare, for example, the following passages : 'The motive . . . is . . . an act in which the agent presents to himself a certain idea of himself . . . as an idea of which the realisation forms for the time his good' (§ 95, p. 99): this may be interpreted not as involving prediction as to the state of attainment, but merely as referring to the adoption of an end. '. . . the presentation of an object with which the man for the time identifies himself or his good, and a consequent effort to realise this object' (§ 140, p. 146). 'The man who calmly faces a life of suffering in the fulfilment of what he conceives to be his mission could not bear to do otherwise. So to live is his good. If he could attain the consciousness of having accomplished his work, if he could count himself to have apprehended—and probably just in proportion to the elevation of his character he is unable to do so—he would find satisfaction in the consciousness, etc.' (§ 159, p. 166).

Let us dwell on the last passage : a course of action is said to be a man's Good although attainment is supposed absent. From such passages taken alone I should infer that Good, in Green's view, is merely an object chosen or adopted as his end by a self-conscious agent, so that Greatest Good would merely mean *object preferred as end to others com-*

pared with it. Thus there would be no real place for illusory belief as to 'greatestness'—Greatest Good is the Good—that is, is the chosen or adopted end.

I do not, however, think this was really Green's view. If we look closer at the passage in § 159, we find in it another possible meaning of Good, viz. Self-satisfaction, which is attached not to the attainment of the end, but to action with a view to it. If the man does not get satisfaction—and Green assumes he does not—at any rate he gets *less dissatisfaction* than from any other course of life, and that, I suppose, is why 'so to live is his good.'

There are many other passages which clearly indicate the ordinary view that the Good sought is really good—good not merely in idea or anticipation —when and so far as an expectation formed when the act is willed, is realised in the effect of the act. For instance, all the passages in which 'good' is identified with 'what satisfies desire.' Compare § 171, pp. 178, 179, with § 131, pp. 135, 136.

I consider, therefore, that there is an unsolved contradiction in Green's view, and that he does not give a decided and unambiguous answer to the question, Is vicious choice due altogether to intellectual mistake?—And I think that perhaps the want of clear distinction between the views (1) that Desire gives the quality of good, and (2) that Satisfaction does so, prevents Green from definitely answering the question, how far vicious choice depends on illusion.

At any rate it is plain that in Green's view the vicious man does not seek true Self-satisfaction, *i.e.* not an object by the realisation of which a self-distinguishing combining consciousness can really satisfy itself. But what is this object? What could satisfy a self-distinguishing combining consciousness, or why is it not satisfied by performing its function of self-distinction and combination, along with the satisfaction of the desires with which it from time to time identifies itself? It has always seemed to me odd that Green never really faces this difficulty.

LECTURE IV

WHAT does Common Sense mean by the Good Will? It may mean 'Will with good Intention, or Motive, or both.' Intention refers to effects as foreseen, say A + B. Motive refers to effects desired, say A. The effects as foreseen may be subjectively right, judged to be on the whole best. If so the intention will be subjectively right or good.—Again, the effects as foreseen may be objectively right or good, though the actual effects are bad.[1] When we say that the 'intention is good,' we commonly mean that the effects as foreseen are both subjectively and objectively good: though they may be inseparable from bad effects not foreseen, so important as to make the whole actual effects objectively bad. But we may merely mean that they are subjectively good: what the agent approves, but not what a reasonable man would approve. I do not think that the distinction is clear in ordinary discourse (cf. 'Well-intentioned,' etc.).

---

[1] Subjective and Objective are used by me in Ethics thus: Subjectively right or good is what is judged by the agent to be so; Objectively right or good is what is so apart from the agent's judgment.

43

Again, Common Sense recognises that Intention may be good, both subjectively and objectively, while Motive is bad, because the effects possibly should not have been desired (so far as desire can be repressed), though rightly accepted, so far as inevitable concomitants of what is intended—take, for instance, the case of malevolent gratification.

The distinction seems to me clear and important. But there is a further distinction. It may be that the effects should not have been desired, but that the agent did not know this. Motive, no less than intention, may be subjectively right, but not objectively. Hence we cannot say that *subjective* means what belongs to the subject; and the proposition—that what I judge to be right must, unless I am in error, be judged to be so by all rational beings who judge truly of the matter—(which involves that if I judge any action to be right for myself, I implicitly judge it to be right for any other person whose nature and circumstances do not differ from my own in some important respects)—this proposition, which is obtained by reflective analysis of our common conception of objective rightness may be applied as a condition of subjective rightness.[1]

But again, a man may have a right general notion of the end, but a wrong conception of the particulars that make it up. (*E.g.* he may aim at Perfection, Realisation of capacities, etc. ; but may consider that a man is more perfect for possessing knowledge or taste—*i.e.* that of two men who have equally good

[1] Cf. *Methods of Ethics*, § 3 of chap. i. Book III.

will, one is more perfect than the other if he has
more knowledge or taste; or he may consider
goodness of will the sole thing needful for perfection.) Here he might be said to be formally
right, but materially wrong. Similarly, he may aim
at general happiness, but take an erroneous estimate
of the particular elements of it: he may overrate one
class of pleasures—*e.g.* the pleasures derived from
material wealth in comparison with others. Thus a
parent devoted to his children may slave to provide
them with wealth, and succeed in enabling them
to drink wine and have fine clothes and furniture
all their days—but he may in this way not do so
much for their happiness as if he had given them less
money and more culture.

It is a different case again (and perhaps the most
ordinary case of well-intentioned mischief) when a
man has a right detailed conception of human
perfection or happiness, but a wrong conception of
the means to it—*e.g.* he may erroneously think that
he will promote the perfection or happiness of certain
barbarous tribes by the mixed application of traders
and missionaries; but in fact the alcohol and
European diseases that the traders bring in may do
more harm than the good done by the appliances of
civilised life, and the missionaries may do more harm
in destroying existing moral sanctions than good in
building up new ones.

Taking these distinctions, then, and applying
them to Green's view, what does he mean by a
Good Will? Is a will good in his view if it

is directed to what the agent conceives to be universal good, though his general notion of it differs
from Green's? For instance, can a Utilitarian in
Green's view have a Good Will? Can a man who
aims at perfection, but conceives it wrongly, or a
man who uses wrong means for the attainment of
perfection conceived rightly or wrongly, have a Good
Will?

I do not find that Green answers any of these
questions clearly and explicitly; but it would seem
that in his view a perfectly good will would involve
a perfectly true conception of the end and of the
means to it. And as regards the degrees of imperfection due to one or other of the defects above noticed,
he seems inclined to sweep away the difficulties of
deciding their relative importance by assuming that
good in effect will always correspond to good motive.

It is (he says) only to our limited vision that there can seem
to be such a thing as good effects from an action that is bad in
respect of the will which it represents, and that in consequence
the question becomes possible, whether the morality of an action
is determined by its motive or by its consequences. There is
no real reason to doubt that the good or evil in the motive of an
action is exactly measured by the good or evil in its consequences,
as rightly estimated—estimated, that is, in their bearing on the
production of a good will or the perfecting of mankind. The
contrary only appears to be the case on account of the limited
view we take both of action and consequences.[1]

This seems to me an arbitrary and unsupported
assumption.

I return to the question: What will afford an
abiding satisfaction of an abiding self? The answer
is given in general terms in the account of *True*

[1] *Prolegomena to Ethics*, § 295, read to end of section.

Good which appears in Book III. But as here given the answer takes various forms, not easily made consistent, and contains, obscurely combined, wider and narrower views of man's true good. It is realisation or full realisation (1) sometimes of capabilities, and (2) sometimes of *moral* capability. Compare § 172, p. 179, 'moral good is the realisation of the moral capability'; but here capability = nature of moral agents.

Let us consider the narrower notion first. *Moral agent*, as already defined, is equivalent to *rational self-conscious agent*, and I do not see why the self-conscious entity should be supposed capable of doing or being anything more than what we already know it as doing or being — *i.e.* self-objectifying, self-distinguishing, and combining. This is all that we know from Book I. either of the Divine or of the human spirit. Now self-objectification and self-distinction seem to be fully realised at present — at least, it is not clear how they could be more fully realised, but it is certainly not the mere extension of combination which forms Green's moral ideal.

If, however, we take 'realisation of capabilities' in a broader and more ordinary sense, how is it to be measured and its elements compared? Some capabilities—some capacities for being pleased—are realised in the voluptuary's life. In fact, in human life, we are always realising capabilities to some extent, in every action, sensation, emotion, thought. And it does not appear that we find 'rest' or 'abiding

satisfaction' in 'realising capabilities,' as we are
always doing this more or less, and never completely.
Again, whenever alternatives are presented for moral
choice, we have to choose between realising one kind
of capability and realising another.   By what criterion
is the choice to be determined ?

Sometimes to answer this question the notion of
Perfection is substituted for Realisation of capabilities.   How Perfection is to be defined and
measured remains equally obscure.   Of this obscurity
I shall have more to say presently ; but at any rate,
Perfection will mean complete realisation of capabilities.   What I now wish to point out is that there
is a fundamental objection to Perfection (or complete realisation of capabilities) as end—namely, that
it is an end admittedly not attained in this mundane
sphere.   This is true even if we take the narrowest
view of it, and regard it as moral perfection or
virtue.   It does not appear that the path of moral
progress, even if pursued with the most stoical contempt for all human good except virtue, is one in
which the effort of the moral agent finds 'rest,' at
least within the sphere of earthly life.   Green, at any
rate, does not maintain that it does : as we saw he says
of the 'man who calmly faces a life of suffering in the
fulfilment of what he conceives to be his mission,'
that 'if he could attain the consciousness of having
accomplished his work, . . . he would find satisfaction in the consciousness,' but adds that 'probably
just in proportion to the elevation of his character
he is unable to do so' : it would seem, therefore,

that he no less than the voluptuary is always pursuing
and never attaining.

Perhaps it may be said that if the 'abiding good'
is not *found* by the man who is seeking perfection
or virtue, it is at any rate approached by him; the
moral aspirant who is daily growing less imperfect,
may not experience the satisfaction of attainment,
but at any rate he is getting towards it.[1] But (1)
what can this avail him if he never actually attains?
Why, in this supreme pursuit, are we to ignore the
proverb that 'A miss is as good as a mile'? And (2)
even granting that the consciousness of approximation
is the best substitute available to him for the consciousness of attainment in this earthly life, I cannot
conceive in what sense this can be regarded as an
'abiding satisfaction,' unless there is a reasonable
prospect of the continuance of his personal existence
after death.

Does then Green supply us with any rational
ground for this expectation? This question is dealt
with in chapter ii. of Book III. (*Characteristics of
the Moral Ideal*), to which I now pass.

In chapter ii. the starting-point taken is the 'gradual
reproduction of the one divine mind in the human
soul.' It is 'in virtue of this principle in him that
man has definite capabilities, the realisation of which,
since in it alone he can satisfy himself, forms his true
good.' It follows of course that the realisation of the
true good must be 'in persons.'

---

[1] Cf. *Prolegomena*, § 239 :—'But of particular forms of life and action we
may say that they are better, . . . because in them there is . . . . a nearer
approach to the end in which alone man can find satisfaction for himself.'

But this does not definitely determine the fundamental question, whether the individual agent may reasonably look for its realisation in himself, or only in other persons hereafter, in 'a development of the human race which individuals unwittingly promote but perish in promoting' (§ 181).

And in fact this is a question on which Green seems to me obscure, partly because the question whether the end is to be realised in *persons*, in perfection of personal character, is not clearly distinguished from the question whether it is to be realised in *the agent in question;* and the question whether I 'partake of the eternal' is not distinguished from the question whether I as an individual am eternal. In Book III. chapter ii., on *Characteristics of the Moral Ideal*, he says :—

Although any other capacity may be of a kind which, having done its work in contributing to the attainment of such a state of being, passes away in the process of its attainment—as the particular capacities of myriads of animals, their function fulfilled, pass away every hour—yet a capacity consisting in a self-conscious personality cannot be supposed so to pass away. It partakes of the nature of the eternal. It is not itself a series in time ; for the series of time exists for it. We cannot believe in there being a real fulfilment of such a capacity in an end which should involve its extinction, because the conviction of there being an end in which our capacities are fulfilled is founded on our self-conscious personality—on the idea of an absolute value in a spirit which we ourselves are. And for the same reason we cannot believe that the capacities of men—capacities illustrated to us by the actual institutions of society, though they could not be so illustrated if we had not an independent idea of them—can be really fulfilled in a state of things in which any rational man should be treated merely as a means, and not as in himself an end. On the whole, our conclusion must be that, great as are the difficulties which beset the idea of human development when applied to the facts of life, we do not escape them, but empty the idea of any real meaning, if we suppose the end of the development to be one in the attainment of which persons—agents who are ends to themselves—are extinguished, or one which is other than a state of self-conscious being, or one in which that reconciliation of the claims of persons, as each at once a means to the good of the other and an end to himself, already partially achieved in the higher forms of human society, is otherwise than completed (§ 189).

If we may infer from this that Green believed in the immortality of the individual, it remains difficult to see *why* he believed in it. Granting that the self-conscious individual man, being a reproduction of the eternal mind, ' partakes of the nature of the eternal,' it is not clear that he partakes of it *qua* individual. Observe, Green says, ' absolute value *in a spirit which we ourselves are,*' not ' *in our spirits.*' The thing of absolute value might therefore remain if our spirits are extinguished. Indeed, when we look closely at Green's argument just quoted, there seems to be some confusion of thought between the different meanings of eternal. Eternal may mean (1) *not in time,* or (2) *perduring through time.*

Now so far as the self-conscious personality was shown to be ' of the nature of the eternal' it was not because it perdures through time, but because ' the series of time exists for it.' So far as it is in this sense eternal we certainly cannot conceive of its extinction, but then no more can we conceive of its perduring or abiding, still less of its progress or development—a notion which involves the idea of its change in time—in fact it is not the individual, *qua* individual, that is thus eternal, but the universal mind whose knowledge it shares and reproduces.

The same distinctions apply to the passage (§§ 184, 185, pp. 193-195) in which he comes nearest to the question of personal survival. In this passage, however, if we look carefully at it, the question which primarily interests Green is not whether the individual John or Thomas has reason to expect continued existence as an individual after death, but whether we have reason to expect that the life of the spirit will always be realised in *some* individual persons. What he is concerned to maintain is, that 'the human spirit cannot develop itself according to its idea except in self-conscious subjects . . . the spiritual progress of mankind is an unmeaning phrase, unless it means a progress of which feeling, thinking, and willing subjects are the agents and sustainers.' Considering the 'promise which the spirit gives of itself, both in its actual occasional achievement and in the aspirations of which we are individually conscious,' we may, he thinks, 'justify the suppositions that the personal life, which historically or on earth is held under conditions which thwart its development, (1) is continued in a society, with which we have no means of communication through the senses, but which shares in and carries further every measure of perfection attained by men under the conditions of life that we know. (2) Or we may content ourselves with saying that the personal self-conscious being, which comes from God, is for ever continued in God. (3) Or we may pronounce the problem suggested by the constant spectacle of unfulfilled human promise to be simply insoluble.'

Now doubtless the consideration of these three
alternatives, the weighing of the *pros* and *cons* for
each of them, is an interesting and elevating speculation; but I fail to perceive that any one of them
meets the difficulty with which I am now dealing.   If

> The high that proved too high, the heroic for earth too hard,
> The passion that left the ground to lose itself in the sky,

present us only with an insoluble problem, I do not
see how the philosopher is to fulfil the task he has
undertaken of showing the effort after an 'abiding
self-satisfaction' to be rational.   Nor, again, do I see
how this is achieved by adopting the second alternative, and supposing that the personal self-conscious
being, now designated as John or Thomas, is to be
'for ever continued in God.'   For God, or the eternal
consciousness—according to the definition given in
Book I.—is necessarily conceived as unalterable ; it is
eternally in reality all that the human spirit is in
possibility, and there are no conceivable perfections
that could be added to it; and the process of man's
moral effort is surely futile if it is to end in nothing
but the existence of that which exists already.[1]   It
may be said that objections of this kind may be
brought against every philosophical theology, unless
it diverges widely from religious common sense :
a plain man cannot but conceive the world-process,

---

[1] It may perhaps be said that I ought not to apply such a conception as
'already existing' to a Being whose existence is expressly stated to be out
of time.   And, though I cannot profess to be able to reason about such
a Being without tacitly conceiving it in some relation to time, I should not
have ventured to use the phrase in the text if Green had not set me the
example—*e.g.* in speaking (§ 173, p. 181) of a 'best state of man already
present to some divine consciousness.'

Divinely ordered, as designed to bring about some good not yet realised, which must be good from a Divine or universal point of view, and yet he cannot conceive the Divine existence as at any time defective or wanting in any respect. I admit the force of the rejoinder; only, unlike Green, I should draw from it the inference that we ought not to use these theological notions, while yet unpurged of such palpable inconsistencies, as the basis of a philosophy of practice. For the purposes of Ethics we have to suppose that the world on which we have to act, is somehow, in some sense, rationally and rightly conceived as imperfect. A Utilitarian has unhappily no difficulty in conceiving this—his difficulty rather is to bear up against his depressing consciousness of this imperfection. But the difficulty exists for the Transcendentalist, and we must press him with it. And when we ask how the imperfect reproduction of the eternal self-conscious thinker, which he regards as the essence of the individual, can be conceived to attain its true abiding good, we may fairly refuse to be put off with the answer that the eternal consciousness remains eternally conscious.

There remains the first answer. Can we find the 'abiding self-satisfaction' which a moral agent is supposed to seek, in the conception of a society of persons who somewhere, somehow, in the indefinite future, are to carry further that movement towards perfection which is so seriously impeded among the human beings whom we know? We might perhaps accept the solution—it being granted on Green's side

that the human spirit can be abidingly satisfied with
movement instead of rest, progress instead of perfection. But it requires us to assume that a 'better
state of humanity' can be taken as a convertible term
for the 'better state of myself' at which, as a moral
agent, I necessarily aim. And in several passages
Green seems to pass backwards and forwards between
these two notions as if they might be used indifferently in his reasonings ; but it is not easy to see how
his moral psychology justifies this procedure. He
has laid it down that 'in all desire, or at any rate in
all that amounts to will,' it is self-satisfaction which
the self - conscious agent necessarily seeks — 'a
certain possible state of himself which in the gratification of the desire he seeks to reach (§§ 170, 175) ;
and since he has also explained how the most characteristic human desires—*e.g.* love, envy, and ambition
—depend on the conscious distinction between the
desirer's own individuality and that of other persons,
I presume that we must maintain this distinction in
interpreting the account above given of 'all desire' ;
and therefore that the 'better state of myself' which
I necessarily seek cannot be the better state of any
other person as such. But if so, we must know
exactly how the one comes to be identified or
indissolubly connected with the other under the
comprehensive notion of the 'bettering of man' or
'humanity.' By what logical process can we pass
from the form of unqualified egoism under which the
true end of the moral agent is represented to us on
one page, to the unmediated universalism which we

find suddenly substituted for it on another ?   I admit,
of course, that the Divine Spirit, so far as it can be
rightly conceived to aim at the realisation or reproduction of itself in men, must be conceived as aiming
at its realisation in ' persons,' not in ' this person,' in
humanity, not in me ; but this only brings out more
forcibly the difference that has to be bridged over
between the aim of my one indivisible conscious self
at its own satisfaction, and this aim of the Divine
Spirit at a satisfaction or realisation which may just
as well be attained in any one else as in me.   My self-
distinguishing consciousness distinguishes itself from
the Divine Spirit as well as from other men ; and
it cannot therefore identify the satisfaction of itself
as so distinguished with the satisfaction of the Divine
Spirit—granting this idea appropriate.   So again, the
mere fact that I am aware of myself as a self-
distinguishing consciousness, and attribute a similar
consciousness to other men, does not necessarily
make me regard their good as my own ; some rational
transition is still needed between the recognition of
them as ends to themselves, and the recognition of
them as ends to myself.

Can this transition be obtained by dwelling on the
essential sociality of men, the universal or normal
implication, through sympathy, of each one's interest
or good with the interests of some others—according
to the plain man's conception of ' interest ' no less than
the philosopher's ?   In some parts of his discussion
(*e.g.* in Book III. chapter iii.) Green seems to rely
to some extent on this line of reasoning, with which

the looser optimism of eighteenth century moralists
appears to have been often entirely satisfied ; but I
think that an exact consideration of it will show its
inadequacy to establish the required conclusion.   For
granting all that is claimed, it only proves that I
cannot realise good for myself without promoting the
good of others in some degree ; it does not show that
my own good is in any sense identical with the good
of others who are to live after me, so that it will
' abide ' in another form when my individual existence
has terminated.

Even if we give up the characteristic of permanence and merely consider whether my good
during life can be identified with the good of
humanity at large, I still fail to see how this identification can be justified by anything that we know of
the essential sociality of ordinary human beings.
The ' better state of himself' as conceived even by a
voluptuary who aims at dining well, is a social state:
his dinner must be a convivial dinner if it is to be
good ; but it does not follow that he contemplates the
waiters who hand round the dishes as ends-in-them-
selves, or has any interest in future good dinners of
which he will not partake.   This is a coarse illustration ; but the proposition that it illustrates seems
to me equally, if less palpably, true of all the ordinary
exercises and functions of cultivated social existence :
the mere fact that I am a social being, that my life is
meagre and starved if I do not enlarge it by sympathy and live the life of the community of which
I am a member, does not necessarily constitute the

good of humanity my good : it brings me a certain
way towards this, but it has not necessarily any force
or tendency to carry me the rest of the way. Granting that ' to any one actuated by it the idea of
a perfection . . . for himself will involve the idea of a
perfection of all other beings, *so far as* he finds
the thought of their being perfect necessary to his
own satisfaction ' (§ 370), it remains true that to most
persons the dissatisfaction caused by the idea of the
imperfection of other beings, not connected with
them by some special bond of sympathy, is at any
rate an evil faintly sensible as compared with the
imperfection of the existence of themselves and those
dear to them. The question therefore arises how far
they should sacrifice their own good or perfection to
promote the perfection of others.

This latter difficulty, no doubt, only becomes a
practical difficulty, if the greatest good of an individual is in any degree incompatible with, or
divergent from, the greatest good of others ; for if
not, whether I pursue my own good or that of others,
I shall do the same thing. Egoism and self-sacrifice
will be when duly enlightened two roads to the same
goal. This latter view we find Green maintains.
He holds that the true good of man is so constituted
that no competition can possibly arise between the
good of one individual and the good of any other.
Now no doubt this, if true, relieves us of many difficulties, gets rid of many problems. But can it be
known to be true, and how ? As to this, two questions arise—as in most ethical controversies. (1)

Can this be maintained consistently with Green's account of True Good and other notions? (2) Is it in harmony with Common Sense? In the next Lecture I shall point out that if so the common sense notions of Justice and Self - sacrifice — naïvely accepted by Green—would require profound alteration, and I shall examine how far this notion of a True Good which is non-competitive can be held consistently with Green's wider notion of good for an individual as consisting in perfection or realisation of capabilities. The question is not an easy one, owing to the difficulty of getting a clear and precise view of Green's moral ideal. For, as we have seen, Green puts forward two views — a wider and a narrower—of this ideal.

LECTURE V

GREEN'S ACCOUNT OF THE MORAL IDEAL

In Lecture III. I examined Green's conception of Moral action in the wider sense, in which it is equivalent specifically to human, as distinct from animal, action, and includes vicious and virtuous action equally. The virtuous and vicious man equally aim at Personal Good or Self-satisfaction. In the last Lecture I began the inquiry into Green's view of the *virtuous* man's aim,—which may be stated to be that by which self-satisfaction is found and not merely sought. What is the general distinction between the content of the good and bad Will respectively? This is the question which Book III. on the Moral Ideal appears to attempt to answer. At the outset, in § 154, p. 161, we are told that the 'real nature of any act of will' depends on the 'specific difference of the objects willed under the general form of self-satisfaction': it is here that we must seek for the distinction between Goodness and Badness of Will. What then is this specific difference?

I may observe that Book III. chapter i., in which this distinction is discussed, is largely controversial; and I have purposely not taken up the controversy, which is mainly directed against views of Mill with which I disagree. The view, for example, which is attributed to the 'modern Utilitarian,' § 155, p. 161, is not exactly mine. When we have got through this controversy, it is, as I said, very difficult to reach a positive statement as to the content of the virtuous man's will, and the object of the virtuous man's aim, the true good, the abiding satisfaction of an abiding self—but *realisation of moral capability*, and *perfection*, are used, and we must try to extract coherent instruction from these vague terms.

As I have indicated, the whole discussion seems to ignore what is, in my view, a fundamental distinction between subjective and objective good and right. (It also ignores the distinction between right and good, but this may be passed over.)

As Good for Green is convertible with Self-satisfaction, it is a distinctive characteristic of the true good that it gives true or abiding self-satisfaction, or rest. This he holds can only be given by complete self-realisation or perfection—that is the wider notion that he sometimes uses; sometimes, however, laying down that the true good must be so far common to all that it does not lie in objects that can be competed for, he finds it in the narrower notion of Virtue or (still narrower) the Good Will or the Will to be good. I will briefly recapitulate my objections to these accounts.

'True good gives abiding satisfaction, or rest.' Why? Why will not continually renascent satisfaction do? What is the objection to the normal condition of human life : desire—fruition—calm, fresh desire—fresh fruition, etc.—supposing the process could go on without any falling off in fruition, or any intermixing of pain ?

But again : by Green's own account the man who seeks perfection does not reach rest—' in proportion to the elevation of his character he does not count himself to have attained.' If it be said that he is approaching it and will attain it hereafter, we have to point out that Green's philosophy affords no ground for expecting the survival of the individual after bodily death. As we found, this appears in examining the argument in Book III. chapter ii. § 189 ; but I may say that it will be even more clear to those who have studied Book I. carefully. For Green's individual, as we there saw, is thought under two distinct notions :— (1) as ' a function of the animal organism, which is being made a vehicle of the eternal consciousness ' ; (2) as ' that eternal conscious- ness itself, making the animal organism its vehicle, and subject to certain limitations in so doing.' Sup- pose the animal organism to come to an end by bodily death, no doubt (2) will remain ; but as it will cease to use the animal organism as its vehicle, we have no ground for supposing that it will still be subject to the limitations to which its action on and use of this organism subjected it. But take away the animal organism and its functions, and the limitations of the eternal consciousness connected with it, and what is left ? Why, simply the eternal consciousness without the limitations.

This Green partly sees. He speaks of 'the conviction of there being an end in which our capacities are fulfilled' as 'founded on our self-conscious personality — on the idea of an absolute value in a spirit which we ourselves are,' not in our individual spirits as such. So again, he suggests that 'We may content ourselves with saying that the personal self-conscious being which comes from God is for ever continued in God.' But he does not seem to see how futile the pursuit of his end thus becomes.

If, as Green maintains, my nature necessarily demands abiding self-satisfaction or rest, is it a sufficient motive for me to 'scorn delights and live laborious days,' and struggle to subdue vicious desires, that when I die, the eternal consciousness will be remaining eternally conscious? For this it will surely do in any case : this kind of 'rest' is surely provided impartially, like sunshine and rain, for the just and the unjust.

As we have already seen, similar difficulties arise when we examine another notion under which Green's end is conceived — the notion of Self-realisation. What is self for Green? Essentially a self-distinguishing, self-objectifying, combining, unifying consciousness. Nothing more, if we consider it apart from the 'solicitations' it receives from the animal organism, which are supposed to mislead it into the pursuit of pleasure.

What then remains for it to realise? Well, it may be answered, it can always extend its knowledge,

combine and unify more phenomena. And certainly
we can form no other conception, on Green's premises,
of a progress in likeness to God—a progress, reproduction or realisation of the eternal consciousness in
us. For God, in Green's metaphysics, is only known
to us as such an agency. But this ideal of purely
cognitive perfection is quite unlike Green's, as
expressed in the other terms : Virtue, the Common
Good, Good-will, etc., and suggested by Holiness.

How then are we to know anything more about
the self-distinguishing consciousness and its self-
realisation ? One answer is, that we know it from
the manifestations of its capabilities in the human institutions of the past. To this (as I have pointed out)
it may be said that all human life that has been, in a
sense is realisation of human capabilities ; but that
does not supply a criterion between pursuit of true good
and pursuit of illusion. The sinner realises capabilities
—in this broad sense—as much as the saint. I lay
stress on this, because it is important to recognise
that one of the subtlest and deepest of the impulses that
prompt intellectual natures to vice is the desire for
full and varied realisation of capabilities, for richness of
experience, for fulness of life. Again, human institutions have been developed not by self-distinguishing
consciousness as such, but by groups of gregarious
animals, possessing such a consciousness, but also
desiring pleasure and avoiding pain. They give no
means for interpreting ' human good ' as something
entirely alien from gratification of the desires of an
animal organism, as Green interprets it.

I now turn to what is certainly the most attractive feature in Green's conception of the end, if only it can be consistently maintained—its non-competitive character, and its consequent freedom from the difficulties in which Hedonism is involved by the occasional incompatibility between the greatest happiness of A and the greatest happiness of B. *I* cannot be accused of under-rating these difficulties; in fact it was a main object of that part of my treatise on *The Methods of Ethics* which deals with hedonistic method to bring them into full view. If Green can consistently maintain an 'idea of a true good' that 'does not admit of the distinction between good for self and good for others,' his system will, in this respect, have a fundamental superiority over Hedonism.

But can he maintain it? It appears to me that he does not even consistently keep to it himself. For his own conceptions of Justice, Self-denial, Self-sacrifice, as he himself expounds them, involve the conception of possible incompatibility between benefit to one man and benefit to another.—Let me show this.

It is true that Green admits that 'we are very far, in our ordinary estimates of good, whether for ourselves or for others, from keeping such a standard before us . . . the conviction of the community of good for all men . . . has little positive influence over our practical judgments'—good being, in fact, 'sought in objects which admit of being competed for.' But he entirely fails to see how the

F

acceptance of the proposed condition of true good,
that it 'does not admit of the distinction between
good for self and good for others,' inevitably alters,
and alters radically, the common notions of virtue,
even the notions to which he himself adheres most
unquestioningly and emphatically in his delineation
of the moral ideal. For instance, in a passage in
§ 212 (pp. 224, 225), of which the ethical feeling is
fine, he describes the refinement in a conscientious
man's sense of justice—how it makes him

> so over-curious, as it seems to the ordinary man of the world,
> in inquiring, as to any action which may suggest itself to him,
> whether the benefit which he might gain by it for himself or for
> some one in whom he is interested, would be gained at the
> expense of any one else, however indifferent to him personally,
> however separated from him in family, status, or nation . . . and
> . . . he will not promote his own wellbeing or that of one whom
> he loves or likes, from whom he has received service or expects
> it, at the cost of impeding in any way the wellbeing of one who
> is nothing to him but a man, or whom he involuntarily dislikes ;
> that he will not do this knowingly, and that he is habitually on
> the look-out to know whether his actions will have this effect or
> not.

This is a fine description, but consider what it
implies. It implies, that in the view of Green's
conscientious man it is possible that he and those
in whom he is interested may be 'benefited,' *i.e.*
obtain good, at the expense of others :—otherwise
why all this scrupulous inquiry?   It implies that
the promotion of one's own wellbeing or that of
one's friends may really involve the cost of imped-
ing the wellbeing of others : otherwise what need
of this resolute impartiality?   It implies, in short,
that Good, as implied in the notions of benefit

and wellbeing, does really consist, at least to some extent, in objects that admit of being competed for; though Green's theory of a true good denies this.

How, after writing this description of an ideally just man, Green could possibly go on to say (§ 232) that 'the distinction of good for self and good for others has never entered into that idea of a true good on which moral judgments are founded,' I cannot imagine. That the distinction ought to be eliminated from our moral judgments is perhaps a tenable proposition; but the statement that it 'has never entered in' seems to me in flat contradiction with his own account of the reasoning and aims of the 'conscientious man,' whom he expressly contrasts with the ordinary man of the world. And surely a moralist who maintains even that the distinction ought to be eliminated, is bound, when he comes to treat of justice, to reconstruct the conscientious man's notions of justice and injustice, and show us exactly what they come to when the distinction between good for self and good for others is eliminated. And I cannot perceive that Green attempts anything of the kind.

There seems to me a similar inconsistency in Green's use of another group of notions, common in ordinary modern moral judgments, but difficult to reconcile with his general conception of virtuous action. He speaks continually—especially in Book III. chapter v.—of the 'sacrifices' made by the virtuous man, of his 'self-sacrificing will,' his 'habitual self-denial,' his 'self-renunciations.' But if all self-conscious agents are always aiming each at his own greatest good or self-satisfaction, if the most virtuous only differs from the most vicious in that he seeks it with a truer insight into its nature, how can he, in the strictness of philosophical discourse, be said to deny or renounce himself in so seeking it? What he denies—according to Green's psychology as expounded in Book II.—is not himself, but those impulses, influences, or tendencies, due to the animal soul, with which the virtuous man, as such, does *not* identify himself (compare *e.g.* § 146). These are 'solicitations,' as we are expressly told, 'by which he is consciously affected, but which are not he': indeed, as we saw, Green is even reluctant to call them his desires. And what, in strictness, can such a man be said to 'sacrifice' when he is seeking his own greatest good with true insight, and with the knowledge that his true good cannot lie in 'objects that admit of being competed for'? What 'sacrifice' is there in giving up things that are no sort of good to one?

In all this I seem to find, in Green's account of moral action, pagan or neo-pagan elements of ethical thought—in which the governing conception takes the form of self-regard—combined with Christian or post-Christian elements, without any proper philosophical reconciliation of the two.

It may be said that these objections are at any rate merely superficial; and that they could be removed by a change of language, leaving the substance of

Green's thought unaffected. I cannot agree; I think that when we examine in detail the content of Green's conception of a true good for an individual, taking the notion of perfection or complete realisation of capacities, we do not find it really so constituted that it cannot possibly come into competition with the true good of any other individual. For this realisation of human capacities is repeatedly stated to include 'art and science' as well as 'specifically moral virtues.' The 'will for true good' we are told (§ 256) is—or rather, includes—'the will to know what is true, to make what is beautiful.' In the 'life of thoroughly realised spiritual capacity . . . we must suppose all that is now inchoate in the way of art and knowledge . . . to have reached completion' (§ 287). The development of 'faculties which find their expression . . . in the arts and sciences' must 'be a necessary constituent in any life which he [the educated citizen of Christendom] presents to himself as one in which he can find satisfaction' (§ 370). But if this be so, is it not idle to tell us that the idea of a true good does not admit of the distinction between good for self and good for others, and that a man's true good does not consist in objects that admit of being competed for,—so long as the material conditions of human existence remain at all the same as they are now? Virtue, no doubt, and the highest virtue—though not every particular virtue—admits of being exercised under any external conditions of life; but the faculties that find expression in the arts and sciences—no. Indeed I should have thought that

a writer like Green, who steadily refuses to take a
hedonistic view of ordinary human aims and efforts,
must regard the 'realisation of scientific and artistic
capacities,' taken in a wide sense, as constituting the
main motive of the keen struggle for material wealth
which educated and refined persons generally feel
themselves bound to keep up, for their children even
more than for themselves. The thoughtful trader
knows that wealth will enable him to provide himself and those he loves with books, pictures, prolonged education, varied travel, opportunities of intellectual society ; and, knowing this, he allows himself
to adopt methods of dealing which sometimes, perhaps,
are hardly compatible with Green's ideal of justice.
Similarly, the hardest choice which Christian self-
denial imposes is the preference of the work apparently most socially useful to the work apparently
most conducive to the agent's own scientific and
æsthetic development.[1]

It may be replied that Art and Science are good,
but Virtue better ; that the self-devotion which leads
a man to postpone to duty the fullest possible realisation of his scientific or artistic faculties, is an
exercise in which a fuller development of his nature
as a whole is attained. I cannot conceive any

---

[1] I think Green unconsciously evades the difficulty which this choice
presents, on his theory, when he speaks (§ 271) of 'the conscientious man
sacrificing personal pleasure in satisfaction of the claims of human brotherhood . . . the good citizen has no leisure to think of developing his own
faculties of enjoyment.' Of course his good man, being anti-hedonistic, has no
theoretical difficulty in sacrificing his own pleasure or enjoyment—or indeed
that of any one else ; but we may still ask whether and why and how far
he is called upon to sacrifice the realisation of his scientific and artistic capabilities. (Cf. also *post*, pp. 94, 95.)

empirical criterion of fulness of development by
which this could be made to appear even probable
as a universal proposition ; but if, for the sake of
argument, I grant it to be true in all cases in which
the occasion for such a sacrifice may be presented, it
can only be because the superiority in importance of
the ' specifically moral virtues,' as compared with

All other skills and gifts to culture dear,

is held to be so great that the alternatives may be
regarded as practically incommensurable.   But if this
be so, it seems to me that the promotion of the
specifically moral virtues — considering the amount
that remains to be done in this direction — ought
in consistency to occupy so large a share of the
practical philanthropist's attention that Green's in-
clusion of art and science will turn out to have
hardly any real significance.

And this would, I think, have been clear to Green,
if he had not somehow allowed his thought to swing
like a pendulum between a wider and a narrower
ideal of true good, sometimes expanding it to Culture,
sometimes narrowing it to Virtue and the Good Will.
When he thinks of full realisation of human capabilities,
he brings in the development of artistic faculties
and the cultivation of taste, as well as the development of scientific faculties and the pursuit of knowledge of all kinds ; when he wants to bring out
its non-competitive character, we find it shrunk to
virtue and goodness of will.   The wider ideal is in
his mind when he speaks of practical social duty—
for instance, when he speaks (§ 245) of the duty of

securing for the poor 'real opportunity of self-development.'   He says that now 'they are left to sink
or swim in the stream of unrelenting competition
in which we admit that the weaker has not a chance.'
Yet the most unrelenting competition does not
interfere with the exercise of virtue on the part of
the weakest competitor : he can will to be good as
single-mindedly and persistently as his most successful
rival—nay, as we know, it is the rich not the poor
whom the Gospel warns of the difficulty of entering
the Kingdom of Heaven.

But further, when we concentrate attention on the
narrower ideal, we find that Green is again in a
similar difficulty as between the formal and material
criteria of virtuous action.   For sometimes a formal
criterion is put forward in language which would
satisfy the most orthodox Kantian, as for example in
§§ 244 and 292 :—'The only good which is really
common to all who may pursue it, is that which
consists in the universal will to be good.'   The good
will is 'the one unconditional good . . . the end by
reference to which we estimate the effects of an action.'
On the other hand, it is explained that 'the good
will' must not be understood to be a 'will possessed
by some abstract idea of goodness or of moral law'
(§ 247), as this would 'amount to a paralysis of the will
for all application to great objects of human interest.'
But if pleasure is rejected and culture narrowed to
virtue, what can these objects of human interest be
except goodness of will in others, as Green says?
'The essence' of the 'perfection of mankind' is 'a

good will on the part of all persons' (§ 294), which, as he remarks, we can only promote indirectly, since 'all that one man can do to make another better is to remove obstacles, and supply conditions favourable to the formation of a good character' (§ 332). But surely we do not get beyond a 'will possessed by some abstract idea of goodness' by multiplying the persons possessed of the idea. The question: What is good? is not adequately answered by saying that it is the will to promote the will to be good in mankind: this solution obviously contains the unknown quantity, which remains undetermined.—Let me try to make this somewhat clearer. Let us take, for instance, the explicit statement in § 286, p. 309 :—

> The good has come to be conceived with increasing clearness, not as anything which one man or set of men can gain or enjoy to the exclusion of others, but as a spiritual activity in which all may partake. . . . Thus the ideal of virtue which our consciences acknowledge has come to be the devotion of character and life, in whatever channel the idiosyncrasy and circumstances of the individual may determine, to a perfecting of man, which is itself conceived not as an external end to be attained by goodness, but as consisting in such a life of self-devoted activity on the part of all persons.

It does not sound badly ; but if we ask ourselves what it means, what answer can be given? Am I to regard nothing as truly good, as an ultimate object of rational aim for me, except this very choice of nothing but this state of will in others ? It goes as Aristotle says εἰς ἄπειρον, and we find that the idea becomes empty and absolutely devoid of practical guidance—i.e. the state of mind which we are directed to aim at in ourselves and others is a state which involves a fundamental unanswered question : Suppose us all willing the good, what should we all will ? We saw that Green sometimes acquiesces in this empty notion—for instance, § 292 : ' the one unconditional good is the good will . . . the end by reference to which we estimate the effects of an action ' ('unconditional' seems to mean ' sole ultimate '), though in other passages, as I said, he seems to avoid this emptiness by including in the content of a good will other effects besides goodness of volition in self and others—*e.g.* knowledge and beauty: 'The will to know what is true, to make what is beautiful.' But if the will directed to knowledge and beauty is a good will, then can it be reasonably denied that knowledge and beauty are good even if not the results of will directed to the ' perfection of human character' as an end ?

It must be observed that in the latter part of chapter ii. of Book III. Green more or less recognises the difficulty of giving a definition of his ideal. Thus he says :—

> From the mere idea in a man, however, ' of something, he knows not what, which he may and should become,' to the actual practice which is counted morally good, it may naturally seem a long step. We have therefore to explain in further detail how such an idea, gradually taking form and definiteness, has been the moralising agent in human life, yielding our moral standards and inducing obedience to them.
>
> Supposing such an idea to be operative in man, what must be the manner of its operation ? It will keep before him an object, which he presents to himself as absolutely desirable, but which is other than any particular object of desire. Of this object it can never be possible for him to give a sufficient account, because it consists in the realisation of capabilities which can only be fully known in their ultimate realisation (§§ 192, 193, p. 203).

But can he give any clear account at all ?   In one

sense, as we saw, all human life that has been, has been realisation of capabilities. Are all parts of it similarly related to good ? If not, what is the criterion ? In a passage in chapter ii. of Book III. Green seems boldly to admit and face the impossibility of giving any definition which does not involve him in a logical circle.

We have said (he remarks) that man can never give a sufficient account of what his unconditional good is, because he cannot know what his capabilities are till they are realised. This is the explanation of the infirmity that has always been found to attach to attempted definitions of the moral ideal. They are always open to the charge that there is employed in the definition, openly or disguisedly, the very notion which profession is made of defining. If on being asked for an account of the unconditional good, we answer either that it is the good will, or that to which the good will is directed, we are naturally asked further, what then is the good will ? And if in answer to this question we can only say that it is the will for the unconditional good, we are no less naturally charged with 'moving in a circle.' We do but slightly disguise the circular process without escaping from it if, instead of saying directly that the good will is the will for the unconditional good, we say that it is the will to conform to a universal law for its own sake or because it is conceived as a universal law ; for the recognition of the authority of such an universal law must be founded on the conception of its relation to an unconditional good (§ 194, p. 204).

His answer to the charge of moving in a logical circle is that the end—the true good—is in full self-conscious realisation of human capabilities (§ 195), but that we have no knowledge of this full realisation—i.e. 'we have no knowledge of the perfection of man as the unconditional good, but that which we have of his goodness or the good will, in the form which it has assumed as a means to, or in the effort after, the unconditional good ;' and he says that 'it is therefore

not an illogical procedure, because it is the only
procedure suited to the matter in hand, to say that
the goodness of man lies in devotion to the ideal of
humanity, and then that the ideal of humanity
consists in the goodness of man' (§ 196).

In answer, I grant that the will to be good is itself
a part of the ideal perfection : my point is that it is a
part the knowledge of which gives us no knowledge of
—no prospect of knowing—the rest, and taken alone,
it fails altogether to give any practical guidance.

With some idea of meeting this answer — as
I suppose — Green falls back on positive morality
and established social institutions.   He tells us
(§ 197, p. 207) that though 'the categorical imperative can enjoin nothing *without liability to exception* but disinterested obedience to itself, it will have
no lack of definite content.   The particular duties
which it enjoins will *at least* be all those in the
practice of which, according to the hitherto experience of men, some progress is made towards
the fulfilment of man's capabilities, or some condition
necessary to that progress is satisfied.'   But how are
we to know these duties ?   If we do not know in
what fulfilment of man's capabilities consists, how
are we to know how progress is made towards it ?
Green answers that 'the system of duties' which the
law of the State or the law of opinion recognises are
'an expression of the absolute imperative to seek . . .
the ideal of humanity,' a 'product of the effort after
. . . an unconditional good' (§ 197, pp. 207, 208).   But
when I examine these duties—say *Neminem laede*,

Suum cuique—I do not find any reference to perfection of character as end. The evils that these rules aim at preventing are pain, and loss of the material means of physical wellbeing, or hindrances in attaining these means; the good that they aim at distributing rightly is of the same kind. And even granting that men established this system of duties in the effort after perfection, why should we suppose that our ancestors, if they did not know what perfection was, could tell the means by which it was to be realised?

Sometimes, as in the earlier part of chapter iii. of Book III., Green seems to think that to prove the sociality of human good as commonly conceived proves its non-competitive character, in the sense above considered. Here we find (§ 199, p. 210) that the 'self of which a man . . . forecasts the fulfilment' is a self with social interests, 'interests which cannot be satisfied without the consciousness that . . . other persons are satisfied.' And we are told that this essential sociality of the self cannot have been developed from animal sympathy which has no element of identity with it; since it involves the conception of others as 'ends in the same sense in which' a man 'is an end to himself' (§ 200). But granting this, it does not show that this sociality of the human individual may not have sprung from sympathy with pleasure and pain, together with self-consciousness and attribution of self-consciousness to others.[1]

[1] Compare what Green says in §§ 201, 207, pp. 212, 219 of the *Prolegomena*.

However, the question of origin is not fundamentally important. It is more important to point out that it is not clear how, either by sympathy or by a self-distinguishing consciousness, my own good is identified with that of others. It is difficult to see why the operation of self-distinguishing consciousness is to obliterate the difference—so far as natural desire goes—between Own good and Others' good. It would rather seem to emphasise and intensify it, since a self-distinguishing consciousness must distinguish itself from other selves. Taking the notion of a common good or wellbeing as we find it historically in the development of society, and granting that the conception of a common good—the good of the family, the tribe, the state—is the root of social institutions, habits of mutual help, and judgments as to particular duties and virtues : does the evidence of history really show that the notion of this common good thus operating is a notion of some abiding good, independent of the conditions of animal life, and that it is a notion of virtue, or perfection (or approximation to perfection) of character? It is the tacit assumption that this is the case which seems to me to vitiate the reasoning of Book III. chapter iii. I do not think the assumption well founded, because I hold that the notion of a common good, so far as it extends beyond the preservation of the community, is determined by a conception of social wellbeing which, if not exclusively hedonistic—since it includes as a permanent element *means* to preservation and happiness—yet at any rate admits of a utilitarian

interpretation more easily than of Green's, when the
question as to Ultimate Good is precisely conceived
and pressed.   (This applies to the conception of the
family, the city, the state, throughout the evolution of
society.)   Thus in chapter iv. § 218, p. 232, Green says
of the 'absolute and common good' that it is *absolute*
as 'independent of the likes and dislikes of individuals.'
There seems to me here a fallacious preclusion of
Hedonism, so far as the appeal is to Common Sense.
Common Sense regards common good as independent
of the likes and dislikes of any individual; but not
therefore of all.   Just as it commends one man dying
for his country but it would be absurd that all should :
there would be no country to die for.   So again,
p. 232, we read that the 'outcome of the process . . .
exhibits itself merely as the intuition of the educated
conscience that the true good must be good for all
men, so that no one should seek to gain by another's
loss.'   (Compare § 240, p. 257, where this is repeated.)   I reply that to the modern conscience it is
surely not manifest that from a mundane point of
view he cannot gain, or that self-sacrifice, *i.e.* sacrifice
of one's own good, is not possible ; it is surely contrary
to Common Sense to say so, and contrary to Green's
own statement.   I admit, however, that the statement is more plausible in relation to the Greek
conscience, and therefore propose in the next Lecture
to examine carefully the comparison in chapter v. of
Book III. between Greek and modern ideas of Virtue.

LECTURE VI

In chapter v. of Book III. Green turns to a historical account of his Moral Ideal with special reference to Greek ethics.

In any discussion of this kind there are two distinct things to consider :—(1) the ordinary morality —what I call Common Sense morality—of an average member of a certain historical society ; and (2) the synthesis of that morality, or the ethical systems formed by the thinkers who — in their effort to reduce the moral thought of their age to coherence— fall into schools.

First, as regards the ordinary morality of the average Greek, Green seems to me quite to fail in showing (as it was his main aim to show) that in ancient Greece—any more than in modern England— the estimation of Virtue, ἀρετή, has always had reference to character and state of will in men, as that which alone has ultimate value. In § 248 we may observe how the erroneous implication gradually becomes more marked. In a sense we should admit with Green, that, under the influence of domestic feeling, the ordinary well-behaved man

80

actually aims, in promoting the good of the family,
at 'persons living decent lives in the future' —
i.e. 'comfortable and not despised lives' — and
that primitive valour had 'its animating principle
in the idea of something which the valorous man and
. . . others . . . were to become'; though this—*i.e.*
the continued existence, the prosperous existence well
supplied with external goods, the honoured existence—was not only or chiefly the existence with a
certain character and condition of will.   But when,
passing to Hellenic ideas of the fifth century, Green
speaks of there being a 'virtue' to be 'exhibited in a
handicraft,' surely we see that character and will
are irrelevant; did this 'virtue' at all depend upon,
or consist in, a desire on the handicraftsman's part to
improve his own character or other people's?—It was
the product of his handicraft that he tried to make
excellent; it was by his success in this attempt that
his own excellency as a craftsman was estimated.   So
again, quoting Aristotle, he says: 'Virtue was a δύναμις
εὐεργετική, a faculty of beneficence;' but was that faculty
of welldoing as popularly conceived, a faculty of promoting, or tendency to promote, virtue ?   Surely the
ordinary Greek understood 'beneficence' as Green himself, in his account of Justice, has been seen to understand 'benefit.'   In short there seems to me no jot of
evidence that the *popular* conception in Greece of
Virtue or Human Excellence either sprang from the
'demand for an abiding self-satisfaction' or recognised
a state of will or character of human beings as the ultimate object in which this satisfaction was to be found.

G

Let us now pass to the ideal of Virtue of the Greek philosophers. This was doubtless, as Green says, not in their view a 'new' idea of Virtue, only a truer and more precise conception of the idea which they found in ordinary thought. But, according to Green, they did represent a 'heightened requirement of conscience.'

We speak (he says) of the change advisedly as consisting not merely in a new theory about virtue, but in a higher order of virtue itself. Socrates and his followers are not rightly regarded as the originators of an interesting moral speculation, such, for instance, as Hume may have started as to the nature of 'moral sense,' or the evolutionists as to its hereditary development. They represent, though it might be too much to say that they introduced, a new demand, or at least a fuller expression of an old demand of the moral nature. Now, though our actual moral attainment may always be far below what our conscience requires of us, it does tend to rise in response to a heightened requirement of conscience, and will not rise without it. Such a requirement is implied in the conception of the unity of virtue, as determined by one idea of practical good which was to be the conscious spring of the perfectly virtuous life—an idea of it as consisting in some intrinsic excellence, some full realisation of the capabilities, of the thinking and willing soul. Here we have—not indeed in its source, but in that first clear expression through which it manifests its life—the conviction that every form of real goodness must rest on a will to be good, which has no object but its own fulfilment. When the same conviction came before the world, not in the form of a philosophy but in the language of religious aspiration —'Blessed are the pure in heart, for they shall see God'—and when there seemed to be a personal human life which could be contemplated as one in which it had been realised, it appealed to a much wider range of persons than it had done in the schools of Greece, and moved the heart with a new power. But if those affected by it came to ask themselves what it meant for them— in what the morality resting on purity of heart consisted—it was mainly in forms derived, knowingly or unknowingly, from the Greek philosophers that the answer had to be given (§ 251, p. 270).

This appears to me a strange medley of the

views of different thinkers, which I will try to
disentangle. First, then, it ignores the special and
prominent characteristic of the teaching of Socrates,
which influences the whole subsequent course of Greek
ethical philosophy, that the difference between virtue
and vice depends primarily on the state of a
man's intellect or knowledge : since, as Socrates
argued with apparently irresistible force, 'every one
wishes for his own good, and would get it if he knew
how to.' As I have said in another place : It no
doubt seems to us an extravagant paradox to treat
men's ignorance of justice as the sole cause of
unjust acts; and to the Greek mind also the view
was paradoxical; but if we would understand the
position, not of Socrates only, but of ancient ethical
philosophy generally, we must try to realise that this
paradox was also a nearly unanswerable deduction
from a pair of apparent truisms. That 'every one
wishes for his own good, and would get it if he
could,' an arguer would hardly venture to question ;
and he would equally shrink from denying that
justice and virtue generally were goods, and of all
goods the finest. It thus became difficult for him to
refuse to admit that 'those who knew what were just
and righteous acts would prefer nothing else, while
those who did not know could not do them if they
would,' [1] which would land him at once in the conclusion of Socrates that justice and all other virtues
were summed up in wisdom or knowledge of good. [2]

---

[1] Cf. Xenophon, *Memorabilia*, III. chap. ix. 5, where Xenophon fully
confirms what Plato's dialogues abundantly illustrate.
[2] *Outlines of the History of Ethics*, chap. ii. § 3, pp. 24, 25.

And—as the Aristotelian author of what stands as the Seventh Book of the Nicomachean Ethics says—Socrates argued on the theory that want of self-control (*i.e.* volition contrary to judgment of what was best) did not exist.

Plato, not abandoning the Socratic ethical inquiry after knowledge of man's true good, but fusing it with a metaphysical inquiry into the essence of Reality, was led to his famous Idealism in the form best known to us, in which the objects of abstract thought constitute the real world, the notion of Good being the highest notion, ' even beyond being.' Hence the unity of virtue for Plato was dependent on the unity of abstract or ideal good, and lay in the fact that the philosophic virtues were all manifestations or aspects of knowledge of true good. It is true that in analysing virtue as it exists in ordinary men, and even in those who are preparing to be philosophers but are not yet perfect in philosophy, Plato recognised appetitive and impulsive elements in man, liable to conflict with reason and requiring to be trained to submission to it; but he none the less held that true philosophy necessarily carried with it all the virtues commonly recognised — the true philosopher must necessarily be truthful, temperate, magnanimous, brave, just, gentle. So that the Socratic doctrine is still maintained, though qualified : it is not will to be good, but knowledge of what is good, which is highest and most essential.

When we come to Aristotle, the inadequacy of mere

knowledge to produce practical virtue is more fully
recognised, and there is a careful analysis of volition
contrary to judgment as to what is best.   But Aristotle's conception of ἀρετή or human excellence is
even more markedly unlike the view given in the
passage above quoted from Green than Plato's is.
The 'unity of virtue'—if 'virtue' is a rendering
of the Greek ἀρετή, as it was in § 248—is for
Aristotle merely a generic unity.   Θεωρητικὴ ἀρετή,
intellectual excellence, or excellence of the faculty of
knowledge, is for Aristotle Speculative Wisdom,
which has no relation to moral virtue, being concerned about eternal truth—objects of thought higher
and nobler than human good and evil; but the
moral virtues are no doubt all involved in his
conception of Practical Wisdom, and may be said to
be unified by this notion.   Aristotle has, however, a
difficulty which he does not succeed in overcoming,
in forming a consistent notion of practical wisdom;
as I have tried to explain elsewhere, the kind
of reasoning which his view of virtuous conduct
requires is one in which the ultimate major
premise states a distinctive characteristic of some
virtue, and one or more minor premises show that
such characteristic belongs to a certain mode of
conduct under given circumstances; since he holds it
essential to good conduct that it should contain its
end in itself, and be chosen for its own sake.   But he
has not failed to observe that practical reasonings are
not commonly of this kind, but are rather concerned
with actions as means to ulterior ends; indeed, he lays

stress on this as a characteristic of the practical or
'political' life, when he wishes to prove its inferiority
to the life of pure speculation.   Though common
sense will admit that virtues are the best of goods, it
still undoubtedly conceives practical wisdom as chiefly
exercised in providing those inferior goods which
Aristotle, after recognising the need or use of them
for the realisation of human wellbeing, has dropped
out of sight; and the result is that, in trying to make
clear his conception of practical wisdom, we find
ourselves fluctuating continually between the common
notion, which he does not distinctly reject, and the
notion required as the keystone of his ethical
system.[1]

At the same time I quite agree that for the
chief schools of philosophers sprung from Socrates,
Virtue or Human Excellence was the whole (or the
main part) of the true good of individuals.   This is
true of Plato, Aristotle, the Cynics, and the Stoics.[2]
And it was no doubt the view of the main
line of philosophers that virtue, to be truly virtue,
must be chosen for its own sake, τοῦ καλοῦ ἕνεκα.
But here the agreement of what I may call the
orthodox schools ended—and in the case of all of
them, it seriously misrepresents and obscures the
relation of knowledge to virtue as conceived by the
ancient thinkers, to lay the stress that Green does on
will, and say that the 'direction of a man's will to
the highest possible realisation of his faculties' was,

---

[1] *Outlines of the History of Ethics*, chap. ii. § 11.
[2] Cf. pp. 105, 106 of *Methods of Ethics*, and chap. ii. of *Outlines of the
History of Ethics*.

in their view, 'the common ground of every form of true virtue.'

Let us concentrate attention on Aristotle; because it is with Aristotle's view that Green is chiefly concerned—and acquainted. We find that in § 254 Green renders Aristotle's definition of 'the true good for man' (εὐδαιμονία, wellbeing) : ' the full exercise or realisation of the soul's faculties in accordance with its proper excellence, which was an excellence of thought, speculative and practical.' It is, I think, misleading to call Aristotle's 'moral excellences' or 'excellences of character' (the ordinary 'virtues') 'excellences of practical thought' without any qualification; for Aristotle recognises a semi-rational element of the soul, capable of obeying reason—and in a thoroughly virtuous man, always obedient to it—and yet capable of conflicting with it; and for virtue there is required a right condition of this semi-rational element as well as of reason.

But, confining ourselves to the thought-element, how are we to conceive the judgment of practical reason by which good conduct in any particular case is determined as an object of knowledge ?—'The pure morality,' says Green, 'which we credit him [Aristotle] with having so well conceived, must have meant morality determined by interest in such a good [i.e. realisation of faculties].' But Green sees that 'interest' in wellbeing thus generally conceived does not get you far towards knowing what conduct in any particular case is virtuous. His answer to the difficulty is that there had taken place already :

. . . such a realisation of the soul's faculties as gave a meaning, though not its full and final meaning, to the definition
of the good.   In fact, however, . . . the same spiritual principle which yielded the demand for an account of what was
good in itself, and the conception of true goodness as determined
by interest in that good, had also yielded a realisation of the soul's
faculties in certain pursuits and achievements, and in a certain
organisation of life.   Already there were arts and sciences,
already families and states, with established rules of what was
necessary for their maintenance and furtherance (§ 254, p. 274).
But the function of ethics, as Aristotle defines it,
is to regulate all other arts.   Hence if Aristotle is
asked how he practically determines the Ultimate
Good, by the conception of which the inferior ends
or goods of other arts and pursuits are to be regulated
or systematised, he can hardly say—he certainly
would not have said—that the mere existence of
these pursuits sufficiently determines it.

No doubt Aristotle takes the definitions of the
particular virtues from Common Sense : indeed, one
of the chief sources of the interest that his work
has for a modern reader, lies in the fact that it gives
us, not merely the moral estimate of the individual
philosopher as regards the qualities of character and
conduct that he analyses, but the social estimate
of his age and country, as it presents itself to the
insight of impartial reflection.   But in his interpretation of Common Sense I find no hint of what Green
suggests in § 255 : namely, that the ' habits of action,
recognised as laudable' under the names of wisdom,
fortitude, temperance and justice, had the value
Common Sense attached to them as conducive to the
' unfolding of his [the rational man's] capacities in
full harmonious activity.'

When (says Green) we come to ask ourselves what are the
essential forms in which, however otherwise modified, the will
for true good (which is the will to be good) must appear, our
answer follows the outlines of the Greek classification of the
virtues. It is the will to know what is true, to make what is
beautiful; to endure pain and fear, to resist the allurements of
pleasure (*i.e.* to be brave and temperate), if not, as the Greek
would have said, in the service of the state, yet in the interest of
some form of human society; to take for oneself, to give to
others, of those things which admit of being given and taken,
not what one is inclined to, but what is due (§ 256).

Here we have Wisdom, Courage, Temperance,
Justice. And Green implies by what follows that
he is conceiving them as conceived by Aristotle.

First, then, as regards the 'will to know what
is true,' I must point out that in the theoretical
excellence of Aristotle—which he places above the
practical—the exercised faculty of knowing what
is true is the important point. There is no evidence
that he placed any value on the *mere* will—which
might exist in a ridiculously unsuccessful researcher
no less than in a Newton.

Again, 'the will to make what is beautiful' is
quite un-Aristotelian. And, so far as I remember,
there is nothing whatever said by Aristotle or any
other Greek philosopher suggesting that the will
to make what is beautiful is a part of human good.
A good deal of loose stuff is talked about the
Greek devotion to beauty. The truth is, that however important the Greeks may have thought Art
as a means of adorning life, there is no evidence
that 'Greek gentlemen' rated the artist's *métier*
high, or that the philosophers, concerned for their
own pursuit, tried at all to exalt it. In Aristotle's

comparison of βίοι, the artist's has no place.   Green is
here (§ 256) modernising very naïvely.

I pass to consider the virtue of ἀνδρεία, commonly
rendered Courage.   Here, according to Green's interpretation, the point is that pain and fear are to be
endured in the service of the State.   The essence of
the virtue is 'self-devotion for a worthy end' which,
says Green, Aristotle 'could only conceive . . . in some
form in which it had actually appeared . . . he knew
it in no higher form than as it appeared in the citizen-
soldier who faced death calmly in battle for his State'
(§ 258).   Now if we are examining the causes of the
special admiration given by Greek Common Sense—
on which Aristotle is reflecting—to valour in war, I
have no doubt that we are right in connecting it
with the social importance of this quality, in an
age when an individual's welfare was more completely
bound up with that of his State than is now the
case, while the very existence of the latter was more
frequently imperilled by hostile invasion.   But I can
find no trace of this view in Aristotle's analysis.
And I think Green gives a wrong impression of
agreement among the Greek philosophers in the
definition of ἀνδρεία.   The truth is that on this
point the opposition between Plato and Aristotle
is very marked, and is very characteristic of the
difference between the preponderantly synthetic
character of Plato's thought and the preponderantly
analytical character of Aristotle's.   In Plato's dialogue
on Courage, Socrates is made to say, in asking what
is Courage (ἀνδρεία) : 'I meant to ask you, not only

who is courageous in war, but who are courageous
in perils by sea, and who, in disease or poverty,
or again in political struggles, are courageous : and
not only who are courageous against pain and fear, but
who contend valiantly against desires and pleasures.'[1]
This is giving an extended meaning to the term :
Aristotle on the other hand narrows it in its
most proper sense to 'death in war.' 'The ἀνδρεῖος
(valiant) is not,' he says, 'concerned with death
under any circumstances—for instance, not death at
sea, or in disease. With what death then ? Surely
death under the noblest conditions; and such is
death in war : for it is death in the greatest and
finest danger. A man, then, will be properly called
brave who is fearless about a noble kind of death,
and things that suddenly bring on death : and the
events of war are especially of this kind.' 'No
doubt,' he goes on, 'the ἀνδρεῖος will be fearless
at sea or on a sick-bed,' but not (e.g.) 'as mariners
are at sea.' For 'experience gives the mariner
confidence ; but the type of man we are speaking
of gives up all hope of safety, and feels grief and
disgust at so ignoble a death.'[2] There is nothing
here said of 'self-devotion' to a 'state' or to a cause :
Aristotle is merely following closely and impartially
the lines of Common Sense, of the ethico-æsthetic
sentiment of his society. He appeals for confirma-
tion to the 'honours given both in republics and in
monarchies': therefore what Green says of the notion

<hr>

[1] Plato, *Laches*, 191 D.
[2] Aristotle, *Eth. Nic.* III. 6, §§ 6-12.

being applicable to a 'citizen-soldier' and implying
'active participation in a civil community' is quite
unwarranted and irrelevant. Even an ordinary
Greek would not have denied that a mercenary of
the Persian king might be as valiant as possible.

So when Green speaks, § 260, of the 'willingness
to endure even unto complete self-renunciation,' he is
using a quite un-Greek and un-Aristotelian notion.
Aristotle simply conceives the brave man as realising
moral beauty in his act. 'The beautiful,' he says,
'is the end for the sake of which the brave man
endures and does whatever is brave.'[1] Green com-
pares Aristotle's account of fortitude with the
Christian's view of this virtue. In all that is
said, §§ 258-261, of the enlargement of the modern
Christian ideal of valour or fortitude[2] there is much
truth, but I must point out that the βίος πρακτικός
is not to be identified with the 'life of rational
self-determined activity'—this would ignore the
distinction from βίος θεωρητικός.

In relation to Green's general view of Good, we
may ask why the 'Christian worker' devotes himself
to the service of the 'hopelessly sick.' Is it to relieve
their pain, or only to make them virtuous—to prevent their pain making them vicious? Then he need
not concern himself with the pain of the virtuous
sick whose fortitude will only be drawn out by it.
But this is a digression.

---

[1] Aristotle, *Eth. Nic.* III. 7, § 6.
[2] We may make a distinction between the two, denoting by valour a
disposition to face danger of any kind without shrinking, and attributing
fortitude to those who bear pain unflinchingly.

I now pass to the notion of Temperance (σωφρο-σύνη). Here the un-Aristotelian interpretation of the καλόν, 'the beautiful' or 'the noble' that Aristotle conceives as the end attained in a particular virtuous act (εὐδαιμονία = wellbeing, being the 'human good' as a whole for an individual) becomes more glaring.

To a Greek who was told that the virtue of temperance was a mastery over certain desires, exercised τοῦ καλοῦ ἕνεκα, there would be no practical doubt what the motive was to be, what was to be the object in which a prevailing interest was to enable him to exercise this mastery. In his view it could only be reverence for the divine order of the state, such a desire to fulfil his proper function in the community as might keep under the body and control the insolence of overweening lust. The régime of equal law, the free combination of mutually respecting citizens in the enactment of a common good, was the 'beautiful thing' of which the attraction might, through a fitting education, become so strong as to neutralise every lust that tended to disqualify a man for the effectual rendering of service to his state, or tempted him to deal wantonly with his neighbour. It was this character of the motive or interest on which it was understood to rest, that gave to σωφροσύνη an importance in the eyes of the Greek moralist which, if we looked simply to the very limited range of pleasures—pleasures of the merely animal nature—in regard to which Aristotle supposes the 'temperate man' to exercise self-restraint, would scarcely be intelligible (§ 263, p. 283 [1]).

Now all this is quite unhistorical. Though Aristotle discusses the virtue of σωφροσύνη at great length, and distinguishes carefully the pleasures to which it relates, and the attitude of the temperate man with regard to them, he never says (and Green almost confesses that he never says) a single word in this connexion about the 'régime of equal law' or the 'free combination of mutually respecting citizens' or

[1] Compare also § 268.

'the foundation of sobriety in a truly civic spirit'—
the whole discussion moves in a region from which
these notions are quite alien. He simply says that
the 'aim of the temperate man is τὸ καλόν'—that is, as
in the case of courage, the quality of his act which
corresponds to the praise commonly awarded to it
—' praise-worthiness' perhaps gives the idea best.
The idea that σωφροσύνη would not be laudable
except in a republic—which is really what Green's
phrases come to—would have appeared to Aristotle
absurd.

As for the corresponding modern notion, I agree
with much of what Green says, §§ 263-269. But I
think it might be more clearly pointed out that
modern thought has come to distinguish several
notions included—so far as recognised—under the
Greek σωφροσύνη. E.g. ' Temperance ' referring to the
agent's physical wellbeing, and ' Self-restraint ' referring to the performance of duty, have come to be
distinguished in a way in which they were not distinguished by Aristotle.

But here I may digress to observe again that in all
that Green says of modern self-denial to the end
of § 270, there seems to me a continual, though unconscious, evasion of a fundamental difficulty. The
end in reference to which desires have to be restrained by 'self-denial' (but again why *self*-denial)
is ' realising the possibilities' of others — for this
people ' shut themselves out from . . . æsthetic enjoy-
ments.' But do they not also shut themselves out
from realisation of their own possibilities ?   If Green

replies that 'moral capabilities' are alone important,
then I answer : How are the poor shut out from the
will to be good ?   The evasion lies in Green's continually speaking of the sacrifice as mere curtailment
of pleasures, which is of course indifferent to the
anti-hedonistic philosopher.   For we read (§ 270) of
sacrifices of all except *moral* capabilities to help the
realisation of possibilities of others.   'The good
citizen,' Green says, 'has no leisure to think of
developing . . . his faculties of enjoyment'; but this
is not only enjoyment—a man who gives up 'search
for knowledge,' 'friendly intercourse,' and so on, gives
up development of faculties ; and thus A's intellectual
development is as much an alternative to B's, as A's
pleasure.   This completer self-denial, we are told, is a
higher ideal than the Greek, because it involves a
fuller realisation of capacities (§ 273).   But when we
ask : Is it of A's capacities or of B's ?—Green does not
fairly meet the question.   He says that A's loss of
'innocent pleasures' is indifferent ; and that the life
of the Greek was not 'morally the better' for its
freedom from limitations.   But the point is : Does A
sacrifice not only enjoyment but development ?   If
not, why not ?   If he does, development is not a
Common Good in the sense of being non-competitive.

However—to return to the comparison of Greek
and modern ideals—I cannot accept Green's interpretation of the Aristotelian ideal because of (1) the
extent to which it ignores the superiority of $\theta\epsilon\omega\rho\iota\alpha$ and
the ulterior ends of $\phi\rho\delta\nu\eta\sigma\iota\varsigma$ or $\pi o\lambda\iota\tau\iota\kappa\eta$ admitted by
Aristotle (Green refers to this, § 287, but does not

appear to me to see its importance); (2) the un-
authorised definition and interpretation of the end in
any practical-virtuous act.   And why did he confine
himself to the virtues of Courage and Temperance?
I think the inappropriateness of his interpretation
of Aristotle would have been more manifest if he had
gone on to the others.   And as Aristotle has a list of
ten ἠθικαὶ ἀρεταί,—besides Justice, which he treats in
a separate book,—it is a little remarkable that Green
should have confined his examination to Courage
and Temperance.   After these, Aristotle gives two
pairs of virtues which are occupied respectively with
the two chief objects of man's more refined and
civilised desire and pursuit—Wealth and Honour;
distinguishing in each case the kind of excellence
which is possible only to a select few from that
which is more widely attainable.   Thus in the case
of Wealth, persons of moderate means may exercise
Liberality, but the more brilliant quality of Magnifi-
cence is only attainable by persons of large estate
and high social position.[1]

And an examination of these would show very
clearly how simply Aristotle is following the ethico-
æsthetic—or even purely æsthetic—sentiment of admiration for certain qualities in the conduct of a Greek
gentleman, and how far he is from conceiving self-
devotion to a social end as essential to the notion of
virtue.   For example his account of Liberality is startling to a modern reader from its want of distinction
between self-regarding and benevolent expenditure.

---

[1] *Outlines of the History of Ethics*, chap. ii. § 20, p, 62.

Compare also his account of μεγαλοψυχία (High-mindedness).

I notice one more point on which Green may mislead. Aristotle, though his definition of human good is primarily non-hedonistic, has nothing of the anti-hedonistic spirit which animates Green throughout. As I have said elsewhere, pleasure, in Aristotle's view, is not the primary constituent of wellbeing, but rather an inseparable accident of it ; human wellbeing is essentially welldoing, excellent activity of some kind, whether its aim and end be abstract truth or noble conduct ; and knowledge and virtue are objects of rational choice apart from the pleasure attending them; still all activities are attended and in a manner perfected by pleasure, which is better and more desirable in proportion to the excellence of the activity.[1] Hence it is not surprising that some members of this school soon came to hold the Aristotelian doctrine in a hedonistic form—as in what now stands as Book VII. of the *Nichomachean Ethics*, but is not, in my opinion, Aristotle's own. If we compare this with Book X. we see what a slight change has made the doctrine hedonistic.

But finally, as an account of the Greek ideal, presented by the philosophers, Green's statement is curiously defective ; he, with some references to Plato, confines himself mainly to Aristotle ; and an uninstructed reader could hardly be blamed for supposing that the transition is immediate from Aristotle to Christianity. The most important system of the

---

[1] *Outlines of the History of Ethics*, chap. ii. § 8, pp. 54, 55.

H

three intervening centuries — the Stoic system — is almost entirely ignored. And Green, in fact, seems almost to have forgotten Stoicism. Thus he tells us (§ 279) that 'Human brotherhood had no meaning for' the Greek philosophers ! But this ignores the 'cosmopolitanism' that was a marked characteristic not only of Stoicism, but also of the earlier Cynicism. No doubt the 'brotherhood' of the philosophers—at any rate till we come to the later Roman Stoics— was limited to the Wise : still it was not limited by polity or race, nor wealth or social position. I think, too, that if we do confine ourselves to Aristotle, it is more difficult than it would be in the case of the Stoics to make Green's view and the Greek philosophers' harmonise. Thus Green says in § 281 : 'The idea of the good and of goodness which first found formal expression in the Greek philosophers . . . implies interest in an object which is common to lla men in the proper sense,—in the sense, namely, that there can be no competition for its attainment between man and man.' But why then the limitation of view referred to in § 270—'To an ancient Greek a society composed of a small group of freemen, having recognised claims upon each other and using a much larger body of men with no such recognised claims as instruments in their service, seemed the only possible society.' Why was Aristotle's ideal restricted to a society of free men in the midst of a large group of enslaved human beings ? Because only so could the leisure necessary to 'realisation of capacities' be gained. And is not this largely true of that 'realising the possibilities of the human soul' which Green has in view ? It always seems to me, too, that the Stoic distinction between *Good and Evil*, and *Preferred and Rejected*, is very much wanted by Green,—for instance, when he says, speaking of Justice, that the 'just man is *impartial* in allotting benefit'—since impartiality can only furnish a rule applicable to *similar* cases.[1]

---

[1] Cf. *Outlines of the History of Ethics*, chap. ii. § 15.

LECTURE VII

GREEN'S TREATMENT OF HEDONISM

IT is sometimes considered that Green's attack on Hedonism is effective, granting his metaphysical doctrine that the Self, like the Eternal Consciousness of which it is a reproduction, is 'outside time.' Now it is doubtless true that Green affirms the Self—the Subject, or Self-distinguishing Consciousness, which is non-natural and therefore free—to be not in time. 'There could be,' he says, 'no such thing as time, if there were not a self-consciousness which is not in time' (§ 52).

At the same time, in both the strictly metaphysical and the ethical parts of his reasoning, Green continually applies terms with a temporal meaning to 'spirits' or self-conscious subjects, and to me at least these time-determinations appear quite essential to his conception of the universe. Take *e.g.* the brief summary in § 180, p. 189, where he says that under certain limitations 'the one divine mind gradually reproduces itself in the human soul. In virtue of this principle in him, man has definite capabilities, the realisation of which . . . forms his true good.' 'They are not realised, however, in any life that has been

. . . lived.' But 'because the essence of man's spiritual endowment is the consciousness of having' such capabilities, the idea of 'a possible better state of himself consisting in their further realisation, is a moving influence in him.' Every feature in this description involves the conception of a spirit changing and developing in time : if I try to apply it to the conception of a self-conscious subject not in time, I find it emptied of all meaning.

I may observe that there is the same difficulty in Kantian ethics. On the one hand, in explaining our consciousness of moral imputation, in justifying the 'judicial sentences of conscience,' Kant tells us that the human subject, so far as he is conscious of himself as a thing-in-himself, considers his existence as not subject to time-conditions, and therefore as an existence in which 'nothing is antecedent to the determination of his will.' Thus the bad man rightly conceives himself as responsible for his bad character, which he makes for himself in a single timeless act. Yet in other parts of the Kantian ethics, the idea of time is essential — consider, for example, the notions of end and motive. And even infinite time is essential. For we are told that 'pure practical reason forces us to assume a practical progress towards perfection as the real object of our will ; ' and 'this infinite progress is possible only if we presuppose that the existence of a rational being is prolonged to infinity.' Either of these doctrines is conceivable by itself; but I do not find their combination conceivable.

Of Green's view on the question of immortality I have already spoken. And in comparing his ethical doctrine with Utilitarianism, or considering his standpoint for judging Utilitarianism, I think we must abstract—as I have shown that he continually does himself—from the conception of the subject out of time.

I now turn to Green's polemic against Hedonism, which is contained chiefly in the following passages :—

Book III. chapter i. §§ 156-170 : *Pleasure and desire.*

Book III. chapter iv. §§ 219-239 : *Pleasure and Common Good.*

Book IV. chapter iii. : *The Practical Value of a hedonistic Moral Philosophy.*

Book IV. chapter iv. : *The Practical Value of Utilitarianism compared with that of the Theory of the Good as Human Perfection.*

As regards the first piece of controversy, I need say but little, as I have dealt fully, in my *Methods of Ethics*, with the Psychological Hedonism of Bentham and Mill, and Mill's proof of Utilitarianism ; both of which I reject. With a part of Green's controversy against Mill—that which is directed against Psychological Hedonism—I am almost entirely in accord—that is to say, I agree with his conclusion that the object of conscious desire and voluntary aim is not pleasure only. And I agree in the main with the explanation he gives of the prevalence of the opposite error—that is, that pleasure normally accompanies the attainment of the desired object, and that hence it is easy to conceive this pleasure as the real object aimed at. But the same analysis which shows me that I do not always aim at my own pleasure, shows me equally that I do not always aim at my own satisfaction. I reject, in the one case as in the other, the conscious egoism of the form in which human choice is conceived—except in the insignificant sense that I am conscious that what I desire and aim at is desired and aimed at by me—a tautological proposition. In fact, I find a considerable difficulty in distinguishing what Green calls self-satisfaction from pleasure. And so far as I can distinguish them,—so far as I can conceive the consciousness of attainment of a desired object separated from all pleasure,—it is something I do not desire.

As I have before said, I have a difficulty in forming a precise conception of what Green means by Self-satisfaction and its relation to the satisfaction or extinction of desire. It would seem that if — as Green conceives — I 'identify myself with a particular desire' in conscious volition, the 'satisfaction' of the particular desire must be at least a partial and transient self-satisfaction; and I have taken this to be his view (cf. § 104) and understood him to mean, when he says that 'self-satisfaction is not to be found in vicious self-seeking,' that *complete* or *permanent* self-satisfaction is not to be found. (This is my interpretation of Green; it goes beyond what he expressly says.) Well, this 'partial self-satisfaction' or 'satisfaction of particular desire' is normally a pleasurable consciousness, and

I can only distinguish the notion of Satisfaction from Pleasure by conceiving the former as the intellectual or cognitive element of the consciousness of attaining a desired end. But it appears to me not in accordance with the common usage of terms to mean by ' satisfaction' this cognitive element alone, abstracted from the pleasant feeling that is normally inseparable from it. No doubt we sometimes have the experience of attaining the desired end, without any consciousness of pleasure when the attainment comes. We desired a Dead Sea apple ; it turns to bitter ashes in our mouth. Here attainment of course carries with it the extinction of the desire ; but should we say that there was any ' satisfaction' ? I think not.

Returning to the polemic against Psychological Hedonism, we find that this recurs again in the discussion in Book III. chapter iv. In fact it is, I think, to be regretted that Green did not separate it more distinctly and completely from his discussion of Utilitarianism as an Ethical doctrine. His view of the connexion between the two partly depends on an ignorance of the course of English ethical thought. This ignorance is shown in his statement as regards Hume (*Prolegomena,* § 3, p. 5) : ' An act of a man's own, necessarily proceeding, according to Hume, from some desire for pleasure.' This, as a historical statement, is a simple blunder due to ignorance. Green must, I think (as editor of Hume), have read, but seems to have quite forgotten, Appendix II. (*Of Self-love*) to Hume's *Enquiry concerning the Principles of Morals*—in which Hume follows Butler in arguing *against* Psychological Hedonism, pointing to 'bodily appetites which necessarily precede all sensual enjoyment,' and mental passions by which we are impelled to seek particular objects without regard to interest : ' Nature,' he says, 'must give an original propensity to fame, ere we can reap any pleasure from it or pursue it from a desire of happiness.' Being in this state of ignorance as to Hume's views, whom he edited, it is not surprising that the anticipation by Hutcheson—a leading opponent of Psychological Hedonism—of Bentham's formula for determining the ' material' goodness of actions should have escaped his notice.[1]

I have made this historical digression because I think it is partly Green's imperfect acquaintance with history which leads him to mix up his polemic against Psychological Hedonism so persistently with his polemic against Ethical Hedonism. This fusion is quite natural in a writer who has before him throughout Mill's Utilitarianism—or rather a more or less incongruous combination of Mill and Bentham [2] —as the doctrine against which he is contending ; but it is liable, I fear, to confuse those who approach the subject through my book.

All this mingled and confusing polemic I propose to ignore. Separating from this the argument against Ethical Hedonism, I find chiefly four points in

---

[1] Cf. Green and Grose's edition of Hume, vol. ii. *Introduction,* § 24.

[2] In § 340 *e.g.* the proof of Utilitarianism which is referred to, belongs to Mill ; but the ' principles' spoken of ignore Mill's recognition of ' infirmity of character' (*Utilitarianism,* p. 14) and his distinction between desire and will (p. 59).

Book IV. chapter iv. :—(1) Duality of Rational Self-
love and Rational Benevolence. (2) Uncertainty of
Hedonistic calculation, as a source of practical weakness. (3) Essential transitoriness of pleasure—pleasure
not an 'abiding' Good. (4) The notion of a 'Sum
of pleasures.'

On the first of these points I need not speak : as
it was the main aim of my treatise on *The Methods
of Ethics* to exhibit this duality unmistakably, and
the need of reconciling the divergent ends : and I
shall recur to it in dealing with Spencer.

The only addition I have now to make is to ask
you to consider how far Green avoids a similar
duality. As we have seen, if we take Green's wider
notion of Perfection, namely, *complete realisation of
capabilities*, and understand this to include (as he
expressly affirms it to include) the development of
Science and Art, of the faculties of knowledge and
of artistic production and appreciation, we cannot
say that our own perfection or approximation to
perfection and others' perfection are not liable to be
presented as alternatives, unless we ignore the facts
of experience and the actual conditions of human life.
And Green's own language, in speaking of Justice,
Self-denial, Self-sacrifice, etc., involves a similar conception of 'Good to one' incompatible with 'Good to
another'—notwithstanding his assertion that True
Good does not consist in objects that admit of being
competed for.

So again as regards (2)—the uncertainty of
hedonistic calculation—I have aimed in *The Methods*

of Ethics at bringing out clearly the uncertainties of hedonistic calculation, and all that I will now observe is, that the uncertainties on Green's view seem to me indefinitely greater,—both more complex and more fundamental,—if a wider conception of the end as the complete realisation of capabilities is taken. All the alternatives presented for practical choice involve different realisations of different capabilities. What criterion does Green offer for preferring one sort of realisation to another? I find none whatever; and if the comparison of quantities of pleasure is difficult and doubtful, the comparison of different realisations of capabilities seems to me indefinitely more difficult and more doubtful.

There remain objections (3) and (4)—objections to the essential transitoriness of pleasure, and to the sum of pleasures; as regards the former of which there seems to be a fundamental and at present irremovable difference between the judgments of value which are passed by different reflective persons.

My own answer to the question of § 357 : Why is the ultimate good and criterion held to be pleasure? is, that nothing but pleasure appears to the reflective mind to be good in itself, without reference to an ulterior end; and in particular, reflection on the notion of the most esteemed qualities of character and conduct shows that they contain an implicit reference to some other and further good. In fact we have already seen that, even according to Green's own account of virtue (*e.g.* of Justice, § 212), this implicit reference is found to be to a

good that is *not* Green's true good which does not
admit of being competed for.   And to a man who
finds himself dissatisfied with the prospect of never-
ending happiness for himself or for the world, because
it has to be enjoyed under the condition of time, and
therefore in successive parts, I can only say that with
the poet

> I hold it good, good things should pass.
> With Time I will not quarrel.

I pass to concentrate attention on the criticism of
a 'sum of pleasures' which is less simple and requires
more distinction and elucidation.   This criticism we
find given in two places—in Book III. chapter iv.
§§ 221 seqq., where it is somewhat discursive and hard
to follow, and more definitely and sharply in Book
IV. chapter iv. § 359.   Looking closer, we see that
it is not the same notion that is being considered in
the two places—in Book III. it is 'sum of pleasures,'
in Book IV. it is 'greatest possible sum.'   That this is
so is not at first clear, as 'greatest possible sum' is
used in the former passage ; but I think it does become
clear on examination.   In the former passage Green
does not attack the notion as 'intrinsically unmeaning' as he does in the latter.   Indeed he says in § 222,
that 'it is not intended to deny that there may
be in fact such a thing as a desire for a sum or
contemplated series of pleasures, or that a man
may be so affected by it as to judge that some
particular desire should not be gratified, if its gratification would interfere with the attainment of that
more desirable object.'   In saying this, I conceive

that he admits all which Ethical Hedonism requires
to be admitted. He asserts, indeed, that a 'sum of
pleasures as felt or enjoyed is a non-entity'; but this
only means that the pleasures cannot be enjoyed
all at once, that 'pleasures do not admit of being
accumulated in enjoyment'; but as no Hedonist
ever dreamt that they could, the question need
not be argued. If Green prefers to talk of 'series'
or 'succession' rather than 'sum,' we need not raise
any difficulties; and thus his objection becomes merely
the objection to the essential transitoriness of pleasure, to which I have already referred.

Apart from this objection to transitoriness, what
Green seems most concerned to argue in this earlier
chapter is the inconsistency of Ethical Hedonism with
Psychological Hedonism as he understands it: since 'if
all desire *is* for pleasure, it rather follows that a sum
of pleasures *cannot* be desired, since it is not a pleasure, and can only be conceived, not felt or imagined'
(§ 221, Analytical summary, p. xxiv.). Now, though
this polemic is not directed against any view that I
hold, I cannot admit the validity of Green's criticism.
I do not admit his statement here that 'a desire to
satisfy oneself, . . . as distinct from desire for a feeling
of pleasure,' is 'necessary even to desire for a sum of
pleasures' (§ 222); nor his statement that 'it is not
the pleasures *as a sum* that attract' a man, because
he cannot 'imagine them as a sum' (§ 228).   I
should answer : Certainly he cannot imagine the
pleasures to be felt as a sum. But so far as they
admit of being quantitatively compared at all—and

Green does not deny that they can be quantitatively compared in some degree, he does not intend to deny that certain courses of action 'tend to make life more pleasant on the whole,' or that 'an over-balance of pain on the whole would result to those capable of being affected by it' from certain other courses of action — pleasures can be summed in thought, *i.e.* they can be thought in the aggregate; and it is as so summed that they attract a man *qua* rational being.

To say that 'desire of pleasure' and 'desire of greatest amount of pleasure' are different, is true; but desire of greatest amount of pleasure or deter-mination to take greatest amount of pleasure as end, is, in my view, the form which the desire of pleasure necessarily takes in a reflective mind, capable of com-paring pleasures quantitatively. If I am asked : Why should I choose action tending to produce a larger sum of less intense pleasures and not a more intense but briefer pleasure ? I answer : If it be granted that pleasure as the end is made up of elements capable of quantitative comparison, it is self-evident that the greater *quantum* of pleasure is to be preferred to the less, and that *ex vi termini* the larger sum made up of less intense pleasures is the greater quantum of pleasure.

Let us now pass to the more definite attack in Book IV. chapter iv. The phrase *greatest possible sum of pleasures* seems, says Green,

to be intrinsically as unmeaning as it would be to speak of a greatest possible quantity of time or space. The sum of pleasures plainly admits of indefinite increase, with the continued existence of sentient beings capable of pleasure. It is greater

to-day than it was yesterday, and, unless it has suddenly come
to pass that experiences of pain outnumber experiences of pleasure, it will be greater to-morrow than it is to-day ; but it will
never be complete while sentient beings exist. To say that
ultimate good is a greatest possible sum of pleasures, strictly
taken, is to say that it is an end which for ever recedes ; which
is not only unattainable, but from the nature of the case can
never be more nearly approached ; and such an end clearly cannot serve the purposes of a criterion, by enabling us to distinguish actions which bring men nearer to it from those that do
not (§ 359, p. 401).

Now, doubtless, absolute time and space, or the
time and space within fixed limits, cannot be increased. The answer of Emerson's Indian to the
philosopher who complained that he had not enough
time, ' I suppose you have all there is,' was from this
point of view incontrovertible. But surely we do
speak of the greatest possible quantity of time and
space obtainable for given purposes under given conditions : I plan the arrangement of my day's engagements to obtain the greatest possible amount of time
for effective study ; I plan the arrangement of my
book-shelves to obtain the greatest possible amount
of space for my books. Surely Green would not say
that it is intrinsically unmeaning to speak of a man
as aiming at the greatest possible length of life.
And when the Utilitarian is aiming at the greatest
possible happiness under certain definitely conceived
conditions — imperfectly known, no doubt, and
especially imperfectly foreseen — it is just the fact
that his rational aim is limited by his foresight that
renders Green's objection on account of ' indefinite
increase ' altogether irrelevant. But the objection
that the series is possibly infinite has no theoretical

validity, even apart from the actual limitation of
foresight; for it may, notwithstanding, be capable of
being made greater or less, and that is all that we
require for a practical criterion.

'To say,' Green goes on, 'that ultimate good is
a greatest possible sum of pleasures' is 'to say that
it is an end which for ever recedes.'   But surely an
end, as a practical notion, *must* be always in the
future : we could not possibly aim at realising it
if it were not.   He says, finally, that it cannot
serve the purpose of a criterion, because we cannot
'distinguish actions which bring men nearer to it
from those that do not.'   That is the argument
I have answered in *Methods of Ethics*, Book II.
chapter iii. § 1,[1] and I still think the answer valid and
adequate.   Green illegitimately imports his special
notion of an end as something to which right actions
only bring us nearer.   I contend that if we once
admit that Ultimate Good may be something capable
of being more or less realised in successive periods of
time, the utilitarian criterion (maximum happiness)

---

[1] 'But unless the transiency of pleasure diminishes its pleasantness . . .
I cannot see that the possibility of realising the Hedonistic end is at all
affected by the necessity of realising it in successive parts.   The argument
seems to assume that by an End must be meant a goal or consummation
which, after gradually drawing nearer to it, we reach all at once : but this is
not, I conceive, the sense in which the word is ordinarily understood by
ethical writers : and certainly all that I mean by it is an object of rational
aim—whether attained in successive parts or not—which is not sought as a
means to the attainment of any ulterior object, but for itself.   And so long
as any one's prospective balance of pleasure over pain admits of being made
greater or less by immediate action in one way or another, there seems
no reason why Maximum Happiness should not provide as serviceable a
criterion of conduct as any Chief Good capable of being possessed all at
once, or in some way independent of the condition of time' (*Methods of
Ethics*, p. 134).

is one that clearly enables us to decide between two courses of conduct, one of which promises a realisation of more of this good and another of less, within the period capable of being foreseen.

To Green's objection that moral approval is impossible without reference to an ideal of a perfect state of existence, I answer: Why? Why cannot approval be given to this preference of *more* good to *less*, without introducing the notion of a possible maximum? In fact it is to such a preference that my approval, and, I believe, the approval of men in general, is given. If I had to wait to convince myself that a perfect state of existence was possible for humanity, before approving or disapproving of human actions, I should be waiting still.

It follows from this that Green's effort to 'make sense of' the Utilitarian theory is laudable but only partially successful: he fails to see that the Utilitarian's Ultimate Good is not like his own a Utopia which we may come nearer to or imitate, but a kind of existence which is continually being realised in some degree. The Utilitarian—with the exception of Mr. Spencer—is *not* thinking of a 'certain sort of social life' such that no one gains pleasure at the expense of another: he does not know and need not know that such a life is possible, nor could the Utilitarian consistently prefer it to a life in which there is more pleasure on the whole, though otherwise distributed. Nor again would he prefer a life with as little pain as possible, supposing that a diminution of pain in any direction involved a greater

I

diminution of pleasure.   In short, Green's effort 'to
make sense' of the Utilitarian theory eliminates or
obscures the quantitative element of the notion of
the end; and the argument which follows in § 361,
to show that the notion (thus rendered indefinite
by Green) is less definite than Green's own 'end,'
becomes unimportant.

In § 362 Green does not dispute the conduciveness
of general virtue to general happiness, but says that
the adoption at an earlier time of Utilitarianism
would not have promoted the development of virtue.
I do not see how he can know this.   If he admits
that Virtue as generally recognised is conducive to
general happiness, how does he know that if men
had been Utilitarians, they would not have found
this out, and promoted virtue accordingly on utilitarian grounds?   But granting that they would
not, that does not prove that the adoption of Utilitarianism *now* would not promote the development
of virtue.   It may be—I think it is—true that
Utilitarianism is only adapted for practical use
by human beings at an advanced stage of their
intellectual development.   'The times past of our
moral intuitions God winked at, but now commandeth
all men to follow calculations of utility.'   Finally, the
contention of § 363, that the 'conception of the good
as human perfection does help us to interpret conventional morality and thus to see the direction in which
we should sometimes go beyond it' (p. xxxiii.), seems
to me a purely dogmatic assertion unsupported by
proofs.   I cannot find in § 363, pp. 405, 406, any

indication of the manner in which the notion of perfection supplies a *rational method* for reforming conventional morality; nor can I find it anywhere in the book. If I could have found it, I would have examined it critically, but I can find nothing sufficiently definite for criticism to bite upon.

LECTURE VIII

GREEN'S TREATMENT OF HEDONISM (*continued*)

I WILL now recapitulate the general discussion in the last Lecture of Green's polemic against Hedonism.

I first dealt with the metaphysical point that the self according to Green is ' out of time,' and therefore ' its satisfaction if sought at all must be sought out of time.' I pointed out that the existence of the human self or subject is characterised by Green himself as a ' gradual reproduction of the eternal consciousness,' and that its true good is said to consist in a ' further realisation ' of capabilities not yet realised (§ 180). Time, therefore, is essentially involved in the conception of the Self so far as ethical. And I noted that Green gives us no ground for conceiving — and hardly himself appears definitely to conceive — the limitations, the finiteness, of the human spirit, as a characteristic belonging to it, except so far as it is conceived under the form of time. Abstract from time and all that belongs to time, and there would seem to be only the eternal consciousness left.

I then passed to consider that part of Green's

controversy—directed primarily against Mill—which
relates to what I call Psychological Hedonism.   Here
I am in agreement with Green as against Mill, in
holding that the object of a man's conscious desire
and voluntary aim is not always his own pleasure ;
but the same reflective analysis which convinces me
of this, shows me equally that I do not always consciously aim at self-satisfaction.   That is, so far as I
can distinguish ' satisfaction ' from pleasure ; but this
I can only do by putting an unusual meaning on the
term and taking it to denote the intellectual element
of the consciousness of attainment of a desired object
—or, if you like, realisation of capacities previously
recognised or felt as needing realisation — as distinguished from the feeling element of such consciousness.   I ought to add that, so far as I make this
abstraction, it is pleasure and not self-satisfaction
so abstracted which I desire and regard as desirable ;
but I do not affirm that a separation between the
two is possible — to me the proposition that I
always desire my own satisfaction, would involve the
proposition that I always desire my own pleasure.
So far as I can analyse my own consciousness both
are equally false—as, for instance, in the case of
desire for posthumous fame, or for the permanence
of the British Empire.

I then, making a brief historical digression, noticed
Green's imperfect acquaintance with the history of
English ethical thought—which makes him always
think, and repeatedly say, that the utilitarian
doctrine of the Chief Good as a criterion was

originally and is most naturally connected with the
hedonistic doctrine that 'pleasure is the sole motive';
in ignorance apparently of the development of
thought represented by Shaftesbury and Hutcheson,
and of the fact that Hutcheson, the leading opponent
of the hedonistic doctrine of motives, yet anticipates
Bentham in his formula for determining material
goodness.   Any one who takes a comprehensive and
impartial survey of the history of English ethical
thought as a whole will see the notion of Good becoming gradually more precisely defined as Pleasure, from
Cumberland to Hutcheson, Hume and Bentham, while
at the same time the disinterestedness of human
desires is maintained with increasing clearness and
definiteness up to Hutcheson ; and is even maintained
by Hume.   Here I noted Green's error of attributing
Psychological Hedonism without qualification to
Hume and to Mill — ignoring Hume's acceptance
of Butler's doctrine of extra-regarding desires, and
Mill's important distinction between the direction
of Desire, and the direction—through habit—of Will.

I next passed to consider Green's attack on Ethical
Hedonism (the doctrine that Pleasure is the Ultimate
Good).   I asked you to distinguish four points
against which the attack is directed.   (1) The Duality
of Rational Self-love and Rational Benevolence.   (2)
The uncertainty of Hedonistic calculation.   (3) The
essential transitoriness of pleasure—pleasure not an
'abiding' Good.   (4) The notion of a 'Sum of
pleasures.'

As regards (1) I pointed out that it was the object

of my *Methods of Ethics* to exhibit clearly this
duality — and its consequences as regards ethical
method. I allowed that the practical objection (2)
has undoubtedly some force. A clear and certain
forecast of consequences must affect a man's will
more than a doubtful or uncertain forecast. I suppose, for instance, that much fewer rich people who
ought not to drink champagne would do so, if they
were quite sure that gout would follow—even at a
long interval. But the degree of weight to be
attached to the objection varies very much with the
individual. There remained the other two theoretical
arguments.

As to (3) what is alleged had to be admitted. Nor
do I now recur to the inquiry how far Green's system
really offers a more abiding good; to his criticism of
Hedonism a mere *tu quoque* would be a poor reply.
The question is as to the force of this criticism. Here
I think there is not much room for argument, when
the question is fairly stated. ' Life is essentially change,
and the good life must be essentially life.' I cannot
in the least understand the objection to a good to be
possessed and enjoyed in successive parts, except as
based upon or springing out of an objection to life
itself. To persons so constituted that they cannot
contemplate never - ending happiness as Ultimate
Good, I can only say that I permanently, deliberately, and contentedly contemplate a prospective *flow*
—needless implication of discontinuity is conveyed
by *series*—of happiness, unending by preference, as
the sole conceivable ultimate good for man.

I passed finally to the fourth objection—the objection to the notion of a 'sum of pleasures.' Here Green's polemical argument appears partly to repeat or depend upon arguments already discussed. Thus he affirms again and again, that if all desire is for pleasure, a sum of pleasures cannot be desired, because pleasure cannot be desired or imagined as a sum. These objections seem to me idle :—it is like arguing gravely that a man cannot desire to live till ninety because he cannot *imagine* but only *conceive* or *think* the number that is a product of 9×10 ! As I have said, I hold that desire of the greatest sum of pleasure, or determination to take greatest amount of pleasure as end, is the form which the desire of pleasure normally assumes in a rational mind. And so far as we can quantitatively compare, in the forecast of practical thought, the pleasures attending respectively alternative courses of conduct, the question how far we can imagine or 'forefeel' them is practically important only because the defect of imagination is the normal cause of the divergence and conflict between prudential reason and non-rational appetites and desires.

Thus, apart from Psychological Hedonism, Green's objection to the hedonistic end as 'sum of pleasures' appears to be partly material, and so far is a repetition of the objection to their transitoriness—'they are not enjoyable as a sum.' Partly it may be a formal or even verbal objection to the use of the term 'sum' as applied to a succession of transient facts that cannot coexist. This is not clearly stated by Green, but I think it was in his mind, and to this the reply is that in ordinary thought and discourse we do continually sum things that cannot co-exist;[1] so far as I know, not even a metaphysician has ever objected to this, except in the single case of pleasures. Putting these objections aside, what is left seems really directed against not 'sum of pleasures' but 'greatest possible sum'; and in answer to this I pointed out that an end as a practical notion must be always in the future, and that as long as any one's prospective balance of pleasure may be made greater or less by immediate action, maximum happiness provides a serviceable criterion of conduct.

I go on now to the polemic directed against myself in Book IV. chapter iv. of the *Prolegomena*—where objection to the 'sum of pleasures' expressly takes the form of objection to 'greatest possible sum.' But I must pause to notice an argument which illustrates the curious want of distinction in Green's mind between 'good in prospect' and 'good in fruition.' An 'enlightened and dispassionate' inquirer, he says,

will be likely to call in question the common assumption that the aggregate of pleasures at any time enjoyed might, *under the circumstances*, be greater than it is. He will see that this assumption conflicts with the principles on which 'the proof

---

[1] Historians, statisticians, and plain men are continually summing facts and events that do not coexist—the deaths in a year from such and such a disease, or the deaths generally, or the births and marriages, or the battles in a war, or the wars in a century, or the Kings of England since the Conquest, or the Prime Ministers of France since the foundation of the Third Republic. We do continually sum the parts of time which by the nature of the case cannot coexist,—the days, weeks, months, in the year,—the years in a century.

of Utilitarianism' has been generally founded. These principles
are that every one acts from what is, for the time, his strongest
desire or aversion, and that the object of a man's strongest desire
is always that which for the time he imagines as his greatest
pleasure, the object of his strongest aversion that which for the
time he imagines as his greatest pain. Now we have clearly no
title to say that any one is mistaken in such imagination; that
anything else would be a greater pleasure or pain *to him at the
time* than that which, being what he is and under the given circumstances, he looks forward to as a greatest pleasure or pain (§ 340).

But why have we 'no title'? There are probably
experiences of the man's own, of which we can
remind him, and certainly experiences of others—and
every man, as a social being, is continually learning
and guiding himself by experiences of others — to
show that imagination, in the state of desire,
exaggerates the expected pleasure; which is continually found, when attainment comes, to be less—
even startlingly less—than it was expected to be.
And this Green seems to admit, for he says:

> The pleasure may turn out to be much less in enjoy-
> ment than in imagination; it may in the sequel lead to the
> most intense pain; but it remains true that for the time, it is
> the pleasure which the man imagines as then for him the greatest,
> and which by inevitable consequence (on the given hypothesis)
> he most strongly desires—it is in fact the greatest pleasure of
> which he is capable (§ 340).

Yet how can this 'remain true'? Is it not, on
the contrary, obvious and certain, that if the man
will be disappointed in fruition and will suffer
intense pain in the sequel, he would obtain a
greater balance of pleasure over pain on the whole
by resisting this particular desire and avoiding the
disappointment and the subsequent intense pain?
And if so, the Utilitarian may obviously convince

the man of this, and lead him to adopt a course of conduct different from that to which the particular desire prompts. And it is just this, and nothing but this, that Bentham—as Psychological Hedonist and Determinist—regards as the function of the Utilitarian moralist in advising individuals.

I now come to the criticism of my own view that §§ 364-371 contain. The misunderstanding of my view on which the treatment of it here is based appears to me to be partly explicable in a writer who had only read—as I believe Green to have only read— certain chapters of my *Methods of Ethics*, especially Book I. chapter iv. (on *Pleasure and Desire*) and Book III. chapter xiv. (on *Ultimate Good*). But I venture to hope that it would have been im- possible to any one who had read the book through.[1] Green begins in § 364 by complaining that I argue ' as if to hold that the ultimate standard of moral valuation is something else than the productivity of pleasure, was to hold that it is something else than productivity of desirable consciousness,' and says that ' it does not appear why a state of consciousness should not be desired ' or deemed desirable ' for another reason than for the sake of the pleasure anticipated in it.'

I answer that Green seems entirely to ignore the line of argument by which I try to make this

---

[1] Holding that I was in part responsible for the misunderstanding which I perceived to have occurred, I endeavoured by some modifications in the third edition to remove that source of misapprehension. (It was the second edition of *The Methods of Ethics*, published in 1877, that Green had before him ; the third edition was published in 1884. Green died in the year 1882, and his *Prolegomena to Ethics* was published in 1883.),

'appear.' Having stated my view that we cannot on reflection maintain anything to be intrinsically and ultimately good, except in so far as it enters into relation to consciousness of some kind and renders that good and desirable : and thus that the only ultimate Good, or end in itself, must be Goodness or Excellence of Conscious Life, I note that when we have so far limited the application of the notion Good to conscious life, it may seem that our result is really identical with what we call Happiness : that to say that all other things called good are only means to the end of making conscious life intrinsically better or more desirable, is in fact to say that they are means to the end of happiness. But I then go on to admit and even emphasise the fact that on the other hand it seems clear that, in ordinary thought, consciousness active and passive is conceived to be preferable on other grounds than its pleasantness. And the explanation of this double view seems to be that when we judge one kind of consciousness to be more pleasant than another, we judge it to be preferable considered merely as consciousness, without taking into account the conditions under which it occurs ; but when we judge it to be better though less pleasant, what we really prefer is no longer the consciousness itself, but something in its conditions, concomitants or consequences. And I illustrate this by reference to some of those ideal objects, for the sake of which it is sometimes thought that a rational being ought to sacrifice human happiness. The mental state of apprehending truth may be preferred to the mental state of half-reliance on generally accredited fictions, although, if the fiction be pleasant, the former state may be more painful than the latter ; and such preference may be independent of any effect which we expect either state to have upon our subsequent consciousness. Here, in my view, the real object of preference is not the consciousness of knowing truth, considered merely as consciousness, because the element of pleasure or satisfaction in this is more than out-weighed by the concomitant pain ; but the relation between the mind and something else, which is whatever it is independently of our cognition of it. This may become more clear if we imagine ourselves learning afterwards that what we took for truth is not really such : for in this case we should certainly feel that our preference had been mistaken : whereas if our choice had really been between two elements of transient consciousness, its reasonableness could not be affected by any subsequent change of belief.

Similarly a man may prefer freedom and penury to a life of luxurious servitude, not because the pleasant consciousness of being free outweighs in prospect all the comforts and securities that the other life would afford, but because he has a predominant aversion to that relation beween his will and the will of another which we call slavery. Here, too, he may perhaps be led to regard his preference as mistaken, if he be afterwards persuaded that there is no such thing as Freedom : that we are all slaves of circumstances, destiny, etc.

So again, one may believe that what pleases one most among works of art is not really the most beautiful, and may prefer the contemplation of the latter to that of the former, as a more elevated exercise of taste.

If such objects, then, as Truth, Freedom, and Beauty, or strictly speaking, the objective relations [1] of conscious minds which we call cognition of Truth, contemplation of Beauty and Independence of Action, are good, independently of the pleasures that we derive from them, it must be reasonable to aim at these for mankind generally, and not at happiness only : and this view seems, though not the prevailing one, to be widely accepted among cultivated persons. [2]

When I compare the cognition of Truth, contemplation of Beauty, volition to realise Freedom or Virtue, with Pleasure, in respect of their relation to Ultimate Good, I would justify my own view that it is Pleasure alone, desirable Feeling, that is ultimately and intrinsically good, by the only kind of argument of which the case seems to me to admit. I would point out that we may be led to regard as mistaken our preferences for the conditions, concomitants or consequences of consciousness, as

---

[1] By 'objective relations of the conscious subject' (cf. Green's note on p. 407) I mean relations of the conscious mind which are not included in its consciousness—what *is* so included is *a belief in the relations*—a belief which may turn out to be erroneous. I see no evidence that Green has understood my argument, since he confounds what I distinguish—*knowing truth* and *believing that we know truth*, and treats 'cognition of truth' as if it was simply a state of consciousness of the knowing particular mind.

[2] Cf. *Methods of Ethics*, Book III. chap. xiv. §§ 1 and 2 in second edition.

distinguished from the consciousness itself, and in
order to show this, I would ask the reader to use the
same twofold procedure that I have regarded as
applicable in considering the absolute and independent
validity of common moral precepts.   I would appeal,
firstly, to his intuitive judgment after due consideration of the question when fairly placed before it ;
and, secondly, to a comprehensive comparison of the
ordinary judgments of mankind.   As regards the first
argument, to me at least it seems clear that these
objective relations of the conscious subject, when
distinguished in reflective analysis from the consciousness accompanying and resulting from them, are not
ultimately and intrinsically desirable, any more than
material or other objects are, when considered out
of relation to conscious existence altogether.[1]

Now, how does Green answer this argument? So far
as I can see, he ignores it.   He answers (§ 364, p. 407)
an argument, involving Psychological Hedonism,
which I do not use ; and which he admits that I do
not use.   He contends that 'to suppose pleasure
. . . to be the object of our desire for supreme or
ultimate good' because it 'carries with it some
anticipation of the pleasure there would be in
satisfaction of the desire' is 'to repeat the mistake,
to which Mr. Sidgwick is so thoroughly alive, of confusing the pleasure which attends the satisfaction of
a desire with the object of the desire, and the anticipation of that pleasure with the desire itself.'
Again Green says (§ 365) that

---

[1] *Methods of Ethics*, Book III. chap. xiv.

it would be unfair to convey the impression that Mr. Sidgwick, in identifying that 'desirable consciousness' which he holds that ultimate good must be, simply with pleasure, is chargeable with confusion between the object of a desire and the pleasure anticipated in its satisfaction. . . . In the common Hedonistic ratiocination—we always anticipate pleasure in the satisfaction of desire, therefore pleasure is the sole thing desired, therefore the sole thing desirable—pleasure must throughout mean pleasure for the person supposed to desire it. . . . It is not upon any such ratiocination that he [Mr. Sidgwick] founds his own conclusion that 'desirable feeling' (by which he understands pleasure) 'for the innumerable multitude of living beings, present and to come,' is the one end ultimately and intrinsically desirable.

Green then goes on to say that I found my own conclusion on an appeal to what I 'call Common Sense.' But the argument which he proceeds to cite from me is *not* an appeal to Common Sense (which I carefully explain to be an appeal to 'a comprehensive comparison of the ordinary judgments of mankind'), but is an appeal to the moral intuition of my readers; and the part of that appeal which now concerns us he misrepresents. For what Green here refers to is an earlier passage in my book [1]—where I say that '*as rational beings* we are manifestly bound to aim *at good generally, not merely at this or that part of it;* we can only evade the conviction of this obligation *by denying that there is any such universal good.*' Now Green quotes only part of this passage, and his reference runs as follows :—

[Mr. Sidgwick says that] 'As rational beings we are manifestly bound to aim at good generally, not merely at this or that part of it,' and in the last resort we can give no meaning to good but happiness, which = desirable consciousness, which = pleasure (§ 365, p. 408).

[1] *Methods of Ethics*, p. 355 of the second edition.

But I do not say that we can '*give no meaning to good but happiness*'; I carefully avoid saying anything of the kind; and in the passages in chapter xiv. of Book III. above referred to, I expressly admit and discuss the view that consciousness may be and is conceived to be preferable on other grounds than its pleasantness.

Green proceeds (in sections 365, 366, 367) to charge me with tautology. Taking the summary on pages xxxiii. and xxxiv. the charge runs as follows :—

> According to Mr. Sidgwick's theory . . . desirable consciousness is the same as pleasure, and his Universalistic Hedonism . . . seems to rest on the position that reason pronounces ultimate good to be desirable consciousness or pleasure, and further, universal pleasure. But 'desirable,' when it is distinguished from 'desired,' seems to be equivalent to 'reasonably to be desired'; and if so, the doctrine will be the circular statement that reason pronounces ultimate good to be the kind of consciousness it is reasonable to seek.

Now I think this charge quite unwarrantable, even taking only the argument in chapter xiv. of my Book III. For the object of a great part of this argument is carefully to distinguish pleasure or happiness—desirable *Feeling*—from other elements of conscious life, which I do not, in a reflective attitude, regard as ultimately desirable.[1] To say that the 'only thing that reason declares to be ultimately desirable is some kind of feeling,' whatever it is, is not a tautology, nor the same thing as saying that it is some kind of conscious life.

---

[1] Compare p. 368, and note 2 on p. 366 in the second edition of the *Methods of Ethics.*

But again, Green's statement of my view leaves out the further determination of the kind of feeling which is given in the definition of Pleasure, and which I fondly supposed that the reader would carry with him from Book II. I there[1] define Pleasure as 'the kind of feeling which, when we experience it, we apprehend as desirable or preferable'—as 'feeling that is preferable or desirable, considered merely as feeling, and therefore from a point of view from which the judgment of the sentient individual is final.' The statement that Ultimate Good is feeling of a certain quality, the quality being estimated by the judgment of value implicitly passed on it by the sentient being at the time of feeling it,—this proposition is certainly not a tautology.

A similar want of understanding of my distinction between 'desired' and 'desirable' appears in Green's subsequent arguments (§§ 368, 369, pp. 412, 413). I do not argue that the reason why 'no one denies pleasure to be a good' is merely 'because he is conscious of desiring it,' for I maintain that we all have experience of desires directed to wrong objects, and also to objects clearly not ultimately desirable —*e.g.* in resentful impulse I desire another's pain, but on reflection I do not judge this pain to be desirable because I desire it, but because it is necessary for the determent or reformation of the offender.

Again, I cannot conceive why 'desirable' should

---

[1] *Methods of Ethics,* Book II. chap. ii. (p. 114 in second edition), and beginning of chap. iii. of Book II.

exclude the 'actually desired,' as is argued by Green on p. 413. Of course we should not apply the idea of 'desirable' as distinct from 'desired,' unless we had empirical evidence [1] that we desire pleasures to some extent out of proportion to their value as pleasures ; but it does not follow that feeling actually desired is not normally, in the main, feeling judged desirable when fruition comes : as overwhelming experience shows to be in fact the case.

[1] Cf. *Methods of Ethics*, Book II. chap. ii. § 2 (pp. 126, 127 in sixth edition).

ON MR. HERBERT SPENCER'S

PRINCIPLES OF ETHICS

LECTURE I

MR. SPENCER's aim is the 'establishment of rules of right conduct on a scientific basis' (Preface to *Data of Ethics*, p. viii.[1]). Before systematically attempting this, he indicates certain important advantages to be derived from it. First, 'supernatural ethics' is disappearing and leaving a gap, and Reason is called upon to supply the hiatus left by the cessation of a belief in Revelation. We need not dwell on this; because, granting that the fact is as alleged, it cannot do more than supply a motive to the study of ethics: from the fact that a need has to be met, a problem to be solved, we gain no guidance as to the method to be adopted in solving it: we cannot even infer without irrational optimism that the problem is one which can be solved.

So far the argument suggests that 'supernatural ethics' met the need of guidance fairly well. Mr. Spencer goes on, however, to indicate certain defects

---

[1] References in the text are to Mr. Herbert Spencer's *Principles of Ethics*, unless otherwise stated.

in current morality—'morality as it is'—from which 'morality as it should be' will be free. Morality as it is has been like a father who 'sternly enforces numerous commands, some needful and some needless,' in an unsympathetic manner. Morality as it should be will resemble a father who maintains needful restraints but sanctions legitimate gratifications; and will gain proportionally in effectiveness. Again, morality as it is has set up an impracticable ideal: morality as it should be will avoid this defect.

I have drawn attention to this, because there seems to me to be a certain ambiguity in the notion of 'establishing moral rules on a scientific basis,' which I am anxious to remove completely before I proceed further. Writers who discuss moral rules either from what Mr. Spencer calls 'the evolution point of view,' or in the earlier manner of the Associationist school, frequently mean by a 'scientific' treatment of morality, merely an investigation of the laws according to which the ethical beliefs and sentiments of our own or any other society have come into existence. Such an investigation is obviously a legitimate branch of Sociology or Psychology; and chapters vii. and viii. of Mr. Spencer's *Data of Ethics*, which treat of the *Psychological View* and *Sociological View*, seem to be largely concerned with speculations of this kind. So far as this is the case, I do not propose to criticise either the method or the conclusions of these chapters; what I wish to point out is, that this species of inquiry, however successfully conducted, has not

necessarily any tendency to 'establish' the authority
of the morality of which it explains the existence;
indeed it has more often, I think, an effect of the
opposite kind.   A scientific explanation of current
morality which shall also be an 'establishment' of it,
must do more than exhibit the causes of existing ethical
beliefs; it must show that these causes have operated
in such a way as to make these beliefs true.   Now
this Mr. Spencer certainly does not attempt; for the
sufficient reason that he does not admit, and could
not, without large deductions, attempt to prove, the
final authority of existing ethical beliefs.   In the
chapters which contain, *inter alia*, his account of the
origin of current moral conceptions, he is continually
criticising them as 'defective,' 'one-sided,' 'vitiated,'
destined to give way to a 'truer ethics.'   He may
explain morality as it is or has been, but what he has
to establish must be morality as it ought to be—
the 'truer ethics.'

Is it, then, possible that Science—*i.e.* Biology,
Psychology, and Sociology—can provide a basis for
ethics so understood, can establish morality as it
ought to be?   Mr. Spencer holds that this may be
done by a contemplation of conduct in general.
Instead of explaining the origin of the sentiments
with which men have come to regard actions, the
accepted rules by which they endeavour to restrain
certain kinds of conduct and encourage other kinds,
we may leave morality aside altogether, and examine
the conduct itself from the point of view of Science:
to see if by mere contemplation of the actual, we can

elicit the ideal. The answer to this question would seem to be that Science shows us, according to Mr. Spencer, in the first place, a supreme or ultimate end, to the realisation of which human actions are universally or normally directed; and it enables us, in the second place, to determine the kind of conduct by which this end may be attained in the highest possible degree.

The lines of reasoning by which these two different results are attained—the establishment of the end, and the ascertainment of the means to the end—are very different; and it is well to keep them quite distinct. We will begin with the establishment of the end, which logically precedes, and which Mr. Spencer is mainly occupied in discussing in the first three chapters of his book. He regards it as fundamentally important to consider that portion of human conduct to which ethics relates—*i.e.* the voluntary actions of human beings, commonly judged to be right or wrong —as a part of a larger whole : that whole being constituted not by the aggregate of merely human actions, even including those commonly judged to be indifferent together with those judged to be good or bad, but by what he calls 'universal conduct — conduct as exhibited by all living creatures.' He defines conduct in this widest sense as the 'adjustment of acts to ends'; acts being more precisely defined as external motions of animate beings. He points out how this adjustment of acts to ends becomes more complex and elaborate as animals become more developed. Conduct exhibits, as we should expect, the character-

istics of evolution generally; the progress from
'indefinite, incoherent homogeneity' to 'definite coherent heterogeneity.'

In the lowest forms of life the 'conduct is constituted of actions so little adjusted to ends that life
continues only as long as the accidents of the environment are favourable'; and so rising from point to
point Mr. Spencer shows how the conduct of the lower
animals as compared with the higher, in a scale
ascending up to civilised man, 'mainly differs in this,
that the adjustments of acts to ends are relatively
simple and relatively incomplete.' What, then, in
the case of these lower forms of life, are we to regard
as the ultimate end, to which the special ends of
catching food, avoiding foes, etc., are subordinate?
Mr. Spencer unhesitatingly says that the 'general'
or 'supreme' end of the adjustments which constitute
life is the continuance and further development of
these adjustments themselves. Life, in short, is for
life's sake; only we are instructed not to measure
life merely by its length, but by what is called its
'breadth' also; that is, we must take into account
the different 'quantities of change' that different
living beings pass through in the same period of time.
We have also, of course, to bear in mind that the
actions of any individual may be partly adjusted to
the initiation, prolongation, and enlargement of other
lives besides its own; and we observe that this is to
a continually greater extent the case as we ascend
in the scale of living beings. Still, notwithstanding
this doubleness of measurement and this complexity

of adjustment, 'quantity of life' none the less remains the ultimate end of ' universal conduct.'

It may be observed that this view is, if I may so say, doubly teleological; we recognise that the external motions of living things are adjusted to a certain kind of end, viz. life, the continuance of the adjustments themselves; and we find further that if we take a certain view of 'quantity of life,' if we estimate it not merely by duration, but consider quantity of change in a given time, this kind of end is more attained as the evolution goes on; *i.e.* the actions of the higher or later beings are more life-sustaining—provided we measure life in this way — than the actions of the lower.

In an article[1] in *Mind* for 1881, Mr. Spencer quotes my remark that ' the frankly teleological point of view from which, in this book, Mr. Spencer contemplates the phenomena of life generally seems worthy of notice ; since in his *Principles of Biology* he seems to have taken some pains *to avoid teleological implications,*' and then makes the following observations :—

That a science which has for its subject-matter the characters of the ends pursued by man, and the characters of the means used for achieving such ends, can restrict itself to statements in which ends are not implied, is a strange assumption. Teleology of a kind is necessarily involved ; and the only question is, whether it is of a legitimate or of an illegitimate kind. [Then after giving an illustration of the two, Mr. Spencer goes on to say :] It is thus with biological interpretations of structures and functions in general. The welfare of the organism, or of the species, is in every case the end to further which a structure exists ; and the difference between a legitimate and an illegitimate teleology is

---

[1] *Replies to Criticisms on " The Data of Ethics."*

that, while the one explains its existence as having gradually arisen by furthering the end, the other gives no explanation of its existence other than that it was put there to further the end.

This is a double misunderstanding: (1) I did not commit the absurdity of charging Mr. Spencer with inconsistency because he viewed teleologically that human conduct which is the subject-matter of moral judgments: what I expressly refer to is the manner in which he contemplates the phenomena of *life generally*. This in *The Data of Ethics* is, as I say, 'frankly teleological'; but (2) I did not say, nor did I mean to imply, that it was illegitimately so: my words were chosen to avoid any such implication— for in fact what I meant to criticise was not the teleology of *The Data of Ethics*, but the forced avoidance of it in *The Principles of Biology*. Compare with p. 83 of Mr. Spencer's article above referred to, the following passage from *Principles of Biology*, chapter v. § 27 :—

We habitually distinguish a live object from a dead one by observing whether a change which we make in the surrounding conditions, or a change which nature makes in them, is or is not followed by some perceptible change in the object. . . . Not only, however, do we habitually look for some response when an external stimulus is applied to a living organism, but we perceive a *fitness* in the response. Dead things also display changes under certain changes of condition, *e.g.* a cord that contracts when wetted, a piece of bread that turns brown when held near the fire. But in these cases we do not see a connexion between the changes undergone and the preservation of the things that undergo them; or, *to avoid teleological implications*—the changes have no apparent relations to further external events which are sure or likely to take place.

The last phrase, we see, avoids mentioning the connexion between changes and preservation. And this avoidance goes on through the chapter. Thus the definitions of life are framed to avoid any mention of 'preservation of organism' :—'The definite combination of heterogeneous changes, both simultaneous and successive, *in correspondence with external coexistences and sequences*' or '*The continuous adjustment of internal relations to external relations.*' I consider that in this chapter the exposition would have been much clearer if Mr. Spencer had not continually tried, by the use of such terms as he here employs, to avoid that recognition of the preservation of the organism as the end of adjustments, which we find in his *Data of Ethics.*

LECTURE II

THE conclusion to which Mr. Spencer's first two chapters lead is that the end which a contemplation of the actions of living beings generally shows us as that to which life is more and more adjusted, as it becomes more and more evolved, is *Quantity of Life, taking Width in as well as Length*—that is, measuring life not only by duration but by amount of change within a given period. And in chapter ii. he tries to show that we call conduct good that tends to preservation of life so understood. Is this then to be taken as the ethical end—the ultimate result which our practical efforts are to aim at realising? Some of Mr. Spencer's language in the first two chapters would suggest this view; since he does not hesitate, in speaking of the lower animals, to describe actions that fail to sustain life as 'conduct falling short of its ideal.' So again in chapter iii. 'good' is taken to mean in its wider use 'adapted to some end,' in its ethical use 'adapted to the preservation of life, or furtherance of complete living.' So that at the end of § 8 we are told that 'the conduct called good rises to the conduct conceived as best,' when 'it simultaneously achieves the greatest totality of life in self, in off-spring, and in fellowmen.'

Now if the arguments in chapter iii. had stopped here, we should have had an Ultimate End or Good defined non-hedonistically. And in fact Life (without breadth) is the ultimate end which certain writers of the evolutionist school are disposed to lay down instead of Happiness; and which, therefore, I have thought it needful to argue against in Book III. of *Methods of Ethics*.[1] I will only now observe, that according to me an ethical end cannot be proved by biology. If biology presents me with a generalisation from lower forms of life to the effect that 'all actions are adjusted to preservation,' I answer that that proves nothing as to the total and complete end; and that mere preservation of life is palpably not adequate to this. To live well, as Aristotle says, we must live somehow; but that does not make life identical with living well.

The view here argued against is, as I say, not exactly Mr. Spencer's; because, according to him, life is measured in breadth as well as length. But it is to be observed, that it is by no means so evident that the motions of living beings are directed to the production of breadth of life, as it is clear they are directed to the maintenance of life. And can we say that the introduction of what Mr. Spencer calls 'breadth' removes the difficulty—that life is better in proportion to 'quantity of change' packed into a given time, apart from consideration of its pleasurable and painful

---

[1] Book iii. chap. xiv. § 3.

quality ? As in my view all depends on the *quality* of life, I do not see how this can be maintained. Now Mr. Spencer does not really maintain it; on the contrary, in face of the arguments leading up to his non-hedonistic biological end, he holds (chapter iii. § 9 to end) that ' the good is universally the pleasurable,' and indeed that ' pleasurable' and ' painful' are the primary meanings of ' good' and ' bad.'[1]

Now here we must distinguish inquiry into the meaning of words from inquiry into ethical principles. I agree with Mr. Spencer in holding that ' pleasure is the ultimate good,' but not in the meaning which he gives to the word ' good.' Indeed if ' good' (substantive) means ' pleasure,' the proposition just stated would be a tautology, and a tautology cannot be an ethical principle. I hold that ' good' in ordinary discourse has blended meanings, but the one that I think most in harmony with usage—among distinct notions—is *desirable, choice-worthy, preferable, to be sought* : at any rate that is required for a non-tautological principle. However, this difference relates to form, rather than substance. Substantially Mr. Spencer gives the most decided preference to ' pleasure' over ' life' as ultimate end. Immediately after the passage before quoted, which seems to take conduciveness to ' totality of life' as the criterion of ' good' conduct, he says there is an assumption involved in this view—namely, that such conduct brings a ' surplus of agreeable feelings'—an assump-

[1] Cf. also the argument of chap. vi. of the *Data of Ethics* (on *The Biological View*), where a hedonistic end is assumed.

tion made by optimists and pessimists alike (compare § 10, p. 28, and § 15, p. 45 of *Data of
Ethics*). He is therefore an Evolutionistic Hedonist,
not an Evolutionist pure. Still he often seems
simply and as a matter of course to treat the two ends
as coincident, and therefore convertible for purposes
of ethical reasoning. I think that after all that has
been said of the importance of viewing human conduct
in connexion with the universal conduct of which
it is a part, this transition from 'quantity of life'
to 'quantity of pleasure' is too rapidly and lightly
made. Pessimism in fact stands in the way, declaring
that life does not bring with it a surplus of agreeable
feeling. Mr. Spencer seems to assume an optimistic
view as to coincidence of life and pleasure which
needs more argument.

I do not mean, as in his reply to me (*Mind*, 1881)
he seems to think, that it is necessary to confute
Pessimism in order to prove Happiness to be
the ultimate ethical end ; as I have argued at the
close of chapter ii. of Book II. of *Methods of Ethics*,
the Utilitarian is under no such obligation. However little happiness there is to be got, we may
always aim at getting as much as we can ; even if we
can only minimise pain for sentient beings, we may
always aim at minimising it as much as possible.
But though the Utilitarian is not bound to confute
Pessimism, Mr. Spencer is bound to do this and more :
he is bound to show the coincidence of the two ends—
Life and Pleasure—at least for practical purposes.

Where the obligation on Mr. Spencer to prove this

arises, is in the transition from the argument in chapters i. and ii. to that of §§ 9, 10, of chapter iii.— from the argument which shows us mere quantity of life as the end which the wider observation of conduct suggests to the view that happiness (maximum pleasure) is the end. For obviously, in proportion as life is shown to contain pain the ends diverge : better quality of life, if that can be arrived at, may outweigh increase in quantity.

In the reply which Mr. Spencer makes to me, I think he still fails to see the full burden of proof that rests on him. He says :—

But now, having pointed out that the conclusions contained in the *Data of Ethics*, in common with the conclusions contained in ethical treatises at large, can reasonably be accepted only by those who hold that life in the aggregate brings more pleasure than pain, or at any rate is capable of bringing more pleasure than pain, I go on to show that the tacit optimism which pervades the work has a wider basis than Mr. Sidgwick recognises. He says that "in Mr. Spencer's view, pessimism is indirectly confuted by the argument—given as an 'inevitable deduction from the hypothesis of Evolution'—which shows that 'necessarily throughout the animate world at large, pains are the correlatives of actions injurious to the organism, while pleasures are the correlatives of actions conducive to its welfare.'" This is true as far as it goes ; but, ignoring as he does all passages concerning the universal process of adaptation, Mr. Sidgwick omits a large part of the evidence favouring optimism. The chapter on the *Relativity of Pains and Pleasures* sets forth and illustrates the biological truth that everywhere faculties adjust themselves to the conditions of existence, in such wise that the activities those conditions require become pleasurable. The pains accompanying the inactions of faculties for which changed conditions have left no spheres, diminish as the faculties decrease ; while the pains accompanying the actions of faculties overtaxed under the new conditions, diminish as the faculties grow, and become pleasures when those faculties have acquired the strength which fulfilment of the conditions requires. This law is alike inferable *a priori* and proved *a posteriori*, and yields a qualified optimism as its corollary—an optimism qualified by the conclusion that the life of every species of creature is happy or miserable according to the degree of congruity or incongruity between its nature and its environment; but that everywhere decrease of the misery or increase of the happiness accompanies the inevitable progress towards congruity. Whence it follows that in the case of mankind, pessimism may be locally true under certain conditions (as those which have fostered the creed which makes annihilation a blessing), while optimism may be locally true under conditions of a more favourable kind; but that with the increasing adaptation of humanity to social life, the excess of pleasures over pains which warrants optimism, must become ever greater.[1]

All this might be true, and yet so long as life is partially painful, it may still be true in any particular case that conduct conducive to maximum quantity of life is not conducive to maximum pleasure. It seems to me that in the chapter on the *Relativity of Pains and Pleasures*, as in other places in Mr. Spencer's writings, we find that, desiring to lead us up to an interesting and important conclusion, he spends useless labour in an ample demonstration of an admitted truism; and having got so far, imagines himself much nearer his goal than he is, and takes the rest of the road in a leap. However, I now proceed to examine the proof which he offers in this chapter of the general proposition that maximum quantity of life is conducive to maximum quantity of pleasure.

That pains and pleasure are, as he says, 'relative to the structures and states of structure of our organism' is a truism, if not to children or uncultured minds, at any rate to persons—to use Hume's phrase —'with the slightest tincture of philosophy.' No one

---

[1] *Mind*, vol. vi. (1881), pp. 85, 86.

doubts that (*a*) the fact that we feel pleasure and pain depends on the constitution and condition of our nervous system; or (*b*) that the constitution of the nervous system — in respect of susceptibility to pleasure and pain—differs in different individuals, and may be presumed to differ still more widely in different species of animals, or again that the condition of the nervous system differs in the same person at different times. We do not require Mr. Spencer's faculty in marshalling the evidence for an induction to prove such statements as these.

Indeed I may remark that in the one case in which he admits that there is to a certain extent 'absoluteness in the relation between positive pains and actions of a given kind,' his conclusion is overstated. 'The painfulness of the feelings produced by forces which tend to destroy organic structures, wholly or in part, is of course common to all creatures capable of feeling . . . there is absoluteness in the relation between positive pains and actions that are positively injurious, in so far that wherever there is sentiency it exists' (§ 64, pp. 175, 178). But there is no reason why *all* actions injurious to the organism should be painful; in fact some—as the absorption of a fatal dose of laudanum—are apparently not so.

However, I will admit the general proposition—of relativity of pleasures and pains to structures and to states of the organism—without further argument. The question is not *whether* pleasures and pains vary with the varying states of the organism, but *how far* they can vary, and what are the laws of change.

We have, as I have shown, a problem presented by
the divergence between the ultimate end obtained
(chapters i. and ii.) by a teleological observation of conduct generally—that is, quantity of life measured in
breadth as well as length, and the ethical end—namely,
maximum happiness or pleasure, unhesitatingly laid
down by Mr. Spencer in chapter iii.   In replying to
me he affirms that the problem is solved by help of
this relativity of pains and pleasures, dealt with
in his chapter x., through the process of adaptation of
life to its environment that is continually going on.

Now observe, the question is not whether this
process of adaptation takes place, but whether we
have sufficient grounds for relying on it to bring
about a coincidence between Life and Happiness so
complete that we may legitimately treat the two as
coincident for ethical purposes,—so that it does not
matter whether we say that actions are good in proportion as they are life-sustaining, or that they
are good in proportion as they are conducive to
happiness.   That is what, as I say, Mr. Spencer's
argument needs.

But what proof does he give in this tenth chapter
of the *Data* ?   All that I can find is in § 67, pp.
182-184—

I have insisted on these general truths with perhaps needless
iteration, to prepare the reader for more fully recognising a
corollary that is practically ignored.   Abundant and clear as is
the evidence, and forced though it is daily on every one's attention, the conclusions respecting life and conduct which should
be drawn are not drawn ; and so much at variance are these
conclusions with current beliefs, that enunciation of them causes
a stare of incredulity . . . ; it is difficult to obtain a hearing for

the doctrine that the kinds of action which are now pleasurable will, under conditions requiring the change, cease to be pleasurable, while other kinds of action will become pleasurable. . . .

And yet as shown in myriads of instances, indicated by the few above given, those natural processes which have produced multitudinous forms of structure adapted to multitudinous forms of activity, have simultaneously made these forms of activity pleasurable. And the inevitable implication is, that within the limits imposed by physical laws there will be evolved, in adaptation to any new sets of conditions that may be established, appropriate structures of which the functions will yield their respective gratifications.

When we have got rid of the tendency to think that certain modes of activity are necessarily pleasurable because they give us pleasure, and that other modes which do not please us are necessarily unpleasing ; we shall see that the re-moulding of human nature into fitness for the requirements of social life must eventually make all needful activities pleasurable, while it makes displeasurable all activities at variance with these requirements. When we have come fully to recognise the truth that there is nothing intrinsically more gratifying in the efforts by which wild animals are caught than in the efforts expended in rearing plants, and that the combined actions of muscles and senses in rowing a boat are not by their essential natures more productive of agreeable feeling than those gone through in reaping corn, but that everything depends on the co-operating emotions, which at present are more in accordance with the one than with the other ; we shall infer that along with decrease of those emotions for which the social state affords little or no scope, and increase of those which it persistently exercises, the things now done with dislike from a sense of obligation will be done with immediate liking, and the things desisted from as a matter of duty will be desisted from because they are repugnant.

This is a good specimen of Mr. Spencer's hasty inferences. When we have got rid of the false generalisation that certain modes of activity are necessarily pleasurable, and have observed that very many acts originally disagreeable become agreeable through habit, we shall, he thinks, adopt the conclusion that 'all needful activities will become pleasurable.' But what grounds have we for supposing that any

such complete result will be produced, in the future
any more than in the past? *Now*, it is admitted,
many needful acts are indifferent, some painful.
Needful labour is largely both; digestion is normally
indifferent.   What is the law from which we can
necessarily infer that all this will be changed?
Mr. Spencer's argument seems to be that given in § 33
of the *Data of Ethics* (quoted from the *Principles
of Psychology*, § 124) :—

> If we substitute for the word Pleasure the equivalent
> phrase—a feeling which we seek to bring into consciousness
> and retain there, and if we substitute for the word Pain the
> equivalent phrase—a feeling which we seek to get out of con-
> sciousness and to keep out; we see at once that, if the states of
> consciousness which a creature endeavours to maintain are the
> correlatives of injurious actions, and if the states of consciousness
> which it endeavours to expel are the correlatives of beneficial
> actions, it must quickly disappear through persistence in the
> injurious and avoidance of the beneficial.   In other words,
> those races of beings only can have survived in which, on the
> average, agreeable or desired feelings went along with activities
> conducive to the maintenance of life, while disagreeable and
> habitually avoided feelings went along with activities directly or
> indirectly destructive of life; and there must ever have been,
> other things equal, the most numerous and long-continued
> survivals among races in which these adjustments of feelings
> to actions were the best, tending ever to bring about perfect
> adjustment.

But granting this to be true, the optimistic conclusion does not follow.   I argued this in my article
on *Mr. Spencer's Ethical System* in *Mind* for 1880.
As I said there : We can only infer that actions
preservative of the individual or the race will be,
generally speaking, less painful than those that have
an opposite tendency ; and that the pains normally
endured will not be sufficiently intense to destroy

life. The connexion, in fact, leaves Nature with a choice of alternative methods in her business of adjusting the actions of living beings to the preservation and continuance of life; she may either attract them in the required direction by pleasure, or deter them from divergent courses by pain: it is undeniable that, hitherto at least, her plan of management has combined the two modes of guidance, and I do not see how the proportion in which the two methods are actually mixed can be ascertained by *a priori* inference—As this suggestion seems to have had no effect on Mr. Spencer, I will expand it somewhat.

First, then, even supposing ' equilibrium' attained between the individual and his environment, it is still quite conceivable that the stimulus to organic actions should be painful, the actions themselves indifferent, and the result merely relief from pain.

I may suggest as an illustration of this the case of hunger, as it is a point on which I have had some controversy. Of hunger, I individually take what may be called an optimistic view. I say, as a matter of personal experience, that the craving for food, after not too long an interval and in a state of health, is not a pain but a neutral excitement. Many persons, however, tell me that their experience of hunger is different; they regard it normally as a pain, and I know of no *a priori* argument, from evolution or otherwise, to show that it is not. There are certainly many organic actions of which we are only conscious as sources of uneasiness. Take for instance the case of digestion, above referred to ; we

get no definite pleasure from it when it goes right,
and considerable definite pain when it goes wrong.
Why should not this be the case with other organic
actions ?

But, secondly, if we are to look ahead, why should
not unconsciousness, 'without one pleasure and
without one pain,' be the ultimate goal of evolution ?
Why should not actions become instinctive or
mechanical ? Experience certainly shows us this
tendency.[1]   And again, why should *more* equilibrium
be attained in the future than has already been
attained in the relation between the individual and
environment ?   Mr. Spencer admits (§ 35) that it is
now only very partial and incomplete. What biological
or sociological ground is there for certainty that the
present derangement will not go on ?   For example,
why should not the pressure for existence, due to the
crowding of population, and the partial remedies
for this, due to the progress of science, continually
force on the individual member of society life under
new conditions, and therefore activities painful from
novelty ?   I submit, therefore, that 'lack of faith in
such further evolution of humanity as shall harmonise
its nature with its conditions,' of which Mr. Spencer
speaks (§ 67), is not due to an inadequate consciousness of causation, but to an adequate consciousness of
what is required for proof.   One who has 'acquired
the habits of thought which science generates,' so far
from regarding Mr. Spencer's conclusion as inevitable,
will see that it is, to a glaring extent, unsupported

---

[1] Cf. Sorley's *Ethics of Naturalism*, chap. vii. § 4.

by the facts. Or shall we say, that acceptance of such conclusion implies indeed 'faith in evolution,' but not a foresight of its consequences resting on legitimate generalisations ?

But further, even supposing it to be true that 'pleasure will eventually accompany every mode of action demanded by social conditions,' it yet does not follow that *maximum* quantity of pleasure will always accompany *maximum* quantity of life—this, however, is required if the two ends are to be treated as coincident in 'establishing morality on a scientific basis.'[1] Quantity of life, therefore, and quantity of pleasure would still remain divergent ends, even if we placed the blindest confidence in Mr. Spencer's argument.

And finally, supposing this difficulty got over as regards the future—supposing that we take a hopeful view, beyond what experience can support, and imagine a Utopia in which all actions conducive to maximum life are also necessarily conducive to maximum pleasure—it would still remain true that at present there is a lamentable hiatus between the two ends. It would seem, therefore, that in establishing morality, for men living here and now, on a scientific basis, we must decide between the two : from the fact that conduct is 'good' in the sense of being conducive to maximum life, we shall not be able to infer cogently that the same conduct is 'good' in the sense of being conducive to maximum happiness ; thus the fact that a certain industrial change

---

[1] Cf. *Methods of Ethics*, Book II. chap. vi. § 4—also Book IV. chap. iv. § 3.

will be attended with an increase of population cannot
be regarded as a final argument for it, if the population is to be less happy.

Mr. Spencer, if I understand him, would answer
this last argument by drawing his distinction between
Absolute and Relative Ethics. He would say that
the coincidence of life-sustaining and pleasure-giving
activities may be assumed in the reasonings of
Absolute Ethics, which constructs a code for an ideal
society ; though not altogether in that of Relative
Ethics, which endeavours to supply guidance for
humanity here and now.   I shall hereafter return to
this distinction, only observing now that the distinction is not directly explained till the close of the
treatise ; and that hence there results a certain difficulty in judging of Mr. Spencer's argument in earlier
chapters. For instance, it is not, I think, sufficiently
indicated in his discussion of Utilitarianism at the
close of chapter iv. on *Ways of judging Conduct*, to
which I will now proceed. The main drift of this
chapter is that 'the various ethical theories are
characterised either by entire absence of the idea of
causation, or by inadequate presence of it.' I will
not dwell on the theological doctrine that 'actions
are made respectively good or bad solely by divine
appointment,' revealed either 'in sacred writings or
in conscience.' I will only say that for earnest and
thoughtful theologians, this can hardly be more than
a half-truth, as it makes meaningless the proposition,
deeply rooted in the religious consciousness, that God
is a righteous God.   Nor will I do more than notice

the historical misrepresentation (§ 19) of implying that
Plato and Aristotle held the view that 'there is no
other origin for good and bad in conduct than law.'[1]
There is perhaps a certain excuse for it, if restricted to the details of conduct, as regards Plato ;
since Plato certainly held that in a well-ordered
State, the lawgiver would determine the rules of
conduct to be observed by ordinary citizens, who
would not know the *rationale* of such rules. But
of course it is manifestly contrary to Plato's view
to suppose that their goodness, or the badness of
violating them, 'originated' in law : their goodness
was due to the philosophic insight of the lawgiver
which would realise in them the best manifestation
of ideal good which the circumstances of human life
would admit.

I must add one word on the criticism of Hobbes
and his school (§ 19), for holding that justice
and injustice depend on law. For this criticism,
though not without force, does not do justice to the
element of truth in Hobbes' view, or penetrate to
the principles from which what is paradoxical and
exaggerated in it is derived. It is unreasonable to
treat Hobbes or his followers as holding that there are
no good or bad consequences of conduct independently
of law : what they do hold is that, without this
coercive power of government, the individual has no
adequate inducements to observe such rules of mutual
behaviour as would be beneficial to all if they were
generally obeyed—*e.g.* to keep covenants. Hence

---

[1] Cf. the Author's *Outlines of the History of Ethics*, chap. ii. §§ 6 and 10.

Hobbes concluded that the 'laws of nature'—as he, after his predecessors, calls these rules—only bind, in the state of nature, to a *desire* that they should be performed, not to actual performance, apart from government. To this view Spencer's argument in § 19 is quite irrelevant. In fact Hobbes' view is only an exaggeration, paradoxically expressed, of the view which Mr. Spencer himself expresses when at the end of the chapter on *Absolute and Relative Ethics* he says that 'these require a certain congruity between the conduct of each member of a society and other's conduct.'

In the criticism in § 19 Mr. Spencer seems to leave out of account the reconciliation of Intuitionism and Utilitarianism, by means of Evolution, which he afterwards gives in chapter ix. § 62 as follows :—

After thus observing how means and ends in conduct stand to one another, and how there emerge certain conclusions respecting their relative claims, we may see a way to reconcile sundry conflicting ethical theories. These severally embody portions of the truth, and simply require combining in proper order to embody the whole truth.

. . . That the intuitions of a moral faculty should guide our conduct, is a proposition in which a truth is contained ; for these intuitions are the slowly organised results of experiences received by the race while living in presence of these conditions. And that happiness is the supreme end is beyond question true ; for this is the concomitant of that highest life which every theory of moral guidance has distinctly or vaguely in view.

So understanding their relative positions, those ethical systems which make virtue, right, obligation, the cardinal aims, are seen to be complementary to those ethical systems which make welfare, pleasure, happiness, the cardinal aims. Though the moral sentiments generated in civilised men by daily contact with social conditions and gradual adaptation to them, are indispensable as incentives and deterrents ; and though the intuitions corresponding to these sentiments have, in virtue of their origin, a general authority to be reverently recognised; yet the sympathies and antipathies hence originating, together with the intellectual expressions of them, are, in their primitive forms, necessarily vague. To make guidance by them adequate to all requirements, their dictates have to be interpreted and made definite by science; to which end there must be analysis of those conditions to complete living which they respond to, and from converse with which they have arisen. And such analysis necessitates the recognition of happiness for each and all, as the end to be achieved by fulfilment of these conditions.

Hence, recognising in due degrees all the various ethical theories, conduct in its highest form will take as guides, innate perceptions of right duly enlightened and made precise by analytic intelligence; while conscious that these guides are proximately supreme, solely because they lead to the ultimately supreme end, happiness special and general.

I may observe that it does not seem *prima facie* obvious that moral intuitions, such as relate to Veracity, Justice, Good Faith, and the moral senti-ments accompanying them, are 'necessarily vague.' It may be said that on Spencer's view they *ought* to be, but it needs careful reflection to see that they *are* so. I would also point out that the Intuitionist view (cf. § 20) is caricatured. The view has never, so far as I know, been put forward by an intuitional moralist, that consequences are to be ignored generally —among his rules have always been the rule of ab-staining from causing pain to others, and the rule of benevolence. What the intuitional moralist has held is, that the rightness of certain acts—*e.g.* Veracity, Good Faith—may be known without a process of inference from their foreseen consequences.—So much by way of preliminary, before I discuss, in the next Lecture, the issue as regards ethical method, between Mr. Spencer and myself.

According to Mr. Spencer, Utilitarianism also, it seems, is characterised by 'inadequate presence of the idea of causation'; and the fundamental objection which he brings against Utilitarians is, that they adopt an empirical and inductive method, instead of deductions to necessary conclusions. They rely on 'observation of results' for determining what conduct leads to general happiness. Now there is no doubt, I think, that Utilitarians do adopt a method to a great extent empirical; but it is mistaken to argue that they do this because they have any indisposition to recognise causation; or because they are ignorant of the elementary methodological proposition that knowledge passes into a higher stage in proportion as it becomes deductive. What Mr. Spencer's utilitarian opponents refuse to recognise is not, I conceive, the importance of scientific deduction in the abstract, but the importance of *his* deductions—at least when regarded as applicable to the whole range of their subject and as capable of superseding and supplanting the empirical method. For here again Mr. Spencer gains an apparently easy triumph (in § 22) by pointing to causal connexions between bad actions and painful consequences, which no Utilitarian has ever denied or overlooked.

LECTURE III

ONE chief difficulty which I find in dealing with Mr. Spencer's argument in chapters v. to viii., inclusive, to which I now pass, lies in the fact that, as we have seen, he takes as established that coincidence between Life and Happiness, which, according to me, he has yet to prove. He has no doubt that the cosmic evolution or progress which has tended continually to make the living more alive, has tended to increase happiness *pari passu*. He seems to hold, therefore, that what the Utilitarian has to do is to trace the characteristics of this evolution, as specially manifested in that part of the actions of living things with which, as a moralist, he is specially concerned ; and that in this way he will attain the truly scientific method which Mr. Spencer wishes to substitute for ordinary empirical Utilitarianism. Now if I am right as to the divergence of the two ends, this method is obviously illegitimate.

The question placed before us at the end of chapter iv. of *The Data of Ethics* is this : Assuming that—as stated at the end of chapter iii.—' the ultimate moral aim' is 'a desirable state of feeling called gratifica-

M

tion, enjoyment, happiness' (more definitely, as I should say, 'greatest possible happiness'), by what method are we to determine the means to this end? The older Utilitarians use mainly empirical methods. They 'ascertain by induction that such and such mischiefs or benefits' will follow from 'such and such acts' (§ 21), and do not 'erect into a method the ascertaining of necessary relations between causes and effects,' and deduce 'from fundamental principles what conduct *must* be detrimental and what conduct *must* be beneficial.' Ethics, in Mr. Spencer's view, ought to transform its method from a mainly inductive to a deductive one; and he appears to imply that the four scientific 'views' which he proceeds to take of Ethics—in chapters v.-viii., entitled respectively *The Physical View*, *The Biological View*, *The Psychological View*, *The Sociological View*—will show us how this transformation is to be effected. In what I have to say I shall, therefore, consider them from this point of view.

Let us take first chapter v. on the Physical View. —The general characteristics of Evolution, regarded on its physical side, are progress from indefinite, incoherent homogeneity to definite, coherent heterogeneity. Accordingly the 'physical view' shows us that the conduct which we call—or at least which we ought to call—moral, has in the highest degree these latter characteristics. Now you will observe that, as regards definiteness and coherence, Mr. Spencer appeals with confidence and with force to common-sense morality : the good conduct is coherent, as contrasted with that which is 'dissolute, unstable, untrustworthy.' And the good conduct is definite and precise, avoids disappointment of expectations, the too much and the too little, etc. But, if the appeal is made to common-sense morality, there is another side to the matter. Conduct may be coherently and definitely framed with a view to the egoistic end; and the conduct of an egoist—*e.g.* an ambitious man —has often greater coherence than that of a man, whom we judge to be better, who adopts a wavering compromise between egoism and altruism. So as regards definiteness, no doubt in many important duties definiteness and precision are valued; but there are others in which a certain indeterminateness — leaving room for the grace of spontaneity — is rather admired; for instance in the case of duties of the affections. This is so even when we are considering the ideal man, much more when we are comparing actual men.

As regards heterogeneity, even Mr. Spencer does not consider that common morality supports his view, but he argues (§ 27) that common morality is wrong. I think there is force in his argument; but I think also he has overlooked a difficulty, from the double point of view of the individual and the social organism, to which I have drawn attention in *Mind*. As I say there, the most prominent characteristic of the advanced development of any organism is the specialisation—or, as Mr. Spencer calls it, 'differentiation'— of the functions of its different parts. Obviously the more this is effected, the more 'definite coherent heterogeneity' will be realised in the organism and in its relations to its environment. But obviously, too, this involves *pro tanto* a proportionally less degree of variety and complexity in the life of each individual member of the society whose functions are thus specialised; and their life becoming narrow and monotonous must become, according to our present hypothesis, less happy. This result has often been noticed by observers of the minute subdivision of labour which is a feature of our industrial progress; but the same sort of *prima facie* conflict between individual and social development occurs in considering most of the great problems of modern politics; such as the relations between rich and poor generally, the relations between governors and governed, and the relations of the sexes.[1]

Here again, instead of meeting the difficulty, Mr. Spencer seems to me (end of § 28) to take refuge in his Utopia. No doubt we may please ourselves by imagining a society in which the individual develops in perfect harmony with his social environment, and becomes more definitely and coherently heterogeneous, and therefore more alive, and therefore happier, in the same proportion as his society acquires the same characteristics. But is there any evidence that history is conducting us to this Utopia? I know none at all adequate. Hence, without denying that definite coherent heterogeneity will be found to characterise the conduct that the moralist ought to approve as a means to general happiness, I deny that these charac-

[1] *Mind*, vol. i. pp. 61, 62.

teristics can give him any material practical guidance. Grant that, as evolution proceeds, the actions of living beings exhibit a progress from indefinite, incoherent homogeneity to definite, coherent heterogeneity; still we have no ground for saying broadly that conduct here and now tends to general happiness in proportion as it exhibits these characteristics. We cannot, therefore, take confidently, as middle axioms of Utilitarianism, the precepts, 'Be definite, be coherent, be heterogeneous.'

It may be said that perfect conduct must be perfectly definite and coherent; if in accordance with reason, it must exhibit the application of some rational principles, whether the Utilitarian or any other, with exactness and completeness. But it should be observed that the antithesis between definite and coherent, indefinite and incoherent, cannot be conceived applicable to the physical world, except from the point of view of imperfect knowledge. For an All-knowing Mind, we cannot but conceive all matter and motion perfectly definite; and all coherent, as each particle attracts all others. The antithesis is only applicable relatively to an imperfect intellect; and relatively to such an intellect as the human, we judge that the indefinite in certain parts of conduct is the better; the play of spontaneous impulse better than the results of reasoning.

Let us now pass to the Biological View. The *datum* which this yields is as follows :—The ideally moral man is one in whom the 'moving equili-

brium,' as Mr. Spencer says, is perfect—*i.e.* in whom
the balanced combination of the actions, internal and
external, of his organism is maintained in face of
external forces tending to overthrow that combination of internal actions which we call his life.
Accordingly, this ideally moral man must be one
in whom the functions of all kinds are fulfilled
'duly' or 'in normal proportion;' hence 'the performance of *every* function is, in a sense, a moral
obligation,' and 'all the animal functions in common
with all the higher functions have their imperative-
ness' (§ 31). At first sight it looks as if we were
going to obtain a principle for practical guidance.
But in the next sentence Mr. Spencer explains that
'in our state of transition . . . moral obligations of
a supreme kind often necessitate conduct which is
physically injurious'; and therefore the proposition,
taken as a practical one, reduces itself to this, that 'it
is immoral so to treat the body as in any way to
diminish the fulness or vigour of its vitality,' when
'considered apart from other effects.' The proposition, therefore, comes out a platitude which no
moralist of any school has ever denied : that it is
our duty *cæteris paribus* to preserve our health in the
highest degree.

It may be said, however, that admitting the
uselessness of this for present practical guidance,
still it does good as pointing out an ideal. My
answer is that the 'ideal humanity' to which the
principle of 'performing every function' would apply
in its completeness is so far distant that it cannot

even afford us an ideal of any practical value; since we cannot tell that by the time we arrive at it the habits of our organism may not have so materially changed, through its adaption to its physical and social environment, that a quite different balance of functions may have become normal. I have no doubt that the ideal man in an ideal society, if he ever comes into being, will not fall into the mistakes that Mr. Spencer eloquently depicts (§ 37, p. 94): he will not, 'when drenched to the skin and sitting in a cold wind, pooh-pooh his shiverings'; he will not 'work too soon after a debilitating illness'; he will not 'burst a blood-vessel through gymnastic feats'; he will not 'sit too long at his office,' 'pore half the night over his briefs,' or otherwise sacrifice health to ends of less importance. But what the rules are which he will have to observe to obtain health I do not know—perhaps his brain will have become indefinitely stronger through heredity and the survival of the fittest, perhaps his need for physical exercise will have become indefinitely less, perhaps chemistry will have learnt to nourish him with an indefinitely smaller amount of indefinitely more digestible food, perhaps medicine will have provided him with infallible prophylactics against colds and fevers and rheumatism. I willingly hope that all these things, or better things than these, may be in store for humanity in the future; but if I knew that they certainly would be, it would do me no good here and now: it would give me no practical guidance beyond the elementary copy-book maxim that I

ought to take care of my health whenever and so
far as it is not my duty to sacrifice it.

Something of the same kind may be said of the
argument which occupies the greater part of this
chapter, showing that 'pleasure-giving acts are life-
sustaining acts,' and that 'painful acts are injurious
to life.' I have already discussed this argument
in its most important theoretical bearing—*i.e.* in
relation to the coincidence assumed by Mr. Spencer
between Maximum Life and Maximum Happiness.
As regards its practical bearing on the present, Mr.
Spencer himself admits that 'guidance by proximate
pleasures and pains' fails throughout a wide range
of cases; that the 'causes of derangement' of the
relation between life-sustaining acts and pleasures,
operating on human beings, have been 'unusually
decided, persistent, and involved'; that 'the guidance
by sensations' has been considerably deranged and the
'guidance by emotions deranged in a greater degree.'

Hence I conclude, as before, that the guidance
afforded by Mr. Spencer's biological law cannot possibly
be such as to supersede the empirical method of
ascertaining effects of actions on happiness : since (*a*)
we cannot tell what the sensations or emotions of the
Utopian will be like when the Utopian comes, and
(*b*) if we could, we could still infer nothing definite
as to the practical value of our own sensations and
emotions as guides to our own happiness.

I may say that if any evidence was wanted of the
vagueness and inadequacy of the guidance furnished
by Mr. Spencer's biological data, such evidence is

amply supplied by himself, in chapter vii., in which
he proceeds to give us his psychological data. We
observe that in the biological chapter, men and
moralists are reprimanded for their neglect of *immediate* pleasures and pains. Probably the answer
of moralists and preachers would be a partial ad-
mission of the charge ; they would say :—Perhaps
we have not told men quite enough that they ought
to observe the warnings of organic pains, and recognise
the value of delight for the sustainment and the
invigoration of life. We are obliged to you for drawing attention to our neglect, and helping to repair it.
But you must make allowance for the necessity of
broad statements and clear emphasis on the parts of
duty commonly neglected. We found that—owing
to that deep and involved derangement of the biological law which you have admitted and scientifically
explained—men were far too much disposed to seek
present pleasures for themselves and avoid present
pains, to the neglect of remote consequences more
important for themselves or for society. Finding the
bow of human nature bent this way, we, in our teaching, tried to bend it back the other way—perhaps a
shade too strongly—in the hope of getting it practically to a tolerably straight condition. For, after all,
the moral progress of man has largely consisted in
his increased tendency to regard remote pleasures
and pains and to overrule the force of the more
proximate.—Should the moralist answer in this way,
he will find Mr. Spencer quite inclined to agree with
him, and to explain the fact scientifically, showing

how foresight increases as creatures rise in the scale
of evolution (§ 42, pp. 106, 107). Hence the guidance of biological and psychological data together is
reduced indeed to a minimum. We can only say
that immediate pleasure is to be sought and immediate pain avoided when there is no reason to suppose
that such pursuit or avoidance will bring with it a
loss of balance of pleasure hereafter—a proposition
which of course no Utilitarian has ever dreamt of
denying. Even supposing Mr. Spencer's criticism
on the 'current conception' to be sound, it has at
any rate no bearing whatever on Utilitarianism.
'The current conception,' he says, 'while it errs
by implying that the authority of the higher over
the lower is unlimited, errs also by implying that
the rule of the lower must be resisted even when it
does not conflict with the rule of the higher, and
further errs by implying that a gratification which
forms a proper aim if it is remote, forms an improper
aim if it is proximate' (§ 43).

I now come to the important account of the
genesis of the moral consciousness (chapter vii. §§ 44-
47). We may observe that *prima facie* this is an
explanation of how our moral sentiments and current
rules have come to be what they are, not a deduction of what our rules ought to be. The distinction
between the two is very important; how far the one
throws light upon the other I will afterwards consider. I proceed now to expound the theory.

'The essential trait in the moral consciousness,'
Mr. Spencer says, 'is the control of some feeling or

feelings by some other feeling or feelings ' — the
' simpler and less ideal by the more complex and
more ideal ' ; again, a cardinal trait in the self-
restraint called moral is a ' conscious relinquishment
of immediate and special good ' to gain ' distant and
general good.' But this is also a cardinal trait of
other restraints not properly called moral ; and the
important point in Mr. Spencer's explanation is the
gradual ' differentiation ' of moral restraint, in the
course of evolution, from these other restraints.
He describes how savage man's impulses are at first
restrained by a vague dread of the anger of other
savages, living and dead (the dead being taken into
account as the ghost-theory develops), and how there
is gradually evolved into distinctness man's dread
of the actual chieftain which becomes the political
sanction ; his dread of the former chieftain's ghost,
gradually promoted to a deity, which becomes the
religious sanction ; and his regard for the praise and
blame of his fellows, which becomes the social
sanction—all these generally harmonising with and
supporting each other. These, however, are not the
moral control, but only preparatory to it (§ 44, p.
118), because, Mr. Spencer says, the evil consequences
the representation of which restrains, are ' factitious,'
not ' necessary and natural.' Still it is from the
restraints generated by these three that the *notion
of moral obligation* is originally derived : as the
results dreaded in these cases — ' legal penalty,
supernatural punishment, social reprobation '—though
' incidental rather than necessary,' are capable of

being more 'vividly conceived' than the results
which, in the course of things, actions 'naturally'
entail : as being 'simpler and more directly wrought
by personal agencies.'

The strictly moral feelings and restraints consist,
according to Mr. Spencer, in the representation, not of
extrinsic and factitious, but of intrinsic and 'necessary
natural' effects ; they have therefore developed later
than the feelings and restraints that originate from
political, religious, and social authorities, and under
conditions which only these other restraints could
maintain. Having thus developed, they have come to
be quite independent of these other restraints in
conscious experience.

Let us concentrate attention on the special feeling
of obligation: this is referred to two elements combined—(1) the consciousness that such feelings have
'higher *authority* as guides to welfare' than the
simpler feelings that they restrain : this is illustrated
by the 'moral authority' of the 'higher self-regarding
feelings.'   But to this is added (2) the 'element of
coerciveness.' [1]   Spencer holds that this is imported
by the association of strictly moral restraint with
political, religious, and social restraint, and will fade
'as the moral motive . . . becomes distinct and predominant' (§ 46, pp. 127, 128).   There is a certain
want of clearness, I think, here.   Mr. Spencer begins
by tracing the 'sentiment of moral obligation or
duty' to the superior authority of moral sentiments
as guides, and says that 'this idea of authoritative-

[1] Cf. Bain, *The Emotions*, chap. xv.

ness is one element in the abstract consciousness of duty'; then he traces a second element, the 'feeling of coerciveness,' which, however (p. 127), seems to be identified with the feeling of obligation itself. There are really two questions as regards the 'transitoriness' which Mr. Spencer attributes to the sense of duty, relating respectively to the idea of 'authoritativeness' and the element of 'coerciveness.' The disappearance of the second would follow naturally from the independence of strictly moral restraint, so far as the coerciveness has only got transferred to moral restraint through association. But why should the first thus disappear? The fact is that this notion of the transitoriness of moral obligation starts Mr. Spencer towards his Utopia, and he travels so rapidly in fancy that the difference between these two elements, 'authoritativeness' and 'coerciveness,' and the corresponding difference between their probable disappearance, is overlooked by his careering imagination. It would seem that after the moral restraint has disengaged itself from the political, religious, and social sanctions, it will still have the character of a restraint, just as the 'higher, self-regarding feelings, prudence and economy.' However, no doubt when Utopia is reached and Man has become perfectly adapted to his environment, he will always like doing his duty; and we reach the result which is stated on p. 129 (§ 46):—

In their proper times and places and proportions, the moral sentiments will guide men just as spontaneously and adequately as now do the sensations. And though, joined with their regulating influence when this is called for, will exist latent ideas of the evils which nonconformity would bring; these will occupy the mind no more than do ideas of the evils of starvation at the time when a healthy appetite is being satisfied by a meal.

Meanwhile there is one result of Mr. Spencer's view of which he hardly sees the full gravity: a sentiment regarded as imported by association, and destined to vanish, cannot now 'coerce us much.' Of this later. For the present we will return to our main question and ask: Do we get any *further guidance* from the account of the gradual growth into independence of truly moral restraint, at first undistinguished from the political, religious, and social restraints—from fear of the anger of an actual live chief, or of a former chief, now dead (a ghost promoted to be a god), or of fellow-members of the tribe—the truly moral restraint being exercised by the representation of the necessary natural painful consequences of bad actions? Does this analysis help us at all towards the performance of the task which Mr. Spencer announced of 'making utilitarian ethics deductive'? I cannot see that it does. We learn, indeed, that the 'element of coerciveness' in our existing consciousness of moral restraint is merely transitory, being imported by association from these other restraints, but this, if true, relates only to the form of the moral conscious- ness: it does not assist us in determining the matter of utilitarian duty. Suppose that so far as we are truly moral, we are to put aside the consideration of what government will do, or public opinion, or God —though why should we, if there are actual pleasur- able or painful consequences? But suppose we do, for the sake of argument—still the question remains : How are we to know 'what is most conducive to general happiness'?

It would seem, therefore, that if we are to get a Deductive Utilitarianism at all, we must get it entirely from the *Sociological View.* Turning to this we find Mr. Spencer saying that 'Ethics from the sociological point of view becomes nothing less than a definite account of the forms of conduct that are fitted to the associated state, in such wise that the lives of each and all may be the greatest possible, alike in length and breadth' (*en passant* observe that here we have the 'biological end' unqualified). As he rightly says, the modifications of conduct necessitated by the social state—imposed on each individual by his relations to others—have come to constitute the chief part of the moral code. And here, as I willingly recognise, Mr. Spencer gets beyond the vague generalities and platitudes which are all that the Biological and Psychological views yielded, and lays down fundamental rules, which, if they can be cogently established with due precision, are undoubtedly important.

These we will presently consider. But at the outset arises the fundamentally important question as to the ultimate end and standard of right conduct, which the conclusion of chapter iii. left open. It there appeared that 'no school can avoid taking for the ultimate moral aim a desirable state of feeling called by whatever name—gratification, enjoyment, happiness. Pleasure somewhere, at some time, to some being or beings, is an inexpugnable element of the conception.' But greatest pleasure to one being or one set of beings may be incompatible with greatest pleasure to another set ; and when we are considering the restraints imposed on the individual's conduct by his relations to other men, it is fundamentally important for us to know how far we are to ask the individual to aim at their happiness rather than his own. Indeed I think it is a defect in the account of ' truly moral restraint' which the Psychological View gave us that the immense difference to the individual between his own pleasures and those of others was left too much in the background.

Let us compare the earlier, not strictly moral, restraints—political, religious, social—and that which Mr. Spencer regards as strictly moral. Firstly, we find, I think, that the difference between them does not lie, as he rather suggests, in the directness and proximity of the former as contrasted with the indirectness and remoteness of the latter. Indeed the contrast is clearly the other way, when we consider the religious restraint especially : the evils that will happen to me from the wrath of heaven in consequence of the day of judgment, are obviously far more indirect and remote than the mischievous effects of my action on others. And even in the case of legal penalties and social disapprobation the same may be said. Nor does it seem to me that we can treat as fundamental the distinction which Mr. Spencer draws between the ' artificial' or ' factitious' consequences the fear of which causes the non-moral restraint, and the ' necessary natural' consequences which the moral restraint represents. For surely if I make myself a nuisance to society, the feelings that will prompt other men to do disagreeable things to me are as ' natural and necessary '—if this latter word is in place at all—as their feeling of the mischief I do them. The essential difference is rather in this, that in the former case it is evil primarily to myself that deters; in ' truly moral' feeling, in the main, it is evil to others, only apprehended by me sympathetically.

We have therefore to meet the question : Why and how far should I concern myself about evil to others, when the sympathetic pain to myself is not such as to outweigh the loss of pleasure involved in submitting to the restraint ? Granting that as society develops, sympathetic pain will affect me more and more, still, for a long time, I am not likely to feel 'remote diffused bad consequences' to others as much as they will feel them. Ought I, as a moral agent, in the long interval that will intervene before this consummation of sympathy is reached, to consider them equally, and if so, why ?

LECTURE IV

THE question asked at the end of the last Lecture is
answered, so far as it can be said to be answered at
all by Mr. Spencer, in chapters xi.-xiv. on *Egoism
versus Altruism, Altruism versus Egoism, Trial and
Compromise,* and *Conciliation.* Briefly, Mr. Spencer's
view is that 'pure Egoism' and 'pure Altruism' are
both rejected—*i.e.* both the formula 'live for yourself
solely,' and the Comtist formula 'live entirely for
others.' A compromise between the two is necessary
at the present stage of evolution, and for some time
to come; but we may look forward to an ultimate
'Conciliation' when, as the poet says,

> Each will find his own in all men's good.

For the present the compromise is that 'general
happiness is to be achieved mainly through the adequate pursuit of their own happiness by individuals;
while, reciprocally, the happinesses of the individuals
are to be achieved in part by the pursuit of the
general happiness (§ 91).' But this general formula
does not recognise the possibility of the two being
presented as alternatives; yet Mr. Spencer cannot

178

and does not deny that they may be so presented. So that notwithstanding the so-called compromise, the necessity of choosing between one's own happiness and the general happiness may arise for the individual in determining the conduct reasonable for him here and now.

Mr. Spencer does not directly face this question; and perhaps the reason why he does not face it is that, in chapters xi.-xiv. he does not, in my opinion, clearly distinguish the question of *Ultimate* End from that of *Proximate* End—or, to put it otherwise, the question of the test, standard, or criterion of right conduct, from the question of practical direction of conduct,—whereas it certainly seems to me that the two questions should be treated quite separately. Thus in chapter xi. (*Egoism versus Altruism*) Mr. Spencer lays stress on the point that 'the acts required for continued self-preservation' of individuals are the 'first requisites to universal welfare.' He points out how the principle of the 'survival of the fittest' in 'the struggle for existence' establishes the advantage, to the whole, of the egoistic competition of individuals each trying to reap the benefits of his better adaptation to his environment; since only by this 'arrangement' is there maintained a continual tendency to the reaching of a higher life, and, therefore, greater happiness on the whole. He shows how the individual who neglects his own health and starves his own capacity for the 'miscellaneous pleasures life offers,' hands down tendencies to misery or incapacities for happiness to his descendants. How

not only posterity but contemporaries gain in happiness by the successful egoism of any individual
directly and indirectly ; for an important condition
of making others happy is to be happy, and the
'inadequately egoistic individual' loses more or less
the ability to be duly serviceable to others. How
again altruism defeats its own end by generating
'unscrupulous egoism' in others : the selfish prey on
the unselfish, and grow more hardened through
success in selfishness ; how again it tends to retard
the 'desirable mitigation of egoism in the average
nature' by the prevention or undue retardation of
marriage on the part of the unduly altruistic.—In
most, if not all, these arguments I recognise much
force; but what I am now concerned to argue is, that
they all assume general happiness to be the ultimate
end, and maintain the superiority of egoism as a
means to this end. The arguments are irrelevant
except to a mind that has already accepted universal
happiness as the ultimate standard and criterion of
right conduct.

On the other hand, in chapter xiii. he certainly
appears to attack Bentham and his followers for holding that general happiness should be the ultimate end
and final standard of right conduct ; and refuses to
admit ' that from the standpoint of pure reason, the
happiness of others has no less a claim as an object
of pursuit for each than personal happiness.' But he
seems to treat this position as identical with the
' theory which makes general happiness the sole (or
almost the sole) *immediate* object of pursuit'; a

theory very remote from Bentham's—whose practical
view was characteristically expressed in the sentence
that ' self-regard alone will serve for diet, though
sympathy is very good for dessert '—and not maintained, so far as I am aware, by any of his leading
disciples. And it is only against this latter doctrine,
which he more frequently and properly designates as
' pure altruism,' that Mr. Spencer's arguments are in
any way effective ; the issue (as he himself states it) is
whether ' equitable egoism ' or ' pure altruism ' will
produce the ' greatest sum of happiness ' on the
whole ; and his conclusion is that ' general happiness
is to be achieved mainly through the adequate pursuit
of their own happiness by individuals,' and really
assumes that greatest happiness is the ultimate end.

I have criticised in another place [1] Bentham's reply
to the fundamental question which remains to be
answered after Hedonism is taken as established :—
After we have decided that the ultimate moral aim
must be ' desirable feeling, pleasure, satisfaction,
enjoyment, happiness to some sentient being,' how
are we to decide which sentient beings are to be
taken into account, and how their happiness is to be
estimated ? This is a question to which Bentham's
Utilitarianism does not give a perfectly clear
answer. He says that actions are to be approved
or disapproved according to their tendency to
augment the happiness of the party whose interest
is in question ; but he does not make quite clear

[1] *Outlines of the History of Ethics*, chapter iv. § 15. (Cf. also the Author's
article on *Bentham and Benthamism in Ethics and Politics*, in the *Fortnightly
Review* for May 1877.)

whose interest is in question for the moralist in Private Ethics as distinct from Legislation. At the close of his life this seems clearly attributable to his belief in the coincidence of the two ends; but it is not clear as regards his earlier view, and is hard to reconcile with his low view of the motives of average humanity. At any rate, however, according to one aspect of Bentham's system, and the one which, handed on to Mill, has been most influential in recent times, the ultimate end and standard for right private conduct is general or aggregate happiness; or to give a precise interpretation to Bentham's phrase, we may say that the party whose interest is in question includes all sentient beings—so far as their feelings are capable of being materially affected by the agent's conduct. And in estimating the respective importance of the elements of this aggregate regarded as an ultimate end, no one sentient being can count for more than another, except so far as the happiness that is, or might be, enjoyed by one, is superior in intensity to that which another is capable of enjoying; it is with this qualification that Bentham's proposition, 'Every one to count for one, and no one for more than one,' is to be understood. As so understood, it seems to me absolutely incontrovertible, and indeed implied in the adoption of general happiness as end.

And on the whole, I am disposed to think that in the polemic against the Utilitarianism of Bentham and Mill in chapter xiii. §§ 85-89, what Mr. Spencer means to attack is *not* the proposition that conduciveness to

general happiness should be taken as the ultimate
standard for determining the right formula of
conduct, but the doctrine that it should be as much
as possible taken as the *immediate end.* I infer this
from a passage (§ 91, p. 237) in which he says :—

> It is a truth insisted on by moralists and recognised in
> common life, that the achievement of individual happiness is not
> proportionate to the degree in which individual happiness is
> made the object of direct pursuit; but there has not yet become
> current the belief that, in like manner, the achievement of
> general happiness is not proportionate to the degree in which
> general happiness is made the object of direct pursuit. Yet
> failure of direct pursuit in the last case is more reasonably to be
> expected than in the first.

But if Mr. Spencer means to imply, as he certainly
suggests to his readers, that the practical directions of
Bentham and Mill are that every one is to make
universal happiness the object of direct pursuit, his
misunderstanding of these authors is so complete
that it can only be accounted for on the supposition
of his having read their writings very partially.
As regards Bentham, it is weak to say that he does
not teach this : he teaches repeatedly and emphatically
the exact opposite of this. Not only does he tell us,
in the phrase quoted above, that 'self-regard alone
will serve for diet,' but he further argues in a
manner not unlike Mr. Spencer's, against the absurd
supposition that each could make the happiness of
others his *primary aim.* Thus he says :—

'For after exception made of the case of children
not arrived at the age at which they are capable
of going alone, or adults reduced by infirmity to a
helpless state, take any two individuals A and B,

and suppose the whole care of the happiness of B confined to the breast of A, B himself not having any part in it, and this to be the case throughout, it will soon appear that, in this state of things, the species would not continue in existence, and that a few months, not to say weeks or days, would suffice for the annihilation of it.

'Of all the modes in which for the governance of one and the same individual, the two faculties could be conceived as placed in different seats—sensation and consequent desire in one breast, judgment and consequent action in another, this is the most simple. If, as has with less truth been said of the blind leading the blind, both would in such a state of things be continually falling into the ditch, much more frequently and more speedily fatal would be the falls, supposing the separation to take place upon any more complex plan. Suppose the care of the happiness of A being taken altogether from A, were divided between B and C, the happiness of B and C being provided for in the same complex manner, and so on; the greater the complication the more speedy would the destruction be, and the more flagrant the absurdity of a supposition, assuming the existence of such a state of things.' [1]

Certainly if there ever was a writer to whom 'altruism' in Mr. Spencer's bad sense—the altruism which inculcates self-sacrifice and self-suppression without limit or reserve—is not to be attributed, it is Bentham. Hence the combination of Benthamite

---

[1] Bentham's *Works*, 1843, vol. ix., *Preface to the Constitutional Code*, p. 6.

Utilitarianism and Comtist Altruism against which Mr. Spencer appears to be arguing in chapter xiii. is the most grotesque man of straw that a philosopher ever set up in order to knock it down.

The case of Mill is different : in fact one of the fundamental differences between Bentham and Mill is due to the powerful influence of Comte on the latter. Mill does inculcate self-sacrifice in particular cases : he knows that under the present imperfect social system a choice will often have to be made between the agent's own greatest happiness and greatest happiness generally, and he demands of the moral man that he shall choose the latter. Hence the confusion of Mill's Utilitarianism and Comte's Altruism is not so grotesque as in the case of Bentham. And yet it is, in a sense, even more inexcusable ; because Mill in his Essay [1] on Auguste Comte, has expressly drawn the distinction between his own doctrine and Comte's; and perhaps the best corrective I can offer of what seem to me to be Mr. Spencer's mistakes and confusions in chapter xiii. is to ask you to read through the passages on pp. 138-146 of Mill's Essay—especially as Mill's view appears to be a more instructive ' compromise ' than any proposed by Mr. Spencer. I cannot think that if he had had these passages of Mill's before him, he could possibly have framed his indictment against Utilitarians in the form it assumes in chapter xiii.

As regards myself—since Mr. Spencer in his reply is obliging enough to designate me as now the 'foremost representative of Utilitarianism as hitherto conceived,'

---

[1] *Auguste Comte and Positivism*, 2nd edit. 1866.

I must just point out that I have recognised clearly, though without either the emphasis of Bentham or the eloquence of Mill, the practical claims of egoism.[1] I think, therefore, that I am justified in saying that Mr. Spencer's apparent antagonism to the English utilitarian school is due to misunderstanding; and that his quarrel in chapters xi.-xiv. is not with the sober, qualified, and guarded 'altruism' of Bentham or his disciples, but with the hard sayings of the prophet and high-priest of Positivism, which I am certainly not prepared altogether to defend. In short, Mr. Spencer has been confounding English Utilitarianism with Comtism.

And yet even for Comte I should like to say a word; even for Comte's suppression of egoistic impulses there is a somewhat better case than Mr. Spencer admits. First, in urging men to 'live for others' unreservedly, Comte did not intend to deny that the principle might be hypothetically carried too far, or that a society of purely altruistic human beings would, as Mr. Spencer argues, be a badly organised machine for the production of human happiness. He did not intend to deny this; but his answer, and the answer of his disciples, to this and all other objections of this kind is that there is no danger: we need have no fear in urging men to be as unselfish as possible, since it is quite certain that they will always remain more than sufficiently selfish. But secondly, in saying that they will always be sufficiently selfish, Comte did not mean that they will always exercise in a due

[1] Cf. Book IV. chap. iii. § 3, of *Methods of Ethics*.

degree a wise and rational regard for self; on the
contrary, one of his grounds for inculcating altruism
so emphatically and unreservedly is the failure of the
merely prudential motives to make men take due care
of their health and bodily vigour ; even doctors, as
he says, disregard their own precepts.   He held that
men would more nearly approach to the ideal of wise
self-regard if they were more strongly moved to take
care of their health, not merely for their own sakes,
but as a matter of social duty, to keep themselves in
full vigour for performing services to others.   There
is, I hold with Mill, exaggeration in all this, but I
cannot doubt that there is an important element of
truth in it ; and that many people are, as a matter of
fact, stirred up to take better care of their own bodily
vigour and prospects of life, by an increased sense of
their importance to others.

   To sum up : I quite accept Mr. Spencer's view as to
the necessity, with a view to the general happiness, of
some such practical 'compromise' between Egoism and
Altruism as he delineates in chapter xiii.—a compromise continually varying, as he says, with the stage in
the evolution that has been reached.   But I urge that
the fact that compromise must be, does not determine
the principle on which compromise is to be planned; for
any individual here and now, the occasions of life may
present alternative compromises—the compromise in
which he pursues the happiness of others so far as it
is consistent with his own, and the compromise in
which he pursues his own happiness so far as it is
consistent with maximum happiness generally.   Mr.

Spencer does not affirm that the two always coincide
—indeed I do not think any writer on Ethics in the
present age ventures expressly to affirm this, taking
only mundane considerations into account.   And if he
does not, all his exposition of the growing implication
of the interest of each with the interests of others and
of the ultimate conciliation of the two, does not relieve
him of the necessity of answering the question of
the individual here and now : Which of the two
alternative compromises am I to take ?

It may be said to me : How do *you* deal with it ?
My answer is, that unless we assume or prove the moral
order of the world, there is a conflict between rational
convictions.—Do I assume it ?   Yes, practically, as a
man ; provisionally, and with due recognition of the
need of proof, as a philosopher.   The assumption is
normal to reflective man, and a postulate of Common
Sense.

However, to return to Mr. Spencer.   Let us suppose
that the compromise which is to be taken is that
framed on the universalistic principle—for this I conceive is what Mr. Spencer would say, when forced to
face the dilemma—let us suppose that the individual
is to be egoistic to that extent to which, at the present
stage of evolution, it is on the whole conducive to
general happiness that he should be so, taking present
and future into account ; we thus come back to the
question, how far it is possible for him to determine
this compromise by any such deductive method as that
which Mr. Spencer advocates as alone truly scientific,
and as the method into which utilitarian ethics ought

to pass.   Can we lay down rules for determining what
conduct must be conducive, and what must be detrimental, to general happiness,—rules so fundamental
as to apply throughout this varying series of compromises, as well as when the final conciliation is
achieved?   This is what Mr. Spencer thinks can be
done, and has been adequately done.[1]

I now turn back to chapter viii.—the *Sociological
View*—and ask again, whether, taking general happiness as ultimate end, Utilitarianism can be made
deductive by Sociology?   At the outset of chapter
viii. in § 49, I notice an assumption which illustrates the rashness of Mr. Spencer's habits of
reasoning—rashness which here reaches, I think,
an express and formal logical fallacy.   He explains
that though the happiness ('quantity of life') of
individuals constitutes the ultimate end, we have to
'put in the foreground the welfare of the society as
a whole,' and to some extent to sacrifice the lives of
individuals to it; since the 'two ends are not harmonious at the outset,' and are 'still partially conflicting.'
But he holds that this can only be in consequence of
the presence of antagonistic societies (cf. § 49, p. 134).
The argument takes the form, *If A is, B is; therefore, if A is not, B is not.*   And the fallacy is not, I
think, merely formal; it indicates a material error
in Mr. Spencer's view which I shall examine when
I pass to Part II.   Not only is it illogical to con-

---

[1] I suppose the 'data' are conceived to be adequately given in outline in
chapter viii. on the *Sociological View*, taken along with the two concluding
chapters on *Absolute and Relative Ethics* and *The Scope of Ethics*, with some
light from chapter ix., *Criticisms and Explanations*.

clude that *because* a certain sacrifice of individual
lives to the life of the community is rendered
necessary by war between societies, therefore all
need for such sacrifice will cease when war ceases :
I should go further and say that there is no ground for
holding that it will cease, or that all the conflict of
human desires and the competition for the means
of human happiness, are due to war. In the older
martial state of things when the Individual is to some
extent sacrificed to the Community, since the happiness of individuals is after all an ultimate end, what
takes place is a sacrifice or diminution of the happiness of *some* individuals for the greater happiness of
others ; and there appears no reason why this kind
of sacrifice should not go on, when the preservation
of the community is no longer threatened by human
enemies. What Mr. Spencer means by 'social antagonisms' would seem to be the state of actual war,
or armed vigilance from time to time interrupted by
actual fighting, between communities. But supposing
'militancy' to have become extinct, and 'industrialism' everywhere dominant, we have no ground for
hoping that industrial antagonisms will not occur,
and we cannot say that they will not be violent.
When armed aggression, either of individual on
individual, or of society on society, has been put
down, the economic conflict of industrial group with
group, of social class with class, may still remain—
I know no ground for hoping that it will cease. It is
necessary to dwell on this, because, when Mr. Spencer
passes (§ 50, p. 137) to 'consider the system of ethics

proper to the state in which peaceful activities are undisturbed,' we have to bear in mind that there are different kinds of disturbance; and, for example, that one industrial group may be reduced to something near starvation by the action of one or more different industrial groups, without anything that we can fairly call 'aggression'—as by a general refusal to employ the services or consume the products of the group in question. In fact we might almost say that the whole dispute between Mr. Spencer's individualism and modern socialism is illegitimately prejudged by the fallacious inference in § 49.

This leads me to notice a fundamental difficulty in dealing with Mr. Spencer's argument in this chapter, due to our not knowing *how* ideal the state is to which his ethics relates. There is a 'final permanent code' which voluntary co-operation implies, and which 'alone admits of being definitely formulated, and so constituting ethics as a science in contrast with empirical ethics' (cf. § 55); still we are now a long way off this, and require temporarily a different ethics. This distinction is more fully developed in the two concluding chapters. But I wish to point out that it hardly seems present to Mr. Spencer's mind throughout : he continually appeals to our experience of man as we know him in support of the particulars of the codes, without suggesting the need of distinguishing between (1) actual men in actual society and the code suitable to them, and (2) ideal men in an ideal society and the code suitable to them. However, in the last two chapters the above statement—that it is only a 'final permanent code' which 'admits of being definitely formulated, and so constituting ethics as a science in contrast with empirical ethics'—is made clear and developed.

Deferring the consideration of the utility of this 'final permanent code' for men here and now, let us briefly consider its chief rules as given in chapter viii. The particulars of the code are sufficiently simple. We have :—

(1) The negative obligations of the old Law of Nature (the *Neminem laede* of the Roman Jurists)— Injure no one, in person, estate, or reputation.

(2) The main positive obligation of the Law of Nature—Observe contracts.

(3) A general duty of positive beneficence—Make spontaneous efforts to further the welfare of others.

Now of course we are all disposed to admit that these rules belong to a 'final permanent code' and will be observed in an ideal community : the question is, whether we know this any more for introducing Sociology—whether Mr. Spencer enables us to know it with a scientific certainty, unlike that which the Utilitarian can attain, who forms his view of the *media axiomata* of ethics from experience. I cannot perceive that we do gain this additional certainty so far as *The Data of Ethics* goes (I defer the consideration of Part IV. on *Justice*). Let us consider (1)—a truism as Mr. Spencer calls it. The 'highest life accompanying completely evolved conduct' excludes, he says, all acts of aggression, 'murder, assault, robbery . . . libel, injury to property, and so forth.' I feel no doubt that so long as men remain anything like what I know, the preservation of society requires that these crimes should be prevented : I know this by a very simple exercise of constructive imagination in which I use my notions of human beings derived from experience.   I do not feel that I obtain any more certainty from taking the 'Sociological point of view' and learning that the 'group will lose coherence' if they are not prevented.   So far as I can feel any doubt about any of the points, the doubt is not excluded by Sociology.

Take Libel, for example ; there is a certain diffi-culty in drawing the line, defining what a man may say to annoy others.   We have to restrict the freedom of one man in order to prevent pain to another, or 'breach of the peace' ; the question is, how far we should go.   And it has been seriously, if not plausibly, urged that the whole of this kind of restraint should be done away with—that society would get on better if plain speaking were allowed : every one's statements would go for what they were worth, be believed or disbelieved according to his reputation and credit, and we should gain valuable information as to each other's character, and useful additional forces to check ill-doing and promote well-doing.   As Godwin says : ' If I have had particular opportunity to observe any man's vices—there may be very sufficient reason for my representing him as a vicious man . . . in order to warn those whom his errors might injure, even though I may be totally unable to demonstrate his vices.'[1]

---

[1] Godwin's *Enquiry concerning Political Justice*, Book VI. chap. vi. 2.

It may be urged that a progress towards publicity, greater mutual vigilance and mutual pressure, is a natural incident of social development; as the Positivists say, we ought to live, and shall come to live, more and more 'in glass houses.' We shall get accustomed in private life, as public men have already done, to the continual free criticism of newspapers : the danger of libel producing a breach of the peace will therefore diminish and become evanescent, as we get more adapted to this closer life of a continually more crowded community.

I have urged these arguments, not because I agree with them, but because I feel that the point is one that can be argued: on the basis of empirical Utilitarianism some such view as this cannot be cogently excluded. But when we ask whether Sociology enables us to exclude it, I think the answer must be that it leaves the matter exactly where it was.

LECTURE V

In considering chap. xv. (*Absolute Ethics and Relative Ethics*) we may first notice that there is a threefold distinction of questions, which is apt, if we do not take care, to lapse into a twofold distinction, from which lapse much confusion results. The three questions are:—(1) What would be right for an individual to do in an ideal society? (2) What is right for an individual to do here and now? (3) What is commonly thought to be right, either in the particular community of which I am a member, or any other?—and there is a certain danger of confounding (2) and (3). According to me, the primary question for which we seek an answer from Ethics is (2), and the answer to (1) is only of practical importance so far as it helps us to answer (2); but (1) is an ethical question, though a hypothetical one; (3), however, is not from a utilitarian point of view primarily an ethical question at all—it is a sociological question; that is, when comprehensively investigated, as embracing the prevalent moralities of different ages and countries, it is sociological rather than ethical. Still a special and limited part of the investigation cannot be excluded

195

from Ethics—namely, the study by any reflective person of the morality of his own age and country, the morality which through education and social life a normal individual finds himself sharing when he begins to reflect. The result of this investigation cannot but have an important bearing on the answer to (2) : What is right for the individual to do here and now ?

At the same time the answers to questions (3) and (2)—from the Utilitarian point of view, in which Mr. Spencer and I agree—are quite clearly distinct. For after I have ascertained what is the Positive Morality, as it is called, established in the community of which I am a member—the commonly accepted moral rules and prevalent moral sentiments—I have still to ask : How far is it my duty to conform to such rules ? This is the question with which I deal, from a utilitarian point of view, in Book IV. chapter v. of my *Methods of Ethics*. In the Intuitional view the distinction between questions (2) and (3) is less, and less clear ; still even in this view it cannot be ignored altogether.

Now Mr. Spencer does not keep clear the threefold distinction of questions. The reason partly is, that, through an eccentricity of language, he is inclined to reduce paradoxically the possibility of giving a definite answer to question (2). This he makes plain, in § 100, by way of a criticism on statements of mine. The whole section should be read, but we may quote here the following passages from pp. 259, 261 :—

In his *Methods of Ethics* (1st Ed. p. 6) Mr. Sidgwick says :— 'That there is in any given circumstances some one thing which

DATA OF ETHICS 197

ought to be done, and that this can be known, is a fundamental
assumption, made not by philosophers only, but by all men who
perform any processes of moral reasoning.'. . . . Instead of admitting
that there is in every case a right and a wrong, it may be contended that in multitudinous cases no right, properly so-called,
can be alleged, but only a least wrong; and further, it may be
contended that in many of these cases where there can be alleged
only a least wrong, it is not possible to ascertain with any precision
which is the least wrong . . . conduct conceived as bad proves
always to be that which inflicts somewhere a surplus of either
positive or negative pain; then the absolutely good, the absolutely
right, in conduct, can be that only which produces pure pleasure
—pleasure unalloyed with pain anywhere. By implication,
conduct which has any concomitant of pain, or any painful consequence, is partially wrong; and the highest claim to be made
for such conduct is, that it is the least wrong which, under the
conditions, is possible—the relatively right (§§ 100, 101).

I do not—as Mr. Spencer suggests—exclude indifferent acts—still less acts of which the moral
character is not definitely cognisable. But I hold
that really indifferent acts, acts of which the consequences—if all the consequences could be foreseen
—are absolutely balanced, are probably very rare:
though acts which relatively to our powers of
judgment are indifferent are not uncommon. This
is one ground for limiting practically the sphere of
moral judgment : another ground being the self-limita-
tion of the principle of aiming at general happiness
by the consideration that happiness will be better
attained if other ends are directly sought, under
restrictions laid down by regard to general happiness.
The issue between us here is really to a great extent
verbal. Mr. Spencer says 'only a least wrong,' meaning that some effects must be painful; but he does
not deny that the less wrong ought to be chosen by a
moral agent; and that is what I mean by calling it

right, and I conceive that my use of the term is in
harmony with Common Sense.   As for cases where it
is not possible to say which is least wrong, we may
quote one illustration from those given in § 103 :—

Here is a merchant who loses by the failure of a man
indebted to him.   Unless he gets help he himself will fail ; and
if he fails he will bring disaster not only on his family but on
all who have given him credit.   Even if by borrowing he is
enabled to meet immediate engagements, he is not safe ; for the
time is one of panic, and others of his debtors by going to the
wall may put him in further difficulties.   Shall he ask a friend
for a loan ?   On the one hand, is it not wrong forthwith to bring
on himself, his family, and those who have business relations with
him, the evils of his failure ?   On the other hand, is it not wrong
to hypothecate the property of his friend, and lead him too, with
his belongings and dependents, into similar risks ?   The loan
would probably tide him over his difficulty; in which case would
it not be unjust to his creditors did he refrain from asking it ?
Contrariwise, the loan would very possibly fail to stave off his
bankruptcy; in which case is not his action in trying to obtain
it practically fraudulent ?   Though in extreme cases it may be
easy to say which course is the least wrong, how is it possible in
all those medium cases where even by the keenest man of business
the contingencies cannot be calculated ?

There is no disagreement between me and Mr.
Spencer as to the great doubtfulness of the details of
Utilitarian Ethics : and I have shown elaborately in
Book II. of my *Methods of Ethics* that the nature of
the method does not admit of 'least measurement' of
quantities of happiness, but I think that in the cases
given by Mr. Spencer as examples in § 103 the 'conservative considerations' urged in *Methods of Ethics*[1]

[1] Cf. Book IV. chap. i. § 1, p. 473 :—'For though the imperfection that
we find in all the actual conditions of human existence—we may even say in
the universe at large as judged from a human point of view—is ultimately
found even in Morality itself, in so far as this is contemplated as Positive ;
still, practically, we are much less concerned with correcting and improving
than we are with realising and enforcing it.   The Utilitarian must repudiate
altogether that temper of rebellion against the established morality, as some-

would more often turn the scale on the side of ordinary
morality than he allows—for instance, I can hardly
conceive a man sincerely thinking it his duty to get
a loan from a friend without revealing his circumstances.   It is assumed to be by deception, and
therefore a breach of the implied understanding of
friendship.   Still I quite agree in the general propositions that there are many doubtful cases in life—
including many of the old 'cases of casuistry' in
which a conscientious Utilitarian would really find
it difficult to decide.[1]

The main issue between me and Mr. Spencer is
as to the value of Absolute Ethics.   And here it is
necessary for me to explain the difference between
the Spencerian doctrine that I had before me when
writing my *Methods of Ethics* and the Spencerian
doctrine presented in *Data of Ethics*.

In *Data of Ethics*, throughout chapters xv. and
xvi., it is recognised that there is an important subject
of systematic study called Relative Ethics; and the
whole inquiry in those chapters is as to the relation
which Absolute Ethics bears to this.   The subject-
matter of Absolute Ethics is the conduct of ideal men
in an ideal society, 'perfect conduct.'   The subject-
matter of Relative Ethics is the 'imperfect conduct'
of actual men in an actual society, which, as producing
some pain, is not in Mr. Spencer's view absolutely right

thing purely external and conventional, into which the reflective mind is
always apt to fall when it is first convinced that the established rules are not
intrinsically reasonable.'
    [1] In such cases I think that a practical rule of some value is, to contemplate
fully the bad consequences of one's action and try to minimise the harm that
they must inevitably do.

but only relatively right, or least wrong. It enunciates 'certain relative truths' and 'ascertains with approximate correctness what is relatively right.' It is paralleled with 'mechanical science fitted for dealing with the real' as contrasted with 'ideal mechanical science.' It is paralleled with Astronomy so far as dealing with the exact position of the stars and ascertaining actual truths concerning them. Mr. Spencer's whole effort here is directed to show that Absolute Ethics must precede Relative Ethics. He points out that, in the case of Mechanics, we require an abstract or ideal science which deals with a hypothetical set of facts simpler than actual facts— supposes levers absolutely rigid, fulcrums without breadth, projectiles that meet with no resistance from the air—and the study of this 'ideal mechanical science' must precede the study of 'mechanical science fitted for dealing with the real.' He points out that similarly, in the case of Astronomy, the 'truths respecting simple, theoretically exact' relations—ideal circles and ellipses—must be ascertained before the truths respecting the complex and practically inexact relations that actually exist. He argues that, similarly, Absolute Ethics, dealing with ideal conduct in an ideal society, should precede Relative Ethics.

All this gives a clear and coherent view; but Mr. Spencer, in connecting his statement with a controversy directed against my view that the primary object of Ethics is not to determine what ought to be done in an ideal society,[1] misunderstands my

---

[1] *Methods of Ethics*, Book I. chap. ii. § 2.

argument. That argument consisted of two parts, the first directed against the more extreme view of Absolute Ethics given in Mr. Spencer's *Social Statics*, the second against the view given in *Data of Ethics*. Mr. Spencer has taken the first part to answer, regarding it as arguing the question argued in the second part, and has altogether ignored the second. In *Social Statics* it is maintained not merely—as in *Data of Ethics* — that Absolute Ethics which ' formulates normal conduct in an ideal society' ought to ' take precedence of Relative Ethics'; but that Absolute Ethics is the only kind of Ethics with which a philosophical moralist can possibly concern himself. To quote Mr. Spencer's words :—

Any proposed system of morals which recognises existing defects, and countenances acts made needful by them, stands self-condemned. . . . Moral law . . . requires as its postulate that human beings be perfect. The philosophical moralist treats solely of the *straight* man . . . shows in what relationship he stands to other straight men . . . a problem in which a *crooked* man forms one of the elements, is insoluble by him (*Social Statics*, chapter i.).

Still more definitely is Relative Ethics excluded in the following passage of the concluding chapter of the same treatise (the italics are mine) :—

It will very likely be urged that, whereas the perfect moral code is confessedly beyond the fulfilment of imperfect men, some other code is needful for our present guidance . . . to say that the imperfect man requires a moral code which recognises his imperfection and allows for it, *seems at first sight reasonable. But it is not really so* . . . a system of morals which shall recognise man's present imperfections and allow for them *cannot be devised, and would be useless if it could be devised.*

I observe that Mr. Spencer, in replying to me, refers to his *Social Statics*, as though he still held

the opinions there expressed ; but I must confess that
I cannot reconcile these passages, and others that
might be quoted from the same context, with the
view of Relative Ethics given in the concluding
chapters of *Data of Ethics*. At any rate, it was in
opposition to the earlier view (in *Social Statics*) and
not to the later one that I thought it fair to adduce
the analogy of geometry and astronomy, and to
suggest the absurdity of a ' philosophical astronomer'
declining to deal with any planets that did not move
in perfect ellipses.   As I have indicated, Mr. Spencer,
in his rejoinder, takes the suggested analogy to relate
to the question whether the study of Absolute Ethics
should precede that of Relative Ethics.   Had this
been my meaning, the reference to astronomy would
have been manifestly inappropriate.   But in fact it
was only in the paragraph succeeding that to which
Mr. Spencer has replied that I began to discuss this
latter question, as is evident from the following
sentences with which my second paragraph opens :
' This inquiry (I say) into the morality of an ideal
society can therefore be at best but a preliminary
investigation, after which the step from the ideal
to the actual remains to be taken.   We have to
ask, then, how far such a preliminary construction
seems desirable.'   I go on to state my objections
to that more moderate view of the claims of Absolute Ethics which is expounded in the treatise before
us.   These objections Mr. Spencer has not noticed ;
in fact his interest in my argument seems to have
ceased exactly at the point at which it began to

be really relevant to his present position. In the first place, granting — a large grant — that Mr. Spencer's ideal society, in which the voluntary actions of all the members cause ' pleasure un - alloyed by pain anywhere' to all who are affected by them, is one which we can conceive as possible, it seems to me quite impossible to ascertain *a priori* the nature of the human beings composing such a society with sufficient definiteness and cer- tainty to enable us to determine their code of con- duct. It has not come within Mr. Spencer's plan to delineate this code in the present treatise, other- wise than in the scantiest and most general way ; but among the meagre generalities that he has given us, I can find nothing that is in any degree important which is not also in a high degree disputable. The most important is undoubtedly the formula of Absolute Justice as the fundamental principle for regulating social co-operation. Of this Mr. Spencer, in the con- cluding chapter, gives the following statement :—

Individual life is possible only on condition that each organ is paid for its action by an equivalent of blood, while the organism as a whole obtains from the environment assimilable matters that compensate for its efforts ; and the mutual depend- ence of parts in the social organism necessitates that, alike for its total life and the lives of its units, there similarly shall be maintained a due proportion between returns and labours : the natural relation between work and welfare shall be preserved intact. . . . That principle of equivalence which meets us when we seek its roots in the laws of individual life, involves the idea of *measure ;* and on passing to social life, the same principle introduces us to the conception of equity or *equalness,* in the relation of citizens to one another ; the elements of the questions arising are *quantitative,* and hence the solutions assume a more scientific form (§ 109).

Here, in speaking of a 'due proportion between returns and labours,' Mr. Spencer does not mean merely—as the analogy of the individual organism might lead us to suppose—that each labourer will receive the means of carrying on his labour in the most efficient manner; his meaning is, as several other passages show, that he will receive a share of wealth proportioned to the value of his labour. But so far as this share is more than our ideal labourer needs for labouring efficiently, I see no ground for affirming *a priori* that he will receive it in an ideal society, since it is quite conceivable that the surplus would produce more happiness if distributed among other ideal persons. To this Mr. Spencer would probably answer (cf. chapter xi. § 69) that unless 'superiority profits by the rewards of superiority' the struggle for existence, to which 'the progress of organisation and the reaching of a higher life' have hitherto been due, can no longer continue. This is doubtless a weighty consideration in dealing with the practical problems of existing societies; but I cannot admit its relevancy in 'Absolute Ethics' until it is shown how we are to get the advantages of the struggle for existence without their attendant disadvantages—that is, without some pain to those who are defeated in the struggle; for all such pain is *ex hypothesi* excluded from Mr. Spencer's ideal society, in which all voluntary actions produce un-alloyed pleasure. Again, I cannot see any validity in the conception of 'equalness,' as governing the relations of ideal citizens, except so far as it means merely that similar persons will be treated similarly; for we cannot know *a priori* how far our ideal citizens will be dissimilar, and therefore reasonably subjected to dissimilar treatment. The progress of evolution, Mr. Spencer elsewhere tells us, is to increase heterogeneity; but how are we to know the degree of heterogeneity which the ideal society will exhibit? This point is very important in reference to a further question, that Mr. Spencer indicates, as to the legitimate ends and limits of governmental authority. I cannot conceive how this question is to be definitely answered, unless we know in what varying degrees political wisdom is distributed among our more or less heterogeneous ideal citizens; and how can we precisely know this?

If we consider Mr. Spencer's two analogies in this chapter—Geometry and Physiology—each of them is, it appears to me, admirably adapted to illustrate what is *not* to be found in his Ideal or Absolute Ethics. (1) Geometry: because of (*a*) the definite conceptions that we can form of our ideal or abstract lines, squares, and circles, so that we can reason about their ideal relations with perfect clearness and precision; and (*b*) the comparatively close approximation between these—almost always capable of being made as close as we like for practical purposes—and the boundaries of the actual spaces with which practical necessities force us to deal. Both these characteristics are conspicuously wanting in Mr. Spencer's Absolute Ethics. Granting that we can conceive as possible a society in which the actions of all the members produce 'pleasure unalloyed by pain anywhere,' we certainly cannot conceive their relations or actions with definiteness and certainty. And, as I say in my *Methods of Ethics*, even if it were otherwise, even if we could construct scientifically Mr. Spencer's ideal morality, I do not think such a construction would be of much avail in solving the practical problems of actual humanity. For a society in which—to take one point only—there is no such thing as punishment, is necessarily a society with its essential structure so unlike our own, that it would be idle to attempt any close imitation of its rules of behaviour. It might possibly be best for us to conform approximately to some of these rules; but this we could only know by examining each particular rule in detail; we could have no general grounds for concluding that it would be best for us to conform to them as far as possible. For even supposing that this ideal society is ultimately to be realised, it must at any rate be separated from us by a considerable interval of evolution; hence it is not unlikely that the best way of progressing towards it will be some other than the apparently directest way, and that we shall reach it more easily if we begin by moving away from it. Whether this is so or not, and to what extent, can only be known by carefully examining the effects of conduct on actual human beings, and inferring its probable effects on the human beings whom we may expect to exist in the proximate future.[1]

---

[1] *Methods of Ethics*, Book IV. chap. iv. § 2.

But (2) Mr. Spencer's comparison with Physiology facilitates criticism still further.   Physiology, he says,

. . . describes the various functions which, as combined, constitute and maintain life ; and in treating of them it assumes that they are severally performed in right ways, in due amounts, and in proper order ; it recognises only healthy func-.tions.   If it explains digestion, it supposes that the heart is supplying blood and that the visceral nervous system is stimulating the organs immediately concerned.   If it gives a theory of the circulation, it assumes that blood has been produced by the combined actions of the structures devoted to its production, and that it is properly aerated.   If the relations between respiration and the vital processes at large are interpreted, it is on the pre-supposition that the heart goes on sending blood, not only to the lungs and to certain nervous centres, but to the diaphragm and intercostal muscles.   Physiology ignores failures in the actions of these several organs.   It takes no account of imperfections, it neglects derangements, it does not recognise pain, it knows nothing of vital wrong.   It simply formulates that which goes on as a result of complete adaptation of all parts to all needs.   That is to say, in relation to the inner actions constituting bodily life, physiological theory has a position like that which ethical theory, under its absolute form as above conceived, has to the outer actions constituting conduct.   The moment cognisance is taken of excess of function, or arrest of function, or defect of function, with the resulting evil, physiology passes into pathology.   We begin now to take account of wrong actions in the inner life analogous to the wrong actions in the outer life taken account of by ordinary theories of morals (§ 105, p. 276).

This is very true ; and it is quite possible to conceive a physiology of the social organism, in which failures to perform functions are similarly omitted. In fact, in treating of politics in my humbler way, I do this.   In delineating organs of government— Legislative, Executive, Judicial—and their relations, I assume, for instance, that the Executive carries out the laws laid down by Parliament ; that the judges decide by a rational procedure whether or not the laws have been broken, and so on ; whereas actually

the Executive may disobey Parliament, judges may
be bribed, etc.   But it is singular that Mr. Spencer
does not see that this kind and degree of idealisa-
tion of the actual social organism does not get
us within reach, or even within sight, of the ideal
society which his principle demands—in which actions
produce 'pleasure unalloyed by pain anywhere.'   For
we have important organs, with functions punitive
and militant, whose actions normally produce pain :
they are, in fact, organised with the view of producing it.   For instance, judges, prisons and
prison-officials, sheriffs, hangmen, armies and navies,
secretaries of war, admiralties, etc.   If we conceive
that part of our organisation which relates to
defence against aggression, external and internal,
altogether removed, because grown altogether useless
in the course of evolution, the average nature of
the human tissue, if I may so say, composing the
social organism must be so completely changed, that
the physiology which deals with it will be altogether
unlike the experimental science which Mr. Spencer
has adduced in his analogy.   And there are many
parts of Mr. Spencer's work in which he seems to
see this.   Compare, for instance, the beginning of
chapter viii. § 48, where he says :—

Not for the human race only, but for every race, there are
laws of right living.   Given its environment and its structure,
and there is for each kind of creature a set of actions adapted in
their kinds, amounts, and combinations, to secure the highest
conservation its nature permits.   The animal, like the man, has
needs for food, warmth, activity, rest, and so forth, which must
be fulfilled in certain relative degrees to make its life whole.
Maintenance of its race implies satisfaction of special desires,

sexual and philoprogenitive, in due proportions. Hence there
is a supposable formula for the activities of each species, which,
could it be drawn out, would constitute a system of morality for
that species. But such a system of morality would have little
or no reference to the welfare of others than self and offspring.
Indifferent to individuals of its own kind, as an inferior creature
is, and habitually hostile to individuals of other kinds, the formula
for its life could take no cognisance of the lives of those with
which it came in contact ; or rather, such formula would imply
that maintenance of its life was at variance with maintenance of
their lives.

Or consider the different formulas of right living
for different creatures which he gives § 48, pp. 132,
133, and the end of chapter viii. § 55, on the successive compromises required for the transitional stages
of society. Thus in § 55 he says :—

During the transitional stages there are necessitated successive
compromises between the moral code which asserts the claims of
the society *versus* those of the individual, and the moral code
which asserts the claims of the individual *versus* those of the
society. And evidently each such compromise, though for the
time being authoritative, admits of no consistent or definite
expression.

To return to Mr. Spencer's analogy :—the kind of
sociology which the analogy of physiology suggests is
that which delineates normal conduct under existing
conditions and at existing stages. If we take a
lion, for instance, the physiology as distinct from the
pathology of the animal assumes its teeth and claws
in a healthy state, but the physiology of a lion whose
actions caused no pain would require us to reconstruct
him with quite different teeth and no claws at all. I
may take a sociological illustration from the notion
of Justice which, as treated in *Data of Ethics*, Mr.
Spencer more than once explains to be the cardinal
point of his ethics, as contrasted with ordinary

Utilitarianism, and ask: Can we, by means of Sociology, get a clearer, better established, more precise view of Justice? Certainly this does not appear from what is given in § 52 of chapter viii. We there learn that 'co-operation can only be maintained by proportioning benefit to achievement,' by 'maintaining directly or indirectly the relation between effort and benefit'—phrases which Mr. Spencer apparently regards as equivalent; and this is to be brought about by 'fulfilment of voluntary agreements.' But one fundamental difficulty in making the principle of requiting desert precise, is due to the divergence between effort and achievement.[1] Equal efforts, experience shows, do not produce equal results; is it just to apportion benefit to result or to effort? And as for attaining this apportionment by free contract, I have pointed out[2] many reasons why free contract does not attain this result. Shall we then restrict freedom in order to obtain a juster apportionment of remuneration to labour? That is the Socialist contention. Or will such restriction do more harm than good from the repression of enterprise, energy, etc.? That is the Individualist contention. A Sociology which would really help us here would be of great use; but I cannot see that Mr. Spencer's does anything for us, as it simply ignores the difficulty. He explains in very scientific language (§ 53) how the social organs, like the organs of an individual organism, have to be 'paid in nutriment for their services to the rest.' But he does not

---

[1] Cf. *Methods of Ethics*, Book III. chap. v. § 6.   [2] *Loc. cit.*

see that this principle gives us a very different result from free contract. What a man earns, in the society that we know, is very different from what is just required to maintain him in efficiency as a worker; or to speak accurately, from what he would get in a division framed on the principle of aiming at the greatest possible efficiency of all organs. Will it be different in the ideal society of the future? If so, how will this difference be arrived at?

So again, as regards the rule of Positive Beneficence (given in this chapter viii. of *Data of Ethics*), according to which men not only refrain from direct or indirect aggression upon one another, and help to complete one another's lives by specified reciprocities of aid, but also make spontaneous efforts to further one another's welfare. Put vaguely and generally, the rule cannot excite hesitation; but when we consider the limitations and restrictions with which the duty of beneficence is hampered at present, and ask ourselves how far they are likely to be diminished, increased, or otherwise modified in the future, the answer is difficult to give; and here again Sociology does not help us. Suppose we take an optimist view, and assume that the future will be better than the present, still in what way will it be better, as regards mutual needs and services? Will 'self-help' predominate more and more, and prudence increase? will there be insurance offices to insure every one against all possible disasters, and will all normal men take advantage of them? Then positive beneficence—outside the range of the services that spring from, testify, and sustain mutual affection—will be reduced to a minimum.   Or shall we see, on the other hand, a great extension of better-directed, better-organised almsgiving? will the needs of the needy be met, the distresses of the distressed alleviated by help given with such judgment, tact, and discretion that it will have no demoralising effect, will not tend to sap the springs of self-reliance and energy?   If we knew scientifically which of these developments was coming, it might give us useful guidance in our present social efforts; but here we get no assistance at all from Sociology, as expounded by Mr. Spencer.   He does not attempt to make definite his vague hypothetical statement that 'if the presence of fellow-men, while putting certain limits to each man's sphere of activity, opens certain other spheres of activity in which feelings, while achieving their gratifications, do not diminish but add to the gratifications of others, then such sphere will inevitably be occupied' (§ 54, p. 147).[1]

I cannot conclude without noticing the confusion which Mr. Spencer introduces (§ 106) in trying to show that his conception of Ethics 'really lies latent in the beliefs of the moralists.'   Of course the conception of an *ideal* man is always latent.   If we delineate virtue and duty, we implicitly delineate a man who realises virtue and fulfils duty—a morally ideal man.   But the whole point of the delineation by, *e.g.*, the Stoics—who made most of the sage—was that an ideal man could live in a non-ideal society.   Of course being a sage he would not behave in a bad community exactly

[1] Cf. *Methods of Ethics*, Book I. chap. ii. § 2, pp. 21, 22.

as he would in a good one : he would not behave like
the truthful, candid, and benevolent fool whom Spencer
contemplates, p. 280 (end of § 106).   It was, for
instance, a disputed question in the Greek Schools
whether a perfect sage should take part in current
politics.   Plato thought not; the Stoics, with some
hesitation, that he would.   But he must behave
somehow ; and that he would under all circumstances
behave like a sage they had no doubt.

LECTURE VI

In the previous five Lectures we have been engaged
in examining closely Part I. of Mr. Spencer's
Principles of Ethics, which contains the general
theory of the subject. I propose to travel more
rapidly over the ground covered by the remainder
of the work, indicating as I go the chapters and
passages that appear to me specially important.

Before I pass to Part II. (*The Inductions of Ethics*)
it will be desirable to examine briefly its relation to
Part I. and to the rest of the treatise, though this will
involve some recapitulation. I must say, frankly, that
I do not think the titles of Parts I. and II.—*Data of
Ethics* and *Inductions of Ethics*—are well chosen to
give the reader an idea of their relation. I will, however, try to explain in what sense these titles are used.
The *Data of Ethics* really gives, as I have said, a
general survey of the subject, and shows the reader
what kind of premises are available for answering
the practical question : What am I to do ? It gives
the relation of Ethics to other sciences, especially
Biology and Sociology, determines the ultimate end

of human conduct, and defines the method to be
adopted in a scientific investigation of the right rules
of human action.   In the last chapter Mr. Spencer
explains that the field for this investigation 'includes two great divisions, personal and social'
(§ 107), the scientific basis of the former being
mainly supplied by Biology, and the scientific basis
of the latter mainly by Sociology.   The first division
comprehends actions which are primarily judged as
affecting the agent himself.   The chief rules for this
are worked out in Part III. on *Ethics of the Individual
Life*, which I shall discuss briefly in the next Lecture.
Mr. Spencer, however, is careful to point out that no
complete separation can be effected between this and
the second division, which comprehends actions which
'must be judged as good or bad mainly by their
results to others.'   The further subdivision of these
is thus explained by Mr. Spencer : 'Actions of this
last class fall into two groups.   Those of the one
group achieve ends in ways that do or do not
unduly interfere with the pursuit of ends by others,'
and are accordingly judged to be unjust or just.
These actions are the subject of Part IV. (*Justice*).
Those forming the other group are of 'a kind
which influence the states of others without directly
interfering with the relation between their labours
and results,' and are accordingly judged as 'beneficent or maleficent.'   These actions, subdivided under
the heads of *Negative Beneficence* and *Positive Beneficence*, occupy Parts V. and VI.   We found further, in
Part I., that under each of these heads a double problem

is, in Mr. Spencer's view, presented to the student of
ethics : it is his business first to determine what the
injunctions of morality must be for an 'ideal man
under ideal conditions,' and then to 'see how such
injunctions are to be most nearly fulfilled by actual
men under existing conditions.' These two lines of
inquiry Mr. Spencer distinguishes as belonging to
'Absolute' and 'Relative' ethics respectively.

The investigation thus sketched out appeared, as we
saw, to be further complicated by the fact that the
ultimate end and criterion of right action was presented by Mr. Spencer in two different aspects : sometimes as 'Life, estimated by multiplying its length
into its breadth '—that is, by taking into account the
quantity of change that living beings go through, as
well as the mere length of their lives ;—sometimes,
again, as Happiness, 'or desirable feeling called by
whatever name.' It is obvious that, so far as life is
unhappy, the actions most conducive to Maximum
Life—for example, economic legislation tending to
promote an increase of population—may be different
from the actions most conducive to Maximum
Happiness. Mr. Spencer holds that — at least in
Absolute Ethics — we may assume the coincidence of life and happiness, on the ground of the
biological truth that everywhere faculties adjust
themselves to the conditions of existence, in such
wise that the activities which those conditions require
become pleasurable. Though actually living creatures
may be more or less miserable owing to incongruity
between their natures and their environment, there

is, he holds, an inevitable progress towards congruity ;
so that with the increasing adaptation of humanity
to social life, the excess of pleasures over pains
must become ever greater. Hence ideal men living
under ideal social conditions—with whom absolute
ethics is concerned—may be assumed to be beings
whose voluntary actions cause 'pleasure unalloyed
by pain anywhere' to all who are affected by them.
This 'qualified optimism' is the indispensable foundation of Mr. Spencer's system ; whatever the human
race may be suffering now, he is convinced that it is
on its way to being blest.

Still, the question at once arises when we are considering the problems of the present : What is to be
done if the two ends—Life and Happiness—do not
coincide, in any particular case, here and now ? and
whose Life (or Happiness) is to be taken as standard
by the individual, if circumstances arise in which a
choice has to be made between action conducive to
his own Life (or Happiness), and action conducive to
the Life (or Happiness) of others ? On the first point
Mr. Spencer's general answer was, as we saw, quite
clearly given in § 15, though in some other passages
he seems to take conduciveness to Life as standard,
even in problems that belong to Relative Ethics—
problems of conduct here and now—without recognising the need of proving that conduciveness to Life, in
the particular case, coincides with conduciveness to
Happiness. But in the passage referred to (§ 15, p.
45) he says, that 'if we call good the conduct conducive
to life, we can do so only with the implication that

it is conducive to a surplus of pleasures over pains,'
and this leaves no doubt that, *on the whole*, we must
understand him to take Happiness as ultimate
End, and Life (in two dimensions) as ultimate End
only on condition that action conducive to increase
of Life is always equally conducive to increase of
Happiness. And, as regards the question : Whose
Happiness? we must understand him to take the
General Happiness as ultimate standard, notwithstanding the argument in chapter xiii. against Bentham. This second point I admit to be arguable, as
much of Mr. Spencer's language implies a different
view ; but, after considering it at length, I have come
to this conclusion, and I hold that the apparent suggestion of a different view is due to a want of clear
distinction between 'ultimate' and 'proximate' End.

If we take the view that it is General Happiness
which is the Ultimate End, Mr. Spencer and ordinary
or empirical Utilitarians agree as to End. There
are then two points on which we may compare him
and them : (*a*) the 'establishment of the End,' and
(*b*) the ascertainment of means to the End. As regards (*a*), although Mr. Spencer's establishment of the
End in chapter iii. of *Data of Ethics* (*Good and
Bad Conduct*) is very unlike mine, I do not think it
is definitely distinguished from that of ordinary
Utilitarianism, and I may observe that it has the
defect—as ordinary Utilitarianism has—of keeping in
the background the difference between Own happiness and Others' happiness. Through this incomplete
distinction, Mr. Spencer's polemic in *The Data of*

Ethics is confused, and there is a gap in his ethical construction — the question : Why am I to seek the General Happiness ? is not definitely answered. Concentrating attention on (*b*)—the means to the End—the distinctive feature of Mr. Spencer's view, as expounded by him, is that, unlike Empirical Utilitarianism, which does not 'sufficiently recognise causation,' he aims at determining what actions must tend to happiness, and what must tend to the opposite. But when we have had fully explained the distinction between Absolute and Relative Ethics, which relate respectively to (*a*) conduct in an ideal society, and (*β*) conduct here and now, it is made clear that Mr. Spencer, as regards (*β*), does not really offer us any other general system than Empirical Utilitarianism. (This will, I think, be confirmed by examining Part V. on *Negative Beneficence*, and Part VI. on *Positive Beneficence*.) The question therefore, *prima facie*, reduces itself to a question as to the value of Absolute Ethics.

I complained that in *The Data of Ethics* Mr. Spencer does not really distinguish enough between the exposition of Absolute and Relative Ethics until the close of the treatise — that is, in some passages (especially in chapter viii. on the Sociological View) he seems to assume that the fundamental rules laid down will be applicable not only to the ideal society, but also at the present stage of social evolution, without explaining how they are known to be so applicable. And I have given reasons for regarding Absolute Ethics according to Mr. Spencer's conception as (1) not capable of being known to us here and now, and (2) of very dubious utility if known.[1] However that may be, what he aims at establishing inductively in Part II. (*The Inductions of Ethics*) is Absolute Ethics and an ideal society to which it primarily relates. The inductions are designed to prove that this ideal society to which Absolute Ethics belongs is the ultimate result to which the evolution of human society and morality is tending, through a series of stages in which Relative Ethics is required.

There are two main theses in this Part II., one negative and the other positive. Negatively, Mr. Spencer seeks to disprove what he, like J. S. Mill and others—by what I regard as a confusion of thought or language—calls indifferently ' the doctrine of the intuitive morality,' and the doctrine ' that men have in common an innate perception of right and wrong.'[2] The second, positive, thesis is that the leading cause that retards the development of morality is the influence of War, and the habits and sentiments which War normally brings with it, in confusing and perverting the ethical ideal. Mr. Spencer has both these theses, the negative and the positive, in view throughout, as the summary in chapter xiv. of Part II. shows, but the latter of the two—the influence of War—is, I think, that in which he is most interested in the greater part of chapters iii. to xi. of Part II. ; the other thesis is rather prominent in chapters xii. and xiii., where the chief aim of his historic instances seems to

[1] Cf. *supra*, Lecture V., and *Methods of Ethics*, Book IV. chap. iv.

[2] Compare my argument in Book III. chap. i. § 4 of *Methods of Ethics* to distinguish between the *Origin*, *Existence*, and *Validity* of moral judgments.

be to show what very queer customs have been, from various causes, supported by ethical or at least 'pro-ethical' sentiments.[1]

Before considering his two main theses, Mr. Spencer has to define more exactly the term 'ethical,' and accordingly in chapter ii. he deals with the question : What ideas and sentiments are ethical ?   He notes the existence of general notions and sentiments—such as those of honour and shame—attached to rules differing from the rules of morality, and yet similarly involving notions of ' duty ' and ' obligation.'   He thinks that these must be included under ethical science.   I quite admit the importance of noting the resemblance between the Code of Honour—or any other body of social rules—and the Moral Code.   But I think it no less important to dwell on the differences ; since no moral person regards the Code of Honour as equally binding with the Code of Moral Duty when the two conflict.   A Christian may fight a duel, from the pressure of the Code of Honour in his society ; but he will ordinarily know that he is fighting from fear of shame, and doing wrong in fighting.   I dwell on this distinction, because in all that Mr. Spencer says in subsequent chapters of the Ethics of Enmity, this distinction is of great historical importance ; since the

---

[1] As regards this distinction I would direct attention to §§ 123, 124 (pp. 335-339) in chapter ii. of Part II. which the student will do well to compare with §§ 44-46 in Part I. chapter vii.   (Part II. was written after an interval of at least a dozen years.)   Comparing the two, you will see that the general view is substantially the same, but the term 'pro-ethical' is new, to express the earlier, not properly moral, restraints ; and, in the later-written treatise, Mr. Spencer's view of the development of morality seems to be somewhat less favourable ; that is, he seems to find *less* of what is strictly moral—cf. pp. 338, 339.

separation of the Christian Church from the world carried with it a clear distinction between the code of what was recognised as the true Morality, the Law of God, and the social code of men of the world.

Granting, then, the general conclusion that an 'idea and feeling of obligation' attaches itself—not only in earlier stages of social development but in our own stage—to rules other than what we ordinarily call moral rules, the question arises : Are we to call these ideas and sentiments 'ethical'? This question Mr. Spencer answers—not very coherently—in § 124. In a wider sense, he is disposed to call any idea and sentiment of obligation 'ethical,' but in a narrower and more proper sense 'ethical' must be restricted to ideas and sentiments which refer to the 'intrinsic results of conduct,' and not to 'ideas and sentiments . . . derived from external authorities, and coercions, and approbations—religious, political, or social,' which should rather be called pro-ethical.   And this view is in harmony with the view given in chapter vii. of *The Data of Ethics*.   He goes on to say that in studying, in subsequent chapters, the details of his induction, we are concerned 'almost exclusively with what is pro-ethical.'   This, though it is no doubt to a great extent true, is, I think, exaggerated.   What Mr. Spencer calls —rather confusingly—the 'ethics of enmity' is no doubt largely, though not entirely, pro-ethical rather than ethical.   And I conceive that, in primitive society, the distinction that is now clear to us between true morality and rules sanctioned by law, or social opinion and sentiment, or false religion, is not applicable ; the

recognised code is the code of custom supported by
social and religious sanctions alike—so far as Religion
is ethical or pro-ethical in its effects—custom harden-
ing into law.

But consideration of the relation of Morality to
Law leads me to a point of serious ethical disagreement between Mr. Spencer and myself. In § 121
(p. 333) he says :

> though a distinction is commonly made between legal
> obligation and moral obligation, in those cases where the law is
> of a kind in respect of which ethics gives no direct verdict ; yet
> the obligation to obey has come to be, if not nominally yet
> practically a moral obligation. The words habitually used
> imply this. It is held 'right' to obey the law, and 'wrong' to
> disobey it. Conformity and non-conformity bring approbation
> and reprobation, just as though the legal injunction were a
> moral injunction. A man who has broken the law, even though
> it be in a matter of no ethical significance,—say a householder
> who has refused to fill up the census-paper, or a pedlar who has
> not taken out a license,—feels, when he is brought before the
> magistrates, that he is regarded not only by them but by
> spectators as morally blameworthy. The feeling shown is quite
> as strong as it would be were he convicted of aggressing on his
> neighbours by nuisances—perpetual noises or pestilent odours—
> which are moral offences properly so-called. That is to say, law
> is upheld by a sentiment indistinguishable from moral sentiment.
> Moreover, in some cases where the two conflict, the sentiment
> which upholds the legal *dictum* overrides the sentiment which
> upholds the moral *dictum* ; as in the case of the pedlar above
> named. His act in selling without a license is morally justi-
> fiable, and forbidding him to sell without a license is morally
> unjustifiable—is an interference with his due liberty, which is
> ethically unwarranted. Yet the factitious moral sentiment
> enlisted on behalf of legal authority, triumphs over the natural
> moral sentiment enlisted on behalf of rightful freedom.

All this seems to me theoretically unintelligent and
practically mischievous. I regard it as theoretically
unintelligent, because it overlooks the distinction
drawn in ordinary consciousness between (1) the

ethico-political judgment on actual law as good or bad, and (2) the ethical judgment on the duty of Order or Law-observance. Modern Common Sense clearly recognises the distinction, holding that it is generally the duty of a private person as such to obey a law judged to be bad; but not always, since 'We should obey God rather than man.' And this view is, I think, clearly sustained by utilitarian considerations: we cannot dispense with the habit of Law-observance, on account of its value for what Mr. Spencer calls the 'cohesion of a group;' therefore any language which ignores the general duty of obeying even bad laws— when laid down by the constitutional authority for making laws—is dangerously revolutionary. To take Mr. Spencer's instance : does he really think that it would conduce to social wellbeing if when *any* set of persons disapprove of a particular law—such as that compelling pedlars to take out a license—they should approve of a breach of the Law? He must not conceive this effect limited to Individualists of his own type : he must consider it applied equally to all conflicting schools and sects. It is surely evident that on such a supposition the difficulty of maintaining order would be increased tenfold. In the summary of the chapter on *Obedience* he repeats these views, and says :—

Decline of political obedience and waning belief in the duty of it, go along with increasing subordination to ethical principles, a clearer recognition of the supremacy of these, and a determination to abide by them rather than by legislative dictates. More and more the pro-ethical sentiments prompting obedience to government come into conflict with the ethical sentiment prompting obedience to conscience. More and more this last

causes nonconformity to laws which are at variance with equity.
And more and more it comes to be felt that legal coercion is
warranted only in so far as law is an enforcer of justice
(§ 166).

Here, again, a distinction is required.   (1) If Mr.
Spencer means that it is a characteristic of political
progress—for which we may reasonably hope increase
and development in the future—that the governed
habitually *judge* the laws they obey, and express
their opinion freely on them, and when they judge
them unjust, combine and agitate for their removal
by constitutional means—I entirely agree.   But (2)
if he means that the habit of disobeying laws which
we regard as unjust and resisting government when
it tries to enforce them, has been growing and may
be expected to grow, 'if from past changes we are to
infer future changes'—then I am bound to say that
his view of history seems to me as superficial as his
political forecast appears gloomy.   In my view, the
most essential characteristic of the modern as distinct
from the medieval state in European history is the
prevalence of order, involving a general habit of
obedience to Law and Government even when disapproved of.   If every one is going to disobey and
resist any interference of government which is not
founded on sound principles, we shall rapidly retro-
grade to medieval conditions; and our hopes of even
reducing and mitigating the baleful effects of militancy
are indeed small.   (Indeed, when we come in Part IV.
to ascertain more fully Mr. Spencer's view of Justice,
we shall probably feel some surprise that Mr. Spencer
pays his rates and taxes as meekly as I believe he

does pay them.) This, however, is a digression, from which I return to the main argument of the chapter.

I shall pass briefly over the thesis which I have distinguished as 'negative'; partly because it is less original, partly because it does not seem to me that Mr. Spencer has a clear idea of what he has to prove in order to refute his opponents. His instances of variation in moral ideas and sentiments are mostly entertaining and sometimes impressive. And so far as his aim is to disprove what I may call the 'finality' of any appeal to Common Sense—that is, to the current ideas and sentiments of one's own age and country—I of course agree with him. But he shows no sign of knowing the views held by the only advocates of an 'originally implanted conscience' who deserve serious consideration. Take for instance Dugald Stewart, who asserts[1] that 'in order to form a competent judgment on facts of this nature, it is necessary to attend to a variety of considerations which have been too frequently overlooked by philosophers; and in particular to make proper allowance for the three following:—I. For the different situations in which mankind are placed, partly by the diversity in their physical circumstances, and partly by the unequal degrees of civilisation which they have attained; II. For the diversity of their speculative opinions, arising from their unequal measures of knowledge or of capacity; and III. For the different moral import of the same action under

[1] *Collected Works of Dugald Stewart*, edited by Sir W. Hamilton, vol. vi. p. 237 (MDCCCLIX).

different systems of external behaviour.' He thus
allows for difference of circumstances, difference of
the meaning of different acts, and difference in knowledge of consequences of acts.   What Mr. Spencer has
to show is that this kind of 'allowance' is inadequate
to explain the facts ; and this he does not try to show.
For instance, the point he brings out about gluttony
in the chapter on Temperance (that what we should
call gluttony is rightly supported by a pro-ethical
sentiment when the supply of food is precarious,—
sometimes scanty, sometimes abundant,—or the need
of food—*e.g.* in very cold climates—is great) obviously
falls under Stewart's first head.   I do not myself
regard Stewart's explanation as adequate : I think it
goes some way, but that there are elements which it
overlooks.   Of these the most important is the limitation of sympathy—which indeed is an important
part of the explanation of the manner in which the
'ethics of enmity' have managed to flourish side by
side with the 'ethics of amity' to the extent to which
they have flourished.   This is strikingly illustrated
by one of Mr. Spencer's examples—the fact that Sir
John Hawkins, who initiated the slave - trade in
Elizabeth's reign, was allowed to put in his coat of
arms 'a demi-moor proper bound with a cord'!

Still Stewart's explanations do go some way ; and
the interesting point to discuss is (1) how far they go,
and (2) what becomes of the doctrine of intuitive
(or 'innate') moral faculty, if they are admitted.
As we shall see, when we pass to Part IV., Mr.
Spencer's real attitude towards the Intuitional theory

of Ethics is less hostile than would appear from Part
II. taken alone ; so I defer further consideration of it
till we come to the passage in Part IV., where it is
more fully, expounded.   In all that he says of it here,
in Part II., he seems to me to commit the blunder of
attacking an indefensible form of the view to which
he is opposed.

I pass now to the ' positive' thesis, which relates to
the effect of war.   I note that Mr. Spencer combines
both theses in an important passage in the concluding
chapter of *The Inductions of Ethics*.   He says :—

While we are shown that the moral-sense doctrine in its
original form is not true, we are also shown that it adumbrates
a truth, and a much higher truth.   For the facts cited, chapter
after chapter, unite in proving that the sentiments and ideas current
in each society become adjusted to the kinds of activity predomi-
nating in it.   A life of constant external enmity generates a code in
which aggression, conquest, revenge, are inculcated, while peaceful
occupations are reprobated.   Conversely a life of settled internal
unity generates a code inculcating the virtues conducing to
harmonious co-operation—justice, honesty, veracity, regard for
others' claims.   And the implication is that if the life of internal
amity continues unbroken from generation to generation, there
must result not only the appropriate code, but the appropriate
emotional nature—a moral sense adapted to the moral requirements.   Men so conditioned will acquire to the degree needful
for complete guidance, that innate conscience which the intuitive
moralists erroneously suppose to be possessed by mankind at
large.   There needs but a continuance of absolute peace externally, and a rigorous insistence on non-aggression internally,
to ensure the moulding of men into a form naturally characterised
by all the virtues (§ 191, end of chapter xiv. of Part II.).

Now on this important passage I have two
remarks to make : (1) that Mr. Spencer's irrepressible
and unwarrantable optimism comes out in the concluding sentence.   This confounds what are, alas !
two very different things : the prevalent moral *code*,

sustained by opinion and sentiment in a society, and the ordinary moral *conduct* of members of the society. Grant—what I shall presently show reason to doubt—that any and all defects of our present moral ideas and sentiments are due to war, still history shows that there has always been a large hiatus between the accepted moral code and the ordinary moral conduct; and Mr. Spencer gives no reason for the optimistic conclusion that this gap will not continue when war has ceased. I remark (2) that a certain ambiguity lurks in the word 'adjusted,' which it is important to bring out. When we are told that men's sentiments and ideas are 'adjusted' to a life of constant war, there are two distinct effects which seem to be intended. It may be meant as Mr. Spencer argues in chapters iii. and iv., on Aggression and Robbery, that the habits of action appropriate to the conditions of war tend to spread further—that continual war produces toleration and even approval of aggression, conquest, revenge, within as well as without the society, that 'in proportion as inter-tribal and international antagonisms are great and constant . . . the ideas and feelings belonging to the ethics of enmity . . . fill with aggressions the conduct of man to man'; that 'societies in which warfare is habitual are characterised by private homicide'; that, again, the habit of plundering enemies and strangers tends—in some tribes at least—to cause robbery within the tribe to be regarded as 'not only legitimate but praiseworthy'; that, similarly, in more modern times long wars, as the

Hundred Years' War between England and France and the Thirty Years' War in Germany, led to general brigandage, plundering of unarmed peasants by soldiers who were their fellow-countrymen, cheating of soldiers by officers, embezzlement of public money by superior officers; that the cheating by kings of their creditors, and the passing of bad money boasted of by shopkeepers, were similarly due to militancy, and that the decrease of dishonesty in our own day is due to the 'progress towards a state in which war is less frequent'; and that, again, revengefulness within a society is proportionate to the habitual conflict with other societies.

I shall try to show that in this induction a one-sided selection of facts has been made. But what I wish now to point out is, that however completely these facts may prove that morality between man and man is *affected* by war between society and society, they have no tendency to prove that morality between man and man is thereby 'adapted' to the needs of a society in this condition of external enmity. This is what we, and Spencer, ordinarily mean by the 'adjustment' or 'adaptation' of an organism to its conditions : namely, that changes are produced in it, rendering it more capable of living and thriving under these conditions. But this is manifestly not the effect in the instances here given. A society does not become better fitted for the struggle for existence with other societies—even for the violent struggle of war—by the prevalence of homicide, robbery, and thieving within it; indeed,

Mr. Spencer's historic instances strikingly show that it becomes worse fitted. There is no time in French history in which the nation as a whole was weaker for conflict with other nations than during the Hundred Years' War, and all German historians look back to the Thirty Years' War as the dark period of national disaster, and depression of national existence, from which it took Germany a century to recover. Even associations for lawless plunder have learnt, as the proverb indicates, that 'honour among thieves' is for the advantage of the associated thieves.

The influence, in short, of war on morality, which Mr. Spencer is mainly occupied in describing in these chapters, is, as he describes it, a force operating *against the adaptation* of the morality of the social organism to the needs of existence, although the universality of this adaptation is the general conclusion that he wishes us to draw from the facts. There can be no doubt that the increase in the cohesion of the tribe or nation, obtained by putting down internal mutual strife, tends to make the tribe or nation stronger for external warfare. It is not by accident that the Romans are known to history as a people with a genius for conquest and at the same time a genius for law. And this consideration must lead us to qualify the conclusion to which the arguments in chapters iii.-v. (*Aggression, Robbery*, and *Revenge*) appear to lead. For it cannot, I think, be doubted that external war tends to develop the superior cohesion which strengthens a society for such war,—partly through the intellectual perception of the dangers of internal strife in face of a common foe, partly because the common peril tends to intensify the sentiment of corporate unity in the nation imperilled.

Mr. Spencer seems in one passage to have a glimpse of this effect of militancy. He says (§ 114, p. 314), 'Dissension being recognised by chiefs as a source of tribal weakness, acts leading to it are reprobated by them'—'weakness' here meaning, of course, weakness in the external struggle with other nations. But there is no reason to suppose that the perception of the weakening effect of internal strife was confined to the chiefs. It is a commonplace to remark that the greater intensity of patriotism in the Graeco-Roman world as compared with the modern world was connected with the greater demands made on patriotism by the continual wars and dangers of war. As Freeman says,[1] 'Every citizen' in an old Greek commonwealth 'might fairly look forward, some time in his life, to witness the pillage of his crops and the burning of his house, even if he and his escaped the harder doom of massacre, outrage, and slavery'; and it is because this was so that these little communities could cherish a warmth of patriotism, an intensity of devotion to country, beyond example in the records of modern States—at any rate except at times when those States are in similar crises of peril. And this leads me to remark that the proposition (§ 137, p. 368) that 'revengefulness within each society is proportioned to habitual conflict with other

---

[1] *Historical Essays*, 2nd series, p. 15 (2nd edition, 1880).

societies' has, so far as I know, no historical basis.
Blood feuds die out in the ancient Graeco-Roman world
as civilisation and 'integration' go on, however warlike the tribe as a whole remains. Modern instances
confirm this. We have heard striking stories in
modern times of sanguinary feuds and revenges
between families in the wilder parts of the United
States of America, and we have never heard of such
things in Prussia. Yet no modern country has been
more free from the influence of foreign war than the
United States of America, and no modern country—
since Frederick William manufactured his army—
more prominent in European conflicts than Prussia.
The reason is, of course, the comparative weakness
of government in the wilder parts of America as
compared with Prussia. Even when we look at Mr.
Spencer's earlier instances, we see that the private
aggression and robbery connected with militancy are
largely due not to the mere reaction of the state of
war on the sentiments and habits of a warring nation,
but to the disorder and partial inhibition of ordinary
governmental functions produced by invasion—as in
Germany in the Thirty Years' War.

And this comparison may be extended. Nothing
that I know of modern nations supports the generalisation that the moral ideal—in respect of justice, honesty,
veracity, etc., as between man and man—is materially
higher in countries where 'militancy' has least predominance, as compared with those where it has
greatest—for instance in the United States of
America as compared with Germany. There are

certain well-known vices to which the eager pursuit of wealth, carried on under conditions of keen industrial competition, offers special temptations, and I know no evidence that the citizens of the United States show greater strength in resisting these temptations than members of the less fortunate European States who believe it necessary for their security to maintain, even in time of peace, large armies raised by compulsory service. It may be replied that we have not anywhere seen freedom from war tried completely and for a long enough time. This is undoubtedly true—to use Mill's logical distinction, it is a case in which we cannot apply the Method of Difference, but only the Method of Concomitant Variations. All I urge is that the Method of Concomitant Variations—as applied to European States and their colonies—does not support Mr. Spencer's thesis.

Finally, let us reflect impartially on the morality of our own age and country. I am far from saying that English morality as regards external aggression is not open to criticism. But I recognise—what Mr. Spencer does not recognise—that the justification or excuse for lawless aggression that I deplore is not without a moral element: it is not aggression pure and simple, but violence in defence of what are conceived to be legitimate claims, which meets with this regrettable sympathy. And this is true in some measure of the approval of war, and the warlike spirit, throughout modern history. When it takes hold of a modern nation, a more impartial analysis than Mr. Spencer's will, I think, almost always dis-

cern in it an element of the spirit of Justice. It is
not fighting simply, but fighting for rights that is
approved and admired.

This leads me to a distinction that Mr. Spencer
rather overlooks in his general view of the conflict
of the Ethics of Enmity and Amity, the distinction to
be taken between (1) the conception of war as right
and good and the qualities leading to success in war
as the highest virtues, when duty to the State is
paramount, and duty to humanity not recognised;
and (2) the conception of war—even offensive war
under certain conditions — as right in our actual
society. The latter is a difficult ethico-political question, which Mr. Spencer's tirades against militancy
(*e.g.* in § 122) do not help us to solve. In the main,
however, he discusses the rules from a point of view
which is sociological, and not strictly ethical, in my
sense—*i.e.* not in relation to practical problems; he
considers what the effect of war or the absence of
war on ethical ideas and sentiments has been in the
past, and may be expected to be in the future : not
what is the right condition of thought and feeling in
respect of war, for States and men here and now.
This, the purely sociological, point of view is the one
that Mr. Spencer professedly takes throughout; and
doubtless, taking his distinction between Absolute
and Relative Ethics and their respective methods, he
might say that it is not his primary business to work
out the rough empirical compromise between the
Ethics of Enmity and the Ethics of Amity, which
is all that we can hope to attain at the present stage

of our development. But if that be his position, I
think he ought to have maintained a greater impartiality of tone than he actually does maintain. We
seem, for instance in chapters i. and iii. of Part II., to
have sociological analysis mixed with the one-sided
rhetoric of a professional advocate of the Peace
Society : cheap sneers at bishops for their warlike
sentiments. Now this is all very well in its way—
for no doubt there is plenty of barbaric feeling
surviving in the so-called civilised world—but it is
not what we expect from a philosopher. Theoretically
it is one-sided, and practically it gives no guidance.
Civilised nations, so long as they are independent,
have to fight ; and, in performance of their legitimate
business—for it is their legitimate business on utilitarian principles—of civilising the world, they have
to commit acts which cannot but be regarded as
aggressive by the savage nations whom it is their
business to educate and absorb. From both points
of view the problems presented by International
Morality are very difficult. But Mr. Spencer gives us
no aid in the difficulty. And the one-sidedness affects
his Sociology as well as his Ethics. For he ignores
—except in an inadequate notice of it in chapter vi.
of Part II.—the whole attempt of the moral consciousness of civilised man to *moralise* war and its effects ;
to limit the approval of war to cases in which,
assuming a society of individuals under no common
government, we should approve it in the case of the
individual. Such efforts have had no doubt but a
partial success, nor do I think they can ever have

VI   INDUCTIONS OF ETHICS   237

more.   War is and must remain a barbaric method of
settling disputes as to right.   But something has been
and may be attained by efforts at moralisation; and
the moralist ought to give such help as general
reasoning can give to these efforts; and sweeping
diatribes of this kind will not help.

Summing up briefly, we see that in *The Inductions of Ethics* Mr. Spencer is mainly concerned with
proving two general conclusions : (1) That men have
in common no 'innate' or 'intuitive' sense of right
and wrong; which he conceives to be shown by the
fact that ' the ethical sentiments prevailing in different
societies, and in the same society under different conditions, are sometimes diametrically opposed,' and (2)
that the influence of war, and the habits and sentiments which war normally brings with it, have continually confused and perverted the ethical ideal of
mankind through the strange mingling of the ethics
of enmity with the ethics of amity.

Of these two theses (which in Mr. Spencer's
view are connected with each other) the second is
certainly the most original and interesting.   The
negative thesis is merely, with a change of form,
the old proposition long ago argued against the
Intuitional moralists by their opponents :—that in
different ages and countries sentiments of approval
and disapproval attach themselves to very different
kinds of conduct.   Mr. Spencer's knowledge of
primitive man enables him to bring fresh and
striking evidence of this proposition.   But, speaking
broadly, no educated person now disputes it : there

is much more freshness and interest in the other
main generalisation.   If we ask why the actual results
of human actions under present social conditions
diverge so widely from the ideal, Mr. Spencer's main
answer is in a word, War.   Current thoughts and feelings about human action, in so-called civilised societies,
are in his view a confused and incoherent compromise
between two irreconcilable elements—the sentiments
and ideas that belong to 'militancy,' and the sentiments and ideas that belong to peaceful, industrial
co-operation.   'Militancy' generates a 'religion of
enmity,' a code in which aggression, conquest,
robbery, revenge, and skilful lying are inculcated and
approved, and thus its moral effect conflicts with and
neutralises the respect for justice, honesty, veracity,
good faith, etc., which a life of peaceful industrial co-
operation—if it could only be relieved from militancy
—would render general and predominant.   Only put
an end to militancy, let industrialism reign unchecked,
and the ideal code will soon become approximately
applicable and accepted.

Readers of Plato and Aristotle will be amused
with this inversion of their ethico-political doctrine.
According to these ancient thinkers, the only class in
the community—except philosophers—that it was
worth while to spend pains in training to virtue was
the class of fighters : a mechanical or commercial life
being—as Aristotle puts it—essentially ignoble and
opposed to virtue.   Now the tables are turned ; and
we are asked to believe that if the producers and
traders could only get rid of the fighters, and purge

themselves of sentiments inherited from fighting ages, they and their purely industrial society would soon be moulded into a form naturally characterised by all the virtues.

This second thesis—which attributes the defects of popular morality to the demoralisation produced by militancy — contains some truth exaggerated into violent paradox. Those defects are attributed to a complex variety of causes ; but most of them fall under two heads—deficiency of average insight into the consequences of actions, and deficiency of sympathy, which renders average men indifferent to the bad effects of actions on others than a special group of human beings.

LECTURE VII

THE ETHICS OF INDIVIDUAL LIFE (PART III. OF THE PRINCIPLES OF ETHICS)

In Part III. we pass from a study of Evolutionary Morality to consider Morality as it ought to be. Part II. is supposed to have shown that 'ethical sentiments and ideas are in each place and time determined by the local form of human nature, the social antecedents and the surrounding circumstances.' How then, Mr. Spencer asks in Part III., shall we 'free ourselves from the influence,' so far as misleading, 'of the particular code we have been brought up under'? We must, he thinks, 'ignore established doctrines' and 'go direct to the facts and study them afresh.' He even wishes to ignore the established meanings of fundamental words—'*Duty* and *obligation*, for example, carry with them the thought of obedience, subordination, subjection to authority; and thus imply that right and wrong conduct are not such by their intrinsic natures, but are such by their extrinsic enactments' (§ 193, p. 477).

But he is not consistent about 'authority.' For he goes on to say, 'Let no one anticipate any loss of authority' in moral precepts from the fresh study of

the facts which evolutionary ethics prescribes. The
explanation is that his own recognition of the
'authority' of reason is fitful and incomplete; and
in criticising others he does not see that it is the
authority of reason that is implied in Common-Sense
morality. Common Sense and the overwhelming
majority of moralists — with only the partial and
qualified exception of Hobbes and Hobbism—agree
in holding that 'right and wrong are such by their
intrinsic natures' apprehended by reason, and not
'by extrinsic enactments.'

In Part III. Mr. Spencer confines himself to *The
Ethics of Individual Life*. He begins as usual with
an attack on moralists and Common Sense for ignoring
in ethical judgments, 'nine-tenths of the conduct by
which life is carried on'—that is, acts conducive to
the life, health and vigour, and pleasure of the agent,
especially the mass of men who are 'unable to conceive that there can be an ethical justification for the
pursuit of positive gratification.' This error, this
'one-sided treatment of conduct,' is said to be mischievous, because (1) 'it alienates multitudes who
would otherwise accept' the teachings of ethics. (2)
'Assuming general happiness to be the end,' the
individual's pleasure is a part of the end, and—as he
is best able to attain it—ought to be a prominent end
for him. (3) Pleasures being 'organically bound up
with the performance of functions needful for bodily
welfare,' neglect of pleasure for oneself 'involves a
lower degree of life, a decreased strength, and a
diminished ability to fulfil all duties.' (4) By main-

R

taining his own health and furthering his bodily and
mental development, a man tends to benefit not only
those around him, but also his descendants, through
heredity.

On this general argument there are four remarks
to make. (1) It is undoubtedly true that common-
sense morality and leading moralists (*a*) do not
inculcate the promotion of the agent's health and
vigour, in proportion to its importance from the
utilitarian point of view; (*b*) do not stamp with
approval—indeed sometimes even discourage—the
pursuit of pleasure for self. Mr. Spencer too much
mixes up these two. We may observe that Kant
makes self-development a duty, though not pursuit
of one's own happiness. (2) The arguments which
Mr. Spencer urges on the other side seem to me
undoubtedly sound in theory; and he may be right
in thinking it practically important to emphasise
them. (3) But his attack is exaggerated. To say
that nearly all the actions of each individual which
directly concern himself only 'are usually supposed
to lie beyond ethical rule,' is a palpable over-
statement. 'Duty to self,' indeed, is traditionally a
chief head in the division of duties. (4) He does
not deal with the practical argument for the one-
sidedness of moralists which I referred to in Lecture
III.—the argument, namely, that it is practically important to lay stress on the duties that men are most
inclined to neglect, and that the pursuit of private
pleasure is not, 'on the average,' among these.

Mr. Spencer seems to me, in his polemic against

current morality and ordinary moralists, to forget that as morality and moralists are evolved like everything else, there is therefore a presumption that they are adapted to their social environment ; and that therefore men's habits and customs of praise and blame, as directed to the conduct of their fellow-creatures, are probably more or less defensible, even when one-sided, as being broadly and generally directed on those qualities of conduct on which—in the present stage of social development—it is most important for social wellbeing to concentrate praise and blame respectively.

A man may (he says) bring on himself chronic rheumatism by daily careless exposure, or an incurable nervous disorder by over-application ; and though he may thus vitiate his life and diminish his usefulness in a far greater degree than by occasionally taking too much wine, yet his physical transgression meets with only mild disapproval, if even that.   But in these cases the transgression is displeasurable, whereas excess in wine is pleasurable ; and the damnable thing in the misconduct is the production of pleasure by it (§ 214).

Obviously, the explanation is not that the moralist regards pleasure as 'damnable' *per se*, but as dangerously seductive.   It may be replied that the moralist ought to rise above this one-sidedness, and consider the effects of conduct on human happiness with scientific impartiality.   I quite agree :   but current morality, with all its limitations, is a fundamentally important part of the complex adjustment of a human society to its environment ; and the moralist ought to study this adjustment, not assuming that it cannot be improved—for the moralist and his criticism are also a part of the adjustment—but in order that his criticism may be thoroughly instructed and circumspect.

I pass on to consider the detail of Mr. Spencer's discussion. Any one reading the introductory remarks of Part III. on the neglect by moralists and Common Sense of the 'ethics of the individual life' may naturally expect to find an unusual novelty and freshness in the practical precepts and counsels which the philosopher proceeds to give, under the heads of 'activity, rest, nutrition, stimulation, culture, and amusement.' If so, he will be rather surprised to find how commonplace, for the most part, these are : though Mr. Spencer makes play with elementary physiology and does not fairly represent current opinion. For instance, we are told in the chapter on Rest that the erroneous belief that for persons of the same sex and age the same amount of sleep is required is current. Well, I never remember meeting an educated person who held this absurd opinion : the statement that 'some people require more sleep than others' is surely as commonplace as the recognition that some people take too much and others too little. The truth is, that most of what Mr. Spencer has to say is familiar to us all, though I admit that it is not ordinarily dwelt on in much detail in systematic treatises on ethics; it floats through literature and conversation in the form of prudential maxims.

He tells us that labour, up to a certain point, is on the whole agreeable and conducive to the individual's happiness—though most human beings, in

the present stage of social development, have to
labour more than they like : that it is wrong to overwork.   That it is important to take enough sleep,
but that there is a ' very general tendency to sleep in
excess'—probably owing to our ' transitional state' :
that, further, Sunday rests and annual holidays are
good for body and mind.   That no doubt civilised
men have a tendency to eat too much—a survival
from the savage period when opportunities for eating
were rather irregular.   But he thinks that this is
rather from desire of the pleasure of eating, or because
the convivial meal is less dull than other hours ; and
not because the guidance of appetite proper is misleading—provided the bodily functions have not been
perverted by ' persistent indoor life or by overwork,
or by ceaseless mental worry or by inadequate clothing or bad air.'   That it is a serious mistake to eat
too little ; that a certain amount of variety in food is
useful as facilitating digestion.   That if we lived a
perfectly normal life we should not want alcohol, tea,
coffee, tobacco, or other stimulants ; but that ' under
existing conditions,' liable as human beings are to
overwork, monotony, and privations, such stimulants
are defensible as preventing waste of tissue and aiding
reparative processes ; also occasionally at convivial
entertainments.   That the ' satisfactions which accompany the superfluous expenditure of energy implied
by amusements' tend to raise the tide of life : but
that most people read too many novels.

Surely most of this is what we have been hearing
all our lives, though no doubt mostly it is not from

the moralist that we have heard it. And we have long since learned that, when and so far as we try to make any of these counsels practical in our own individual cases, we do so by reference to our personal experience aided by the experience of others — especially of a physician. Nor does Mr. Spencer suggest any other course so far as regards Relative Ethics—which is concerned with right conduct under actual conditions. The question then is, what is the value here of the deductive method, on which he has laid so much stress? What are the results attained by it in dealing with the 'Ethics of the individual life,' and are they strictly attained by scientific deduction? 'From the point of view of absolute ethics'—as we may remember—'actions are only right when they produce pleasure unalloyed by pain anywhere': therefore labour is only right when it is 'immediately pleasurable' as well as 'conducive to future happiness.' Accordingly, Mr. Spencer has no doubt that in the ideal state of society every man will like the work he has to do; no one (he implies rather than asserts) will have any tendency to eat or drink or sleep too much—these tendencies at present come from the imperfect adaptation of our present transitional state. More explicitly, 'from the point of view of absolute ethics' stimulants of every kind, tea and coffee as well as alcohol—or 'at any rate the daily use of them'—must be 'reprobated.' Here, for the first time, I find a definite deduction (§ 215). 'A stimulant, alcoholic or other, is neither tissue-food, nor heat-food, nor force-food. It simply affects the

rate of molecular change.'   Now 'in a being fully fitted
for the life it has to lead, the functions are already
adjusted to the requirements'; therefore, 'it does not
seem that any advantage can be obtained by changing the established balance.'   I am not concerned to
disprove the conclusion, but there seems to me a
begging of the question in the premises.   'In a being,'
says Mr. Spencer, 'fully fitted for the life it has to
lead, the functions are already adjusted to the requirements.'   But why should not a part of the
adjustment be such a modification of vital changes
as stimulants bring about?   Of course if we assume
that it is perfectly adjusted without stimulants, it
will follow at once that stimulants are superfluous :
but what right have we to make this assumption
with regard to a being of whom we know so little as
Utopian man?   With this single exception, the conclusions of Absolute Ethics that I have mentioned,
are obvious immediate inferences from Mr. Spencer's
assumptions with regard to the ideal condition ; and
all of them, I think, entirely fail to furnish practical
guidance.

But the arbitrariness of this deductive method
seems to me most strikingly shown by another characteristic of the Utopia—namely, that a considerable
space in the individual's life will be filled by amusements.   Why this is so, I cannot gather : I should
have thought it more in accordance with Mr. Spencer's
general line of deduction to assume that a being with
his functions perfectly adjusted to his requirements
and his environment would enjoy his regular work so

much that he would not want any amusements. If
Mr. Spencer had argued in his *a priori* way that
'amusements' were all very well in our present
transitional state, but that—like tea, alcohol, tobacco,
and a sense of moral obligation—they would have no
place in that perfect adjustment through which every
activity of a human being was attended by pleasure
totally unalloyed with pain—would not this *a priori*
argument be as sound and as plausible as any of the
others ?

The topic of amusements, however, furnishes me
with an occasion for passing back from Utopia to the
inferior world in which we live. I have said that in
dealing with matters that belong to Relative Ethics—
that is, in giving practical advice to his contemporaries
—Mr. Spencer's treatment is often rather surprisingly
commonplace, considering the need for a fresh study
of the facts on which he lays stress. This is the case
with most of what he says on activity, rest, nutrition,
stimulation. But I did not mean that he was always
disposed to come round to agreement with Common
Sense, and especially in the chapter on *Amusements*
there are novelties deserving of attention. However,
where he is original, I am obliged to say that he
satisfies me as little—in respect of methodical (and so
far as possible) scientific treatment of the questions—
as he does where he is commonplace. Partly, he seems
to me to commit the elementary mistake of being too
much guided by his own likes and dislikes, and laying
down rules for mankind accordingly, without a sufficient knowledge of the facts or a sufficiently com-

prehensive view of the varieties of human habits and
sentiments.   For instance, he condemns field sports,
football and boat races, and has doubts about chess,
owing to the extreme pain that it gives a man to
be beaten by somebody else.   In these points my
personal sympathies are largely with Mr. Spencer,
but I think there is a want of comprehensiveness
and considerateness of view.   In the case of field
sports, I understand the deduction that the sports-
man must be inadequately sympathetic with human
beings.   But is it true that football—Rugby football
—is 'more brutalising than sport'?   Personally, I
have always hated football, because the frequent
incident of being kicked on the shins, or finding
myself in the midst of a ball of struggling human
beings, is disagreeable to me.   But if others get keen
pleasure on the whole, I do not see why the moralist
should interfere, especially a moralist who is not
going to be stern (§ 196).

Observe, the important question is as to method.
We noted how Mr. Spencer announced in Part I. that
Ethics, as he designed to treat it, was to be deductive
and thus superior to the merely empirical reasoning
of ordinary Utilitarianism—was to show what conduct
must be beneficial or mischievous.   But we noted, too,
how at the close of Part I. it was explained that it
was to Absolute Ethics—concerned with rules of right
conduct in an ideal society — that this deductive
character belonged : the Relative Ethics, which gives
precepts and counsels to men here and now, must—it
was admitted—be largely empirical.   Hence, when in

Part III. Mr. Spencer gives practical advice in detail, I admit that he quite consistently uses empirical reasoning. My point is, that, perhaps from his contempt for this inferior method, he seems to me to use it rather hastily and rashly, generalising from very limited experience. He says, for instance, in speaking of games of skill :—

> It should be added that such drawbacks as there are, from the emotions accompanying victory and defeat, are but small in games which involve chance as a considerable factor, but are very noticeable where there is no chance. Chess, for example, which pits together two intelligences in such a way as to show unmistakably the superiority of one to the other in respect of certain powers, produces, much more than whist, a feeling of humiliation in the defeated ; and if the sympathies are keen this gives some annoyance to the victor as well as to the vanquished (§ 227).

No doubt it is never so pleasant to lose a game as to win it. But surely the importance attached to the pain of defeat here implies a morbid sensitiveness in the player : surely it is an elementary stage in the moral training which most men go through to become comparatively indifferent to this pain compared with the pleasures of conflict and the exercise of skill. A more important case of the same defect is found in what Mr. Spencer says of gambling in the same section :—

> Of course, such ethical sanction as is given to games cannot be given where gambling or betting is an accompaniment. Involving, as both do, in a very definite way, and often to an extreme degree, the obtainment of pleasure at the cost of another's pain, they are to be condemned both for this immediate effect and for their remote effect—the repression of fellow-feeling

Surely this is too sweeping, and only applies to gambling for high stakes. Where the loss is small in

proportion to the loser's income, common experience
shows that the pleasure of excitement outweighs the
pain of loss.   The really important objection to gambling lies in the dangerously seductive character of
this peculiar pleasure of nervous excitement, re-
sembling in its effect the use of alcohol and other
stimulants in excess.

I have left to the last a critical observation referring to the relation between Part III. and what
follows, namely, that—as Mr. Spencer's own arguments
continually bring home to us—though the *life* is
individual, the *ethics* are inevitably only partially so.
This is true even as regards the earlier chapters of
Part III., in which we are considering action and rest
as conducive to health and efficiency.   We must and
do consider a man's efficiency for his social function :
consider that the mere voluptuary leads a comparatively
useless life, and that it is a man's duty to maintain
his health and efficiency with a view to rendering
services to others.   And this comes out still more
clearly when we pass to the topic of Culture.   The
duty of self-culture, as analysed by Mr. Spencer,
includes as a main part the duty of ' acquiring fitness
for carrying on the business of Life ' : this, he says,
' is primarily a duty to self, and secondarily a duty
to others.'   But the business of life is for man a social
business ; and for one who accepts—as Mr. Spencer
on the whole does—*general* happiness, it is surely unwarrantable to treat the ' duty to others ' as secondary
in dealing with this topic.   And even in dealing with
his second part of the duty of culture—the develop-

ment of the fitness for 'utilising those various sources
of pleasure which Nature and Humanity supply to
responsive minds'—the importance of contributing
through self-culture, along with the natural play of
sympathy and sociality, to the higher pleasures of
other men, cannot properly be neglected.

When, finally, we come, in chapters viii. and ix.,
to the topics of Marriage and Parenthood, even Mr.
Spencer has practically to recognise that the egoistic
view must take a subordinate place.   Doubtless
marriage and parenthood are fundamentally important from an individual's point of view, as sources of
joy and happiness normally when rightly dealt with;
and of the deepest misery and sorrow through mistakes in dealing with them.   But even Mr. Spencer
feels that this whole topic has to be primarily treated
from a social aspect, in view of the social need of
maintaining, and within due limits increasing, the
numbers of the human race; with due regard to
the health and efficiency of the population thus
maintained and increased; and he puts this consideration in the forefront.

LECTURE VIII

JUSTICE (PART IV. OF THE PRINCIPLES OF ETHICS)
CHAPTERS I. TO VIII.

I pass now to Part IV. (entitled *Justice*) of the *Principles of Ethics*, which in the author's view is the most important after Part I., and was accordingly published in 1891, before Parts II. and III.—though twelve years after *The Data of Ethics*—with a preface in which its special importance is expressly stated. It is, however, rather a politico-ethical than an ethical treatise; that is, the first seven chapters are ethical, the last seven mainly political, the intervening fifteen concerned with a subject which may be regarded as common ground between Ethics and Politics — the determination of the rights of individuals as they would be maintained by a law that realised justice. In the present and the succeeding Lecture I shall confine my attention mainly to the ethical part of the treatise. I begin by recalling a criticism that I urged against Part I. (*The Data of Ethics*)—namely, that it assumed too easily a practically complete coincidence between Life and Pleasure or Happiness—it assumed, that is, that actions conducive to Maximum Life would also be conducive to Maximum Happiness

—ignoring, as I said, the possibility of life being
increased at the expense of happiness. This fundamental assumption Mr. Spencer maintains in Part IV. ;
and I shall try to show that at important points this
duality in the conception of the End, and the liberty
he reserves to himself of passing from Life to Happiness and back to Life according to the convenience
of his argument, are sources of serious confusion.

He sets out (in chapter i. on *Animal Ethics*) by
stating as the 'ultimate end not only of human conduct
but of animal conduct at large,' the 'greatest length,
breadth, and completeness of life'; while 'relatively
to the species' acts are said to be 'good' which are
'conducive to the preservation of offspring or of the
individual.' Such acts, he says, may be 'egoistic or
altruistic.' And thus, in Mr. Spencer's view, there are
two cardinal and opposed principles of animal ethics—
assuming for simplicity that we take the preservation
of a single species as end—each having its own proper
sphere. (1) 'Within the family group—during early
life—most must be given where least is deserved,'
while (2) 'after maturity is reached benefit must
vary directly as worth'—'worth' being measured by
'fitness for the conditions of existence.' The second
of these principles or laws is limited by the first,
since, so far as adults act for the sustentation of their
children, they do not receive from their own acts
'benefit' in proportion to their 'work'; and it is
limited (3) by a further consideration :—

If the constitution of the species and its conditions of existence are such that sacrifices, partial or complete, of some of its

individuals so subserve the welfare of the species that its numbers are better maintained than they would otherwise be, then there results a justification for such sacrifice (§ 249).

This limitation suggests two questions :—(*a*) Why is it limited to maintenance of numbers of the species ? If, as Mr. Spencer declares, the end is 'greatest length, breadth, and completeness of life of members of the species,' any sacrifice of individual life conducive to this end, and not merely sacrifices conducive to maintenance of numbers, ought to be approved. (*b*) What does 'justified' mean ? Shown to be in harmony with Justice ? If so, a wider and more comprehensive principle of Justice is required.

However, I will not dwell on this now, as this third point does not appear to be in Mr. Spencer's view an equally 'essential' one (§ 250). At least he expressly lays down only 'two essential but opposed principles of action by pursuance of which each species is preserved,' belonging to the domestic and social spheres respectively ; and he holds that, in considering Justice, we are concerned only with the second. It appears to me that this limitation of view to the social sphere is likely to lead to error, when an attempt is subsequently made to determine the formula of Justice, to define and analyse the sentiment and idea of Justice among human beings, and to trace their growth ; for the Common Sense of mankind certainly recognises that relations established by law or custom within the family, may be either just or unjust ; and that even keeping within legal limits a parent may be just or unjust in the treatment of his

children; and it would therefore seem desirable that
the application of the notion and sentiment in the
domestic sphere should not be left out of account in
a general discussion of Justice. And in fact when
Mr. Spencer comes in later chapters (xx. and xxi.) to
treat of the mutual rights or claims of husbands and
wives, and of parents and children, the inadequacy
of the principle of Justice formulated in his earlier
chapters becomes manifest.

For the present, however, let us 'consider the
law of the species as composed of adults only.' Considering this first in the case of 'sub-human life,'
Mr. Spencer lays down as the 'law of sub-human
justice' that 'each individual shall receive the
benefits and the evils of its own nature and its
consequent conduct.' In a certain sense, this law is
said to 'hold without qualification in sub-human life';
in another sense, it is explained that 'sub-human
justice is extremely imperfect, both in general and in
detail.' In general, it is imperfect 'in the sense that
there exist multitudinous species the sustentation of
which depends on the wholesale destruction of other
species'; which, according to Mr. Spencer, implies
that 'the species serving as prey have the relations between conduct and consequences habitually
broken.'

But surely the existence of a predatory species is
a part of the conditions of existence of the species
preyed upon; and if the former eats up the latter, it
would seem that the latter's unfitness to the conditions
of its existence would be demonstrated, and Spencerian

Justice perfectly realised in its annihilation.   It may
be said, as Mr. Spencer goes on to say, that 'enemies
are causes of death which so operate that superior
as well as inferior are sacrificed,' and that other
'accidents'—'inclemencies of weather,' 'scarcity of
food,' 'invasions by parasites' — fall 'indiscrimi-
nately upon superior and inferior individuals.'   Here,
however, the term 'superior' seems ambiguous: it
may mean (1) more highly organised, or (2) more
qualified to preserve itself and its species under
hypothetical conditions—*e.g.* with extremes of frost
and heat, exceptional famines, foes and parasites left
out—or (3) more qualified to live under actual conditions, though not sufficiently vigorous to resist the
destructive forces.   The two former meanings seem
hardly relevant when we are basing ethical principles
on biological laws ; for the adaptation of the species
in accordance with biological laws must be adaptation
to an actual, not an ideal, environment.

If 'worth,' as Mr. Spencer says, is simply to be
measured by 'fitness to the conditions of existence,'
then the individual most highly organised and
most qualified to live in mild climates, if well
supplied with food and protected from foes and
parasites, ought surely to be regarded as less 'worthy'
than a less developed organism, if the latter manages
to live in the conditions in which it actually finds
itself, while the former does not.   And this a study
of the geological record of past life shows us to have
been largely the case : more highly organised types
have perished while types lower in the scale of

S

organisation have survived. But if so, if superiority
is strictly measured by capacity for living under actual
conditions, I do not see how sub-human justice can
be said to be 'imperfect,' according to Mr. Spencer's
statement of its law, because it is not finely graduated.
Suppose that in a given region two-thirds of a certain
species of animal are killed by extreme cold ; each of
those individuals is none the less 'subject to the
effects of his own nature,' because some may be
hardier than others. The point is that no one is
hardy enough.

I notice these points chiefly to show how very
unlike Mr. Spencer's so-called 'principle of sub-human
justice' — that what is qualified to live under its
conditions of existence deserves to live—is to anything that has ever been current as a principle of
Justice in human relations. It is indeed not without affinity to the political maxim, connected with
Machiavelli's name, that a true statesman will
adopt any means to keep himself in power or to
maintain his State ; but this maxim has not usually
been called, even by those who have accepted it, a
'principle of Justice.'

But further, the individualistic 'law of sub-
human justice' is also qualified by the conditions
of gregariousness. This qualification Mr. Spencer
admits and explains fully, though he does not seem
to me quite to realise all the importance of its bearing
on his argument. He points out that each member of
a herd of gregarious animals receives the benefits and
evils not only of 'its own nature and consequent con-

duct,' but of the nature and consequent conduct of some or all of the other members of the herd, and it may happen that even ' an occasional mortality of individuals in defence of the species furthers . . . preservation of the species in a greater degree than would pursuit of exclusive benefit by each individual.' This last 'limitation of sub-human justice' is, however, regarded as solely due to the coexistence of living enemies of the species in question. The limitation seems to me arbitrary and dogmatic. There is no attempt to show that there are not other conditions which may make the sacrifice of individuals tend to preservation of the species.

This point is illustrated by consideration of the instances which Mr. Spencer brings in support of a condition of wider range—anticipatory, as we shall see, of his formula of Justice—which he lays down as ' absolute for gregarious animals,' *i.e.* the condition that ' each member of the group while carrying on self-sustentation and sustentation of offspring, shall not seriously impede the like pursuits of others.' This condition, in the case of some gregarious creatures, even becomes a law enforced by sanctions. Thus, we are told,

A 'rogue' elephant (always distinguished as unusually malicious) is one which has been expelled from the herd, doubtless because of conduct obnoxious to the rest—probably aggressive. It is said that from a colony of beavers an idler is banished, and thus prevented from profiting by labours in which he does not join : a statement made credible by the fact that drones, when no longer needed, are killed by worker-bees. The testimonies of observers in different countries show that a flock of crows, after prolonged noise of consultation, will summarily execute an offending member. And an eye-witness affirms that among rooks, a pair which steals

the sticks from neighbouring nests has its own nest pulled to
pieces by the rest.

Here, then, we see that the *a priori* condition to harmonious
co-operation comes to be tacitly recognised as something like a
law ; and there is a penalty consequent on breach of it (§ 254).

But in these illustrations Mr. Spencer seems to me
to put together cases that should be carefully distinguished.   In a case like that of the rooks, it is
abnormal action on the part of a member of the
group, tending to interfere with the sustentation of
other members, which is punished by those other
members.   The normal rook does not steal the
materials of its nest from the nests of other rooks.
But the case of the drones in a hive is different, as
the drone is normally distinct from the working bee.
I dwell on this, because Mr. Spencer's ' sub-human
justice ' is intended to lead up to human justice ; and
while the punishment of the thievish rook is certainly
analogous to the enforcement of the individualistic
law of actual civilised societies, the wholesale destruction of drones suggests a drastic treatment of those
who ' neither toil nor spin ' such as the most blood-
thirsty socialist would shrink from publicly recom-
mending.   (I observe, too, that when Mr. Spencer
says that ' conditions such that by the occasional
sacrifices of some members of a species, the species as
a whole prospers,' are ' relative to the existence of
enemies,' he seems to ignore this normal destruction
of drones by working bees.)

However, let us pass to ' human justice ' (chapter
iii.), which Mr. Spencer states to be ' a further development of sub-human justice,' the two being 'essentially

of the same nature' and forming 'parts of a continuous whole.'   We read as follows in § 257 :—

> Of man, as of all inferior creatures, the law by conformity to
> which the species is preserved, is that among adults the individuals
> best adapted to the conditions of their existence shall prosper
> most, and that individuals least adapted to the conditions of
> their existence shall prosper least—a law which, if uninterfered
> with, entails survival of the fittest and spread of the most adapted
> varieties.   And as before, so here, we see that, ethically con-
> sidered, this law implies that each individual ought to receive
> the benefits and the evils of his own nature and consequent
> conduct; neither being prevented from having whatever good
> his actions normally bring to him, nor allowed to shoulder off
> on to other persons whatever ill is brought to him by his
> actions.

Here, since 'benefits' must be understood as
'things tending to preservation,' 'prosper' ought to
mean 'shall be preserved and shall produce offspring.'
'*The* law' seems too strong; if 'adapted' means
'adapted to self-preservation,' it is even by Mr.
Spencer's own account *a* law, not *the only* law,
because an individual may be adapted to self-
preservation, but not to the preservation of the race
or the community.   So again when he says that the
law thus originating is 'obviously that which commends itself to the common apprehension as just,'
it is certainly not the whole of what so commends
itself.   We do not think it just, on reflection,—not
in accordance with Divine Justice,—that a man should
suffer for what is not due to wilful wrongdoing.

We should examine carefully the phrases quoted
in § 257 :—

> When of some one who suffers a disaster, it is said—'He has
> no one to blame but himself,' there is implied the belief that he
> has not been inequitably dealt with.   The comment on one

whose misjudgment or misbehaviour has entailed evil upon him, that 'he has made his own bed, and now he must lie in it,' has behind it the conviction that this connexion of cause and effect is proper.   Similarly with the remark, 'He got no more than he deserved.'   A kindred conviction is implied when, conversely, there results good instead of evil.   'He has fairly earned his reward,' 'He has not received due recompense,' are remarks indicating the consciousness that there should be a proportion between effort put forth and advantage achieved—that justice demands such a proportion.

All these phrases are compatible with the view that it is on intention and moral effort, not on achievement, that desert depends.   Indeed Mr. Spencer seems to recognise this when he speaks of the 'consciousness that there should be a proportion between effort put forth and advantage achieved.' Yet afterwards (§ 269) he speaks with entire disagreement of the proposition laid down in Mr. Bellamy's 'communistic Utopia,' that 'each shall make the same effort, and that if by the same effort, bodily or mental, one produces twice as much as another, he is not to be advantaged by the difference.'   I quite agree with Mr. Spencer in thinking that it would be practically disastrous to adopt this rule ; but I recognise—what he fails to recognise— that it is in accordance with the prevalent view of ideal justice.   This view, however, being accompanied with a recognition of the impracticability of realising such justice under the actual conditions of human society, takes the form of a conception of Divine rather than human justice.

I pass to an effect of gregariousness which Mr. Spencer admits to be important, but treats, I think, too lightly.   In the case of man, the operation of the

law that among adults the individuals best adapted
to the conditions of their existence shall prosper
most, and that individuals least adapted to the conditions of their existence shall prosper least, is
modified in a manner only 'faintly indicated among
lower beings.' For 'as communities become developed' the 'limits to each man's activities necessitated by the simultaneous activities of others' become
more and more 'recognised practically if not theoretically'; also in the case of this 'highest gregarious
creature' the principle of individualistic justice has to
be qualified, to a greater extent than in the case of
lower gregarious creatures, by admitting the sacrifice
of individuals for the benefit of the community. This
highest creature is distinguished by the characteristic
of fighting his own kind; and 'the sacrifices entailed
by wars between groups' of human beings have been
'far greater than the sacrifices made in defence of
groups against inferior animals.' But 'the self-
subordination thus justified, and in a sense rendered
obligatory, is limited to that which is required for
defensive war.' It may, indeed, be contended that
'offensive wars, furthering the peopling of the Earth
by the stronger, subserve the interest of the race.'
But, in Mr. Spencer's view, 'it is only during the
earlier stages of human progress that the development of strength, courage, and cunning are of chief
importance; . . . the arrival at a stage in which
ethical considerations come to be entertained is the
arrival at a stage at which offensive war ceases to be
justifiable.' And he holds that even defensive war,

and the qualifications of the abstract principle of justice which it involves, belong to a transitional condition, and 'must disappear when there is reached a peaceful state.' Such qualifications, therefore, belong to 'relative' not 'absolute ethics.' In absolute ethics the law that 'each individual ought to receive the benefits and evils of his own nature' is true without qualifications; and that it is 'obviously that which commends itself to the common apprehension as just' is affirmed by Mr. Spencer.

It seems to me that the effects of gregariousness, in the highly developed form in which it appears in the human race, are inadequately conceived in this reasoning, and the supposed effects of evolution somewhat arbitrarily assumed. Also, in the consideration of war and its consequences Sociology and Ethics are too much mixed up. Even accepting his view of war, it is too hastily assumed that the necessity of subordinating the welfare of the individual to that of the species arises solely from war. Granting that it would be for the advantage of the human race that war should disappear, it does not follow that it will disappear; it might similarly be better for sub-human life that beasts of prey, poisonous serpents and insects, and the innumerable hordes of parasites should dwindle and die out, but Mr. Spencer's faith in sub-human evolution does not lead him to assume that this will be its ultimate result. Granting again, that industrialism will put an end to militancy, it is not shown that conflicts of interests among industrial groups—such as we see at present in apparently growing intensity—will not continue, and that the exigencies of such conflicts will not impose on individuals a severe subordination to the interests of their respective groups.   Granting, finally, that such industrial conflicts are ultimately to cease, it seems rash to assume that when this consummation is reached Mr. Spencer's individualistic principles of justice will be found reigning unchecked ; for it may be that this result will be brought about by an implication of interests and a development of sympathy which will render all men 'members one of another' to a degree beyond our present experience ; so that when any one suffers the rest will inevitably suffer with him, and the rule that ' each is to bear the evils of his own nature' will become impracticable or unmeaning.   If an Individualist can thus 'fancy warless men,' and indeed confidently predict that the world is becoming warless, why has not the Socialist an equal right to predict unselfish men, among whom the competition will be who shall do most good for others, and who will acquiesce in receiving in return only what is necessary for their efficiency ?   We can imagine a very high development of ' qualities adapted for the social state' under these conditions.

I turn to examine Mr. Spencer's account of the development from a psychological point of view, first of the *Sentiment of Justice*, and then of the *Idea of Justice*.   He begins with what he calls the ' egoistic sentiment of Justice,' which appears to be irritation at interference with the pursuit of egoistic ends. The term seems to me a misnomer : such resentment of interference is rather a condition of the

sentiment of justice than itself such a sentiment in
any degree.

Mr. Spencer goes on to explain how the 'altruistic
sentiment of justice' comes into existence by the aid
of a 'pro-altruistic sentiment having several com-
ponents.' This exposition is, in the main, a repetition of the account given in *The Data of Ethics*
(in the chapter on the Psychological View) of the
growth of moral sentiments generally, applied to the
particular case of Justice. 'The dread of social dislike, the dread of legal punishment, and the dread of
divine vengeance . . . form a body of feeling which
checks the primitive tendency to pursue the objects
of desire without regard to the interests of fellow-
men' (§ 264). The theory, however, is improved by
the addition of a still earlier deterrent—'dread of retaliation.' Then, society being held together by the
'pro-altruistic' sentiment formed in this way, the
development of sympathy through gregariousness thus
maintained produces the genuine 'altruistic' sentiment of justice.

Accepting this account as largely true, I think it
requires some qualifications. First, I do not understand Mr. Spencer to affirm that a tribe of entirely
unsympathetic *men*—as distinct from monkeys—ever
existed. Gregarious men, we may assume, developed
out of gregarious monkeys—our ancestor was not
man before he could talk—and the development of
sympathy through gregariousness begins, I conceive,
in the pre-human stage. Again, I would observe
that 'social reprobation' is partly due to sympathy

with the resentment of the sufferer from aggression, though partly also to the fear of similar aggression. The two elements blend, as I think direct reflection will show. So, I conceive, the action of the chief in preventing aggression is only partly due to the egoistic desire for the maintenance of his power, to which Mr. Spencer attributes it. He doubtless acts partly as the organ of the community, under the influence of public opinion—sympathy aiding in impelling him to do what others desire him to do.

To sum up Mr. Spencer's view :—Resentment of interference combining first with fear of retaliation of others if interfered with, of social reprobation of such interference, of human and divine punishment for it ; combining secondly with sympathy with the annoyance caused to others by such interference : the idea of a limit to each kind of activity up to which there is freedom to act gradually 'emerges and becomes definite.' The idea of Justice that thus emerges contains two elements. 'Inequality is the primordial ideal suggested. For if the principle is that each shall receive the benefits and evils due to his own nature and consequent conduct, then since men differ in their powers, . . . unequal amounts of benefit are implied.' On the other hand, the recognition of the need of 'mutual limitations to men's actions' involves the conception of Equality ; since 'experience shows that these bounds are on the average the same for all.' But the appreciation of these two factors in human justice has long remained unbalanced. Thus Mr. Spencer says that in the Greek conception of justice

—which admitted slavery as just—'there predominates
the idea of inequality,' and 'the inequality refers not
to the natural achievement of greater rewards by
greater merits, but to the artificial apportionment of
greater rewards to greater merits.' On the other hand,
in the dictum of Bentham that 'everybody is to count
for one, nobody for more than one,' the idea of
inequality entirely disappears.   It has, in short, been
left for Mr. Spencer to give the true conception of
Justice by 'co-ordinating the antagonistic wrong
views,' and showing that the ideas of equality and
inequality 'may be and must be simultaneously
asserted,' being 'applied the one to the bounds and
the other to the benefits.'   The Formula of Justice,
so conceived, may be precisely expressed as follows :—
Every man is free to do that which he wills, provided he infringes not the equal freedom of any other
man.

Here, in examining the historical conception of
Justice, we must, first, I think, note a distinction
which Mr. Spencer overlooks between what I call Ideal
and Conservative Justice—*i.e.* between the conception
of the rights that have actually come to be established in any society, and the conception of the rights
that ought to be established.   Throughout the chapter
on *The Idea of Justice* (chapter v.) there seems a
want of clearness of distinction between the two.   No
doubt the two elements are not distinguished, or only
faintly, in primitive thought; but they are distinguished
long before the termination of Graeco-Roman thought
by means of the conception of *Jus Naturale*.   Further,

in the development of the idea of Justice, Non-interference seems to me less prominent, and Equality
more prominent, than Mr. Spencer supposes.   In
the Greek view of Justice — as indeed he notices
(§ 268)—inequality is an element; but it is not Mr.
Spencer's inequality, but rather an inequality that
involves equality of proportions.   It is the inequality
that belongs to distribution according to Desert, but
not the inequality that results from *Laisser-faire*.
And this is surely more in accordance with Common
Sense.   Mr. Spencer is imperfectly acquainted with
Aristotle, or he would have noted the prominence of
Equality in Aristotle's conception of Justice and in
Greek Common Sense as interpreted by Aristotle.[1]

Mr. Spencer discusses in an Appendix[2] the relation
between his own view and Kant's, and quotes the
following statement of Kant's *Universal Principle of
Right* :—' Every action is *right* which in itself, or in
the maxim on which it proceeds, is such that it can
coexist along with the Freedom of the Will of each
and all in action, according to a universal Law.'   He
next proceeds to point out the connexion, positive
and negative, between his own view and Kant's.
Mr. Spencer is quite right as to the fundamental
difference between Kant's doctrine, prescribing
Freedom absolutely, and his own doctrine, which
prescribes Freedom as means to general happiness.
This of course introduces a fundamental difference
in the criticism of either view.   The difference

---

[1] Cf. *Outlines of the History of Ethics*, chap. ii. § 11, p. 65.
[2] *Principles of Ethics*, vol. ii, Appendix A, p. 438.

between the older Utilitarians and Kant is a difference
of principle ; the difference between the older Utilitarians and Mr. Spencer is only a difference of method.
Kant's conclusion, says Mr. Spencer,

is reached by a 'search in the pure Reason for the sources of
such judgments'—forms a part of the 'metaphysic of morals';
whereas, as shown on pp. 67, 68 of the original edition of *Social
Statics*, the law of equal freedom there shadowed forth and subsequently stated, is regarded as expressing the primary condition
which must be fulfilled before the greatest happiness can be
achieved by similar beings living in proximity. Kant enunciates
an *a priori* requirement, contemplated as irrespective of beneficial
ends ; whereas I have enunciated this *a priori* requirement as one
which, under the circumstances necessitated by the social state,
must be conformed to for achievement of beneficial ends.

In what he here says Mr. Spencer seems to me to
be right; but I think he is wrong as to the second
difference between himself and Kant, which he states
thus :—

Kant, by saying that 'there is only one innate right, the
birthright of freedom,' clearly recognises the positive element
in the conception of justice; yet . . . the right of the
individual to freedom is represented as emerging by implication
from the wrongfulness of acts which aggress upon this freedom.
The negative element, or obligation to respect limits, is the
dominant idea ; whereas in my own case, the positive element
—the right to freedom of action—is represented as primary ;
while the negative element resulting from the limitations imposed by the presence of others, is represented as secondary.
This distinction may not be without its significance ; for the
putting of obligation in the foreground seems natural to a
social state in which political restraints are strong, while the
putting of claims in the foreground seems natural to a social
state in which there is a greater assertion of individuality
(*Principles of Ethics*, ii. pp. 438, 439).

Now, Kant is giving, not the ethical formula of
right action, but the formula of right legal coercion—
that is, A's freedom may only be coercively limited, in
order to protect the freedom of others. But this is

also Mr. Spencer's view.   He does not mean, any more than Kant, that a man ought to do just as he likes, and that we ought to approve of anything a man does, so long as he does not infringe the freedom of others ; for he may neglect the ethics of individual life, and the duty of positive and negative beneficence. He means, like Kant, that we ought to disapprove of any one's being interfered with.   A man is not necessarily right in doing what he ought to have a legal right to do.   This becomes important when we ask— as we have to ask from either thinker—for a precise definition of Freedom ; and Mr. Spencer makes it clear at once that he does not mean by law of equal freedom, merely that every one must allow others the same liberty he claims for himself.

For (he says) the truth to be expressed is that each in carrying on the actions which constitute his life for the time being, and conduce to the subsequent maintenance of his life, shall not be impeded further than by the carrying on of those kindred actions which maintain the lives of others.   It does not countenance a superfluous interference with another's life, committed on the ground that an equal interference may balance it.   Such a rendering of the formula is one which implies greater deductions from the lives of each and all than the associated state necessarily entails ; and this is obviously a perversion of its meaning.

If we bear in mind that though not the immediate end, the greatest sum of happiness is the remote end, we see clearly that the sphere within which each may pursue happiness has a limit, on the other side of which lie the similarly limited spheres of action of his neighbours ; and that he may not intrude on his neighbour's spheres on condition that they may intrude on his. Instead of justifying aggression and counter - aggression, the intention of the formula is to fix a bound which may not be exceeded on either side (§ 273).

What is aimed at is not merely maintenance of equal freedom, but prevention of interference with

272 ON MR. SPENCER'S ETHICS   LECT.

'the actions which constitute' the life of each and
'conduce to the subsequent maintenance of his life.'

It must be observed that Mr. Spencer is scarcely
justified in speaking (at the beginning of § 273) of
misapprehension of a formula, when what is really
meant is that the formula is inexact. After giving
an apparently simple and precise formula, he says
that is not what he meant, and substitutes a loosely
expressed different one. What he goes on to say
of advance from 'the incorrect to the correct
interpretation' seems to me somewhat to con-
found *the rule*, and *the manner of enforcing it*.
He says the early idea of justice 'is that of a
balancing of injuries' (§ 274). Freedom to kill and
maim, however, was never an interpretation of justice :
but self-protection had a larger range in ruder times,
and no doubt retaliation confounded retribution and
reparation, and took a barbaric view of reparation.
Still the Lex Talionis—an eye for eye—did not mean
that the first eye might be legitimately gouged by
any one who did not object to lose his own.

How, then, is the Formula of Justice proved?
There seem to be three lines of argument adopted :—
(1) The evolutional argument from general biology.
Any species, and therefore the human species, is improved by the struggle for 'existence'; and therefore
by each individual bearing the burdens and receiving the benefits of his own nature. This argument I
answered before. It seems to me to underrate the
effect of 'gregariousness' in the human family.

(2) In § 276 it is attempted to be shown that

History exhibits a gradual growth of this conception of Justice into distinctness. It does not seem to me that this is proved by the fact—if it be a fact—that entirely pacific tribes 'quickly develop' an aversion to killing and robbery: since an aversion to killing and robbery would be recognised as normal by any antagonists of Mr. Spencer no less than by himself, and would be as decidedly prohibited in a socialistic as in an individualistic community. Nor do I see any evidence that 'militancy' in modern nations has prevented a recognition of the equal claims of members of the nation; consider, for instance, the pre-revolutionary movement in the eighteenth century. Nor that the 'Hebrew commandments' recognise Mr. Spencer's formula more than any other. Nor that the Christian Golden Rule is relevant; being again—with the limitations required to make it rationally acceptable —acceptable equally by all schools. And certainly the general tone of Christianity is rather socialistic than individualistic; *e.g.* in the parable of the rich man and Lazarus, we are told of the 'mammon of unrighteousness.' Mr. Spencer has more right to urge the affinity of his view with the doctrine of Natural Law, as held by a succession of thinkers from the Roman Jurists to the eighteenth century; but we must observe, that until the eighteenth century it never based the Right of Property on the Right of Freedom.

(3) Fortified by this historic survey, Mr. Spencer seems disposed in § 278, which is important for his

reconciliation of Intuitive and Utilitarian Method, to
affirm the Law of Equal Freedom to be self-evident
a priori, though 'relatively vague' and requiring
'methodic criticism.' In answer to this I have to
say primarily, that it is not self-evident to me; and I
claim my mind to be a result of evolution as much as
Mr. Spencer's. And it is difficult to see how the
appeal to Evolution which Mr. Spencer makes can
settle a controversy of this kind, on the ground that
our present beliefs are the result of a long series of
human experiences; for the disagreement and controversy are just the result of the long series of experiences. Even if it were proved that the majority were
on Mr. Spencer's side, still the minority might appeal
to history to prove that minorities have often been
right. But Mr. Spencer does not contend this: indeed he says expressly (§ 275), in stronger language
than I should use, that 'nothing less than scorn' will
be shown for his doctrine by those 'brought up in
the reigning school of politics and morals.' The
reigning school must, I suppose, represent the pre-
ponderant latest result of evolution—which, therefore,
seems opposed to Mr. Spencer. Nor can it be said:
Schools perhaps, but not Common Sense — for he
complains equally of prevalent Common Sense (§ 271).
If it be said: Still Common Sense accepts it as
an ideal—I should reply : (*a*) If so, it is certainly
accepted *along with* the conflicting principle of the
requital of desert; it is not ideally just that a man
should suffer for no fault of his own : (*b*) Is experience of past human life likely to have produced a

trustworthy intuition as to ideal relations?—Why should it have produced such an intuition?

> We have not ... only reasons (Mr. Spencer says in § 280) ... for concluding that this *a priori* belief has its origin in the experiences of the race, but we are enabled to affiliate it on the experiences of living creatures at large, and to perceive that it is but a conscious response to certain necessary relations in the order of nature.

> No higher warrant can be imagined; and now, accepting the law of equal freedom as an ultimate ethical principle, having an authority transcending every other, we may proceed with our inquiry.

It is difficult to see how it can transcend the principle: Promote general happiness. What Mr. Spencer means is that it is a paramount prescription of necessary *means* to the end.

In his application of the formula, especially in chapter viii. (*Its Corollaries*), I have first to notice a certain danger of confusion between *legal* and *moral* rights, and between legal rights as actually established and legal rights that ought to be established. Some moral rights, if recognised at all, are at the same time recognised as ideally legal rights; but not all: *e.g.* members of a family have a moral right to affectionate services from each other, which it is universally regarded as undesirable to enforce by law. To take Mr. Spencer's instances: When it is said that a working man has a 'right to labour,' it is meant that he ought to have a legal right; but when it is said that the public has 'a right to know' facts, it is not commonly meant that any one should be under a legal obligation to furnish the required information; only that those who furnish it should be approved and those who refuse it disapproved. Again, when

Mr. Spencer speaks of a 'confirmed and indeed contemptuous denial' by Bentham and others of rights apart from the State, he can hardly mean that they refuse to admit the conception of legal rights that ought to be established, other than those that are established —the charge would be peculiarly absurd as applied to Bentham, the great theoretical reformer of law. If Mr. Spencer merely means that there are no legal rights apart from the State, that is of course Bentham's view ; but Bentham has never dreamt of saying that there are no moral rights.

So again, the concluding sentence of this chapter —'Further, it will become apparent that so far is it from being true that the warrant for what are properly called rights is derived from law, it is, conversely, true that law derives its warrant from them' (§ 283)— seems to me seriously ambiguous. If he means by *warrant* 'reason why the legislator should establish them,' good; but if he means 'reason why private citizens should obey them,' this is dangerously revolutionary, since it seems to deny that the mere fact of a command being issued by the established legislature in a State is any reason for obeying it.

Mr. Spencer does not say expressly that all the ' rights' which he regards as corollaries from the law of equal freedom ought to be established by law. But he seems to imply this ; since he says (§ 283) that his corollaries not only ' one and all coincide with ordinary ethical conceptions,' but that they ' one and all correspond with legal enactments.' I propose in the next Lecture to examine carefully, in particular cases,

how far this correspondence goes.   I think, however,
that in several cases the deductions from Mr. Spencer's
principle are not performed with sufficient exactness :
that if they were made more exact, the discrepancy
between the results obtained by his deductions and
the established laws of civilised society would be more
marked.   This would not, indeed, necessarily invali-
date Mr. Spencer's conclusions ; since, firstly, actual
law may be wrong, and secondly, it may be right but
not ideal, a compromise inevitable at the present
stage of social development ; for Mr. Spencer's idea of
Justice, as he is careful to state, is 'appropriate to
an ultimate state, and can be but partly entertained
during transitional states.'   But it would be an
advantage to have the three things—the ideal rights
of an ideal society, the legal rights as they ought to
be here and now, and the actual legal rights—more
clearly and fully compared.   As it is, I fear that the
reader will not always thoroughly distinguish the
three questions: (1) How far can we know the relations
of members of an ideal society ?   (2) How far ought
we to imitate these relations here and now ?   (3)
What changes in our actual law would this imitation
involve ?

LECTURE IX

I PROPOSE in this Lecture to attempt a systematic examination of Mr. Spencer's 'Deductive Utilitarianism' in the department of Justice. This is, both in his own view and mine, most important,—it is here that he conceives the main practical issue to lie between his own view and the more empirical Utilitarianism that I represent. We both agree that the greatest happiness of the aggregate of persons affected by actions is the ultimate end; and we also agree in the practical conclusion that in the main, and speaking broadly, the service that any one sane adult should be legally compelled to render to others should be merely the negative service of non-interference, except so far as he has voluntarily undertaken to render positive services,—provided we include in the notion of non-interference the obligation of compensation for previous interference, whether intentional or careless, or of preventing mischief that would otherwise result from some previous act. This, speaking broadly, is the principle on which law and the administration of Justice is mainly based in modern States; and I have no doubt that it is a practically sound basis in the main.

278

The difference between me and Mr. Spencer is that he declares that his formula for Justice may be treated as an absolute or ultimate ethical principle, having an authority transcending every other; and that the particular legal rights that ought to be established in an actual state may be ascertained by simple deductions from this principle. As we have seen, he even goes further. He says :—

. . . rights, truly so called, are corollaries from the law of equal freedom, and what are falsely called rights are not deducible from it.

In treating of these corollaries, as we now proceed to do, we shall find that, in the first place, they one and all coincide with ordinary ethical conceptions, and that, in the second place, they one and all correspond with legal enactments. Further, it will become apparent that so far is it from being true that the warrant for what are properly called rights is derived from law, it is, conversely, true that law derives its warrant from them (§ 283).

There are, then, three points to which I shall specially direct your attention :—(1) I shall criticise closely Mr. Spencer's deductions from his fundamental formula. (2) I shall point out the divergences between the corollaries from this formula and the actually established rules of law. (3) I shall show that these divergences, in most if not in all cases, are supported by considerations such as those by which empirical Utilitarianism is guided.

The Principle of Justice, as we saw, is, according to Mr. Spencer, the Law of Equal Freedom : every man is to be free to do that which he wills, provided that he infringe not the equal freedom of other men. Let us examine the meaning of the term Freedom. Primarily it signifies the negation of physical coercion or confinement. A is not free if B moves his limbs or physically prevents his moving them according to his will; and he is not free if he cannot get out of a building because B has locked the door. But Freedom is also—and this is specially important for us—opposed not merely to physical restraint, but to the moral restraint caused by the fear of pain resulting from the action of other human beings. Here, however, there is some dispute as to whether the 'other human beings' are *any human beings* or only *Government*. To put it briefly : Is the state of anarchy or no-government a state of Freedom? Hobbes regarded it as being so : he regarded the State of Nature as miserable indeed, from the intense mutual fear felt by those living in it ; but yet as a state of unlimited liberty.

But it is surely paradoxical to say that it is contrary to liberty to be restrained by dread of the magistrate, and not contrary to liberty to be similarly restrained by the fear of lawless violence. Freedom, then, must be taken to exclude pain, actual or threatened, that acts as moral restraint, and also, of course, physical disablement. Now the greater part of the pain that human beings are moved to inflict on each other is coercive either in its intention or in its effect. So that if our aim is to prevent violations of Freedom as much as possible, we should prevent *most* voluntarily inflicted pain. But we cannot say that on this ground we should prevent *all* such pain. For instance, not pain that there is mutual agreement to allow ; for consent excludes coercion. Hence,

when Mr. Spencer says in chapter ix. that 'considered
as the statement of a condition by conforming to
which the greatest sum of happiness is to be
obtained, the law [of equal freedom] forbids any act
which inflicts physical pain or derangement,' he
clearly goes too far.   Clearly it only forbids acts that
cause a balance of pain on the whole; and only this if
we give to Freedom quite an unusual extension of
meaning.   Take, for instance, the case of some rough
game, such as Rugby football.

It is true, as Mr. Spencer explains, that the legal
protection of the individual from pain and annoyance
has become more complete and refined as civilisation
has progressed, still no cogent argument is shown for
regarding it as 'unqualified' in a system of absolute
ethics—except on the assumption, which Mr. Spencer
makes no attempt to prove, that *no* action causing
physical pain or derangement can possibly be conducive to the greatest sum of happiness.   But granting
that the principle is to exclude all pain or annoyance
as far as possible, reflection will show that it is a
delicate matter to apply the rule in the case of mental
annoyance ; because we cannot prevent mental annoyance to A, without seriously interfering with the
freedom of action of B.

From the principle of preventing mutual coercion
and pain as much as possible, the Right to Free Motion
and Locomotion is a simple corollary, and the complete
establishment of this right within the limits of a civilised State is undoubtedly a result of the process of
civilisation in modern times.   But if we are to deal

with the corollary with precision, we must distinguish different things which Mr. Spencer puts together. Mr. Spencer treats Slavery and Serfdom as the great historic instances of infringement of the right. But Slavery is much more than an interference with free motion and locomotion ; it is interference —or rather a protected right of general interference— with the free action of the individual, with the view of directing that action to the attainment of the purpose of the slave-owner.   It ought, therefore, to come under a more general head ; and indeed the only point in it which presents any difficulty or requires to be handled with any care, is the case of slavery arising out of contract.   This I will refer to again under the Law of Contract.   Even in the case of serfage, though here 'attachment to the soil' was more important, still it is not to be regarded as mere interference with locomotion, but rather as an incident of the right on the part of A to direct the labour of B to A's profit.

With regard to chapter xi.—*Rights to the Use of Natural Media*—I would ask : What does the principle of Equal Freedom mean in determining the relation of man to his material environment ?   To make our conceptions definite, let us take the case of the surface of the earth.   It is obvious that the maximum freedom—if we take the word simply in its ordinary meaning—is attained by simply protecting each man while using any portion of land for the satisfaction of his needs and desires—say by lying on it, walking on it, picking wild strawberries, etc.—without excluding

any other from similarly using the land at the same
time or afterwards. (Actually legislation does treat
roads, commons, etc., in this way.) But it is no less
obvious that maximum utility is not to be attained in
this way ; but only by allowing exclusive use for a
time. Without exclusive use of land, man could not
have emerged from savagery. But if so, how is it
possible to apply the law of equal freedom ? For if
A is allowed exclusive use of a portion of land, the
freedom of B, C, D is necessarily *pro tanto* restricted
with regard to it. It is not enough to say that B, C,
D have equal freedom to appropriate similar land ; the
point is that appropriation inevitably limits freedom
for the sake of utility. And in fact—even if for simplicity we concentrate attention on land hitherto
unoccupied, land (say) in a new colony—the equal
freedom to appropriate similar land will soon be im-
paired if appropriation is fully allowed.

But there is a further difficulty which I have
noticed in my *Principles of Political Economy* :
I there point out that we have to ask first, Under
what limitations land should be allowed to pass into
private ownership ? and secondly, Why and how far,
after this transition has taken place, Government
should still exercise a special control over this
particular kind of property ? As regards the first
question, it is obvious that such portions of land as
are manifestly more useful to the community when
thrown freely open to common use should be retained
in public ownership, and under governmental management : *e.g.* roads, navigable rivers and inland lakes,

natural harbours, public parks, commons, etc. So, again, there are strong reasons why the land required for railroads or other similar monopolies should not be allowed to pass, except temporarily, out of public ownership : and a general right should be reserved of taking back from private owners any land that may be needed for public uses, at its market-value, as determined independently of such need, with a slight addition by way of compensation for any special utility that it may have for its owner.[1]

In my *Political Economy* I was considering the question from the practical point of view of what Government ought to do.   What I am now considering is the jural principle involved.   It seems to me that the idea of mere equal freedom, mere protection from mutual encroachment, is clearly inapplicable : as we try to apply it, it changes—if I may so say—in our hands into the idea of governmental regulation with a view to the common interests of the aggregate of human beings concerned.   No doubt, in this conception of common interests, equality of claims on the part of individuals composing the community comes in, and is recognised as demanded by Justice, but it is equality of claims not to Freedom but to Utility.   Again, in this governmental regulation which we see to be required, the principle of individualism, of leaving the individual free to adapt his material environment to his need, occupies, indeed, an important place ; but it does not come in as an 'ultimate ethical principle, transcending every other,' but

---

[1] Cf. *Principles of Political Economy*, Book III. chap. iv. § 12.

as subordinate, and subject not only to the general
principle of Utilitarianism, but to the particular end of
making the land, and labour spent on it, most useful
to the community.   Justice itself, in short, compels
us to supplement it by the principle of equal claim of
all, *not* to Freedom, but to the Utility derived from
the land, or to the land itself as a source of utility.

And the remarkable thing is that in chapter xi.
Mr. Spencer's notion of Justice does go through this
change ; although he hardly seems aware of it.   Here
the proposition that ' the liberty of each should be
limited only by the like liberties of others,' suddenly
becomes (§ 297) the proposition that ' men have equal
claims to the use of land,' although it is clear that
this ' equality of claims ' does not in any way determine
how much freedom should be allowed to each in using
land—indeed, as Mr. Spencer goes on to argue, it is
satisfied by ' the people's supreme ownership of the
land,' and he considers that it is implied in the right
of ' expropriation by State-decree ' claimed by modern
States.

The right of an existing holder of land (he says) can be
equitably superseded, only if there exists a prior right of the
community at large ; and this prior right of the community at
large consists of the sum of the individual rights of its members
(§ 298).

The last phrase seems to me misleading if the
' right of the individual ' is understood to be a deduction from the law of equal freedom, since the
question is whether the life of the community may
not be better maintained by restricting the freedom
of individuals.   The general happiness is no doubt

composed of the happinesses of individuals; but it may be better promoted by restricting the freedom of individuals. If so, the 'right' to restrict may belong to the aggregate, not deduced from 'rights' of individuals but from a consideration of their common interests. In any case, if ownership by the community satisfies the individual's claim to equality—and Mr. Spencer's argument here seems to imply this—the question still remains open as to the extent of the individual's right of property. And, in fact, as the next chapter shows, the difficulty of satisfactorily deducing this from the Law of Equal Freedom is very great.

Mr. Spencer thinks (§ 299) that there are 'three ways in which under savage, semi-civilised and civilised conditions, men's several rights of property may be established with due regard to the equal rights of all other men.' (1) Tacit consent 'among the occupiers of a tract' to appropriation of wild products—but, as his instance shows, the assent may give a varying amount to the individual. (2) Tacit assent—'in the semi-settled stage'—to the ownership of food grown on an appropriated portion by any one. (3) There *might* be, in civilised societies, a contract by which cultivators should give a share of the produce to non-cultivators, though 'we have no evidence that such a relation . . . has ever arisen.'

Mr. Spencer must be aware that none of these suggestions amounts to a justification of the actual right of property. For there is no proof, for landless men now, that such assents were given by their predecessors; and granting that they were, no proof is attempted that these previous assents could bind the present landless ones. (Mr. Spencer might have studied Locke with advantage on this latter point.) Accordingly when he turns to find an opponent, he ignores the modern Socialist who claims that an equitable right of property—involving, as it does, equality of opportunity — can only be secured by common ownership of land and the instruments of production; and he directs his attack against 'many in our days' who 'think it wrong that each man should receive benefits proportionate to his efforts.' There may be 'many' such; but certainly they scarcely count in current political controversy. What modern Socialism claims is, that the present system of private property prevents the worker receiving full natural return for his work; against this Mr. Spencer's defence of Individualism is surprisingly weak.

Mr. Spencer supports his defence here of the Right of Property by an Appendix on Land Nationalisation,[1] in which his chief argument is that since 1601 the landless have received some £500,000,000 from poor-rates charged on land, which would, he suggests, be a high price for 'land in its primitive unsubdued state.' This does not seem to me very relevant to the 'equal claims' of existing human beings. It seems more reasonable to hold that the poor-rates paid in the past are rather a compensation to past poor; and it might fairly be urged that they were inadequate compensation for the injustice done to

---

[1] *Principles of Ethics*, vol. ii. p. 440, Appendix B : *The Land Question.*

them.   Suppose we were considering whether slavery
should be abolished, we should not take into account
money spent by slave-owners in keeping slaves alive
whom they might have killed.   If the poor were
wronged by being kept out of the land, a pittance
doled out under conditions of discredit seems inadequate to balance the past wrong, let alone the
present.   Also, Mr. Spencer's estimate ignores 'un-
earned' increment of value, due not to labour but to
increase of population.   It is an obvious inference
from his fundamental principle that the existing
rental, so far as not due to labour—*e.g.* ground rents
in towns—should be regarded as due to the poor.
But this is the doctrine of 'Ransom,' against which
Mr. Spencer argues very strongly when it takes the
form of free libraries (§ 271).   Even in the form
of poor-rates he seems in chapter viii. (§ 282) to disapprove of it.   Throughout his political discussion,
he assumes right of property as it seems to me
without justification.   At any rate, his argument
admits that Justice may require compensation to be
given in certain cases.   How is the compensation
due to those who have spent their labour *bona fide*
on things not properly theirs, to be determined?
Surely for consideration of this question, we require
a conception of Justice entirely different from Mr.
Spencer's;—'conformity to normal expectation,' or
something of the kind.   I may refer again to what I
say in my *Methods of Ethics*, Book III. chapter v.
(especially pages 293, 294), of Conservative and Ideal
Justice and the difficulty of reconciling the two.

Mr. Spencer is mainly concerned with one form of
Ideal Justice, but in working this out he has—in this
matter of compensation—to use a notion of Conservative Justice without deducing it from a principle.

Again, even as against the Communist, Mr.
Spencer's argument does not seem to me completely
valid when we are considering Absolute Ethics.

With a human nature (he says) such as has been known
throughout the past and is known at present, one who, by
higher power, bodily or mental, or greater endurance of work,
gains more than others gain, will not voluntarily surrender the
excess to such others ; here and there may be found a man who
would do this, but he is far from being the average man. And
if the average superior man will not voluntarily surrender to
others the excess of benefit gained by his superiority, the implication is that he must be obliged to do this, and that the use
of force to oblige him is justifiable. That the many inferior are
physically able thus to coerce the few superior is agreed on both
sides ; but the assumption of the communists is that the required
coercion of the minority who are best by the majority who are
worst would be equitable (§ 301).

What the Communist holds is that this need not
be true if men were placed under a different system
of laws and education adapted to the laws. By what
reasoning does Mr. Spencer prove that this may not be
so, when we reach the final stage—what right has he,
I ask again, in dealing with Absolute Ethics, to assume
men on the one hand warless, on the other hand as
selfish as now ?

When we pass to consider Incorporeal Property (in
chapter xiii.) the argument is changed in a double way,
which Mr. Spencer hardly enough recognises. On the
one hand, it is easier to show that on the principle
of ' each individual receiving the benefits and evils of
his own nature,' an author (*e.g.*) has a right to ex-

clusive use of the products of his labour, than that
the occupier of land has, since the author does not
interfere with the opportunities of others. On the
other hand, so far as the examples (other than
those relating to property) have previously gone,
this was secured by preventing interference with
'actions conducive to maintenance of life.' In this
case the protection of the right requires interference
of a novel kind—the prevention of imitation. If
the question is argued on the *a priori* lines which
Mr. Spencer prefers, ought not the immense amount
of beneficial imitation *not* protected by law to be
considered? An ingenious writer, M. Tarde, has
argued that the fundamental characteristic of social
man, and mainspring of social progress is Imitation.
Would it not be plausible to lay down a 'Right to
Free Imitation' as indispensable to the improve-
ment of a gregarious animal? It would be quite as
plausible as much of Mr. Spencer's reasoning.

Further, existing law certainly does not support
Mr. Spencer's view; for his conclusion is that

in fact a production of mental labour may be regarded as
property in a fuller sense than may a product of bodily labour;
since that which constitutes its value is exclusively created by
the worker. And if so, there seems no reason why the duration
of possession in this case should not be at least as great as the
duration of possession in other cases (§ 306).

It is easy to give a utilitarian explanation and
justification of the actual differences in the treatment of different kinds of property; but difficult to
give one on the principle of Equal Freedom, owing
to the general importance, in the case of material

property, of encouraging care as well as industry—
which does not apply to immaterial property.   The
distinction between the case of Patents and other
incorporeal property is rightly drawn in § 306 :—

The inventor's claim, for several centuries legislatively
enforced, has of late come to be more carefully regarded; and
by great reduction of fees, the impediments in the way of
obtaining legal protection have been reduced.   To which add
that there has been a like growing recognition in the laws of
other countries, and a much greater one in America; with a
resulting superiority in labour-saving appliances.

A restriction of the right thus set forth and justified must be
named.   It is a truth, made familiar by modern experience,
that discoveries and inventions, while in part results of individual
genius, are in part results of pre-existing ideas and appliances.
One of the implications also made familiar by modern experience
is, that about the period when one man makes a discovery or
invents a machine, some other man, possessed of similar knowledge and prompted by a like imagination, is on the way to
the same discovery or invention; and that within a moderate
period this discovery or invention is tolerably certain to be
made elsewhere—possibly by more than one.   A long continued
exclusive use of his invention would therefore be inconsistent
with other equitable claims likely to arise; and hence there is
need for a limitation of the period during which he may rightly
receive protection.   Over how many years the protection should
extend is a question which cannot be answered here, and, indeed,
cannot be answered at all in any but an empirical manner.   To
estimate the proper period account should be taken of the
observed intervals of time commonly elapsing between similar or
identical inventions made by different men.   There might fitly
be some recognition of the prolonged thought and persevering
efforts bestowed in bringing the invention to bear; and there
should also enter into the calculation an estimate, based on
evidence, of the probable interval during which exclusive use of
the invention should be insured to make possible an adequate
return for labour and risk.   Obviously the case is one in which
the relations of the individual to other individuals and to
society, are so involved and so vague, that nothing beyond an
approximately equitable decision can be reached.

Passing over the Right to Reputation (dealt with
in chapter xiii.) let us note that *Rights of Gift*

and Bequest (chapter xiv.) cannot be justified by Mr. Spencer's formula. And granting that so far as the right of property is admitted, the right of gift is admitted, I do not see that a right of bequest therefore follows. It is argued in § 309 : 'The right of gift implies the right of bequest, for a bequest is a postponed gift, etc.' Surely this contains a *petitio principii*— it assumes that the effect of ownership continues after death. I do not see how the Right of Property justifiable by the Law of Equal Freedom would imply it. What Mr. Spencer has to show is, that a man's freedom is interfered with by refusing him the right of determining what is to be done with any portion of his material environment after death.

It is to be observed that in § 310 Mr. Spencer argues that, 'strictly taken,' the right of bequest cannot include the right of determining what is to be done with a man's property after his death, because ' presented in its naked form the proposition that a man can own a thing after his death is absurd,' but if so, it seems equally absurd that he should determine who is to have it.[1]   Mr. Spencer, however, qualifies this by allowing (*a*) bequest in trust for the benefit of children (but why then allow alienation from children ?); (*b*) bequest of personalty though not realty to definite uses ; but here, he says, ' an empirical compromise seems needful.'

One who holds land subject to that supreme ownership of the community which both ethics and law assert, cannot rightly have such power of willing the application of it as involves permanent alienation from the community (§ 312).

[1] Cf. the Author's *Elements of Politics*, chap. vii. § 1.

But why not, so far as it may be permanently
alienated by a series of gifts to individuals ?   Of
course the land might be taken by the community ;
but why not with compensation ?   Mr. Spencer goes
on to say :—

In respect of what is classed as personalty, however, the case
is different.   Property which is the product of efforts, and
which has resulted either from the expenditure of such efforts
upon raw materials for which equivalents (representing so much
labour) have been given, or from the savings out of wages or
salaries, and is thus possessed in virtue of that relation between
actions and their consequences on the maintenance of which
justice insists, stands in another category.   Such property being
a portion of that which society has paid the individual for work
done, but which he has not consumed, he may reasonably contend that in giving it back to society, either as represented by
certain of its members or by some incorporated body, he should
be allowed to specify the conditions under which the bequest is
to be accepted.   In this case, it cannot be said that anything is
alienated which belongs to others.   Contrariwise, others receive
that to which they have no claim ; and are benefited, even when
they use it for prescribed purposes ; refusal of it being the
alternative if the purposes are not regarded as beneficial.   Still,
as bequeathed personal property is habitually invested, power to
prescribe its uses without any limit of time, may result in its
being permanently turned to ends which, good though they
were when it was bequeathed, have been rendered otherwise by
social changes (§ 312).

The fact is that the law of equal freedom is
inadequate for the deduction of the Rights of Bequest
—Utilitarianism comes in, clearly.

The Right of Exchange (chapter xv.), so far as
ownership extends, is, as Mr. Spencer says, a corollary
from the Right of Gift, and easily deducible directly
from the law of equal freedom.   But the case is different
with contract to render future services.   Mr. Spencer
hardly seems to recognise the difference between

making a contract and *enforcing* it.[1] He does not
seem to notice the general limitation of enforcement
of contract in actual law, but he does notice (§ 315)
one 'exceptional case' as to which his argument
seems hardly cogent :—

> While we observe that law has in this case gradually come
> into correspondence with equity, we may also fitly observe one
> exceptional case in which the two agree in forbidding a contract.
> I refer to the moral interdict and the legal interdict against a
> man's sale of himself into slavery. If we go back to the biologi-
> cal origin of justice as being the maintenance of that relation
> between efforts and the products of efforts which is needful for
> the continuance of life, we see that this relation is suspended by
> bondage ; and that, therefore, the man who agrees to enslave
> himself on condition of receiving some immediate benefit, tra-
> verses that ultimate principle from which social morality grows.
> Or if we contemplate the case from an immediately ethical point
> of view, it becomes manifest that since a contract, as framed in
> conformity with the law of equal freedom, implies that the con-
> tracting parties shall severally give what are approximately
> equivalents, there can be no contract, properly so called, in
> which the terms are incommensurable ; as they are when, for
> some present enhancement of his life, a man bargains away the
> rest of his life. So that when, instead of recognising the sale of
> self as valid, law eventually interdicted it, the exception it thus
> made to the right of contract was an exception which equity also
> makes. Here, too, law harmonised itself with ethics.

I would ask here (*a*) Why does slavery traverse
the ultimate principle ? For the immediate benefit
may be preservation of life ; and a slave may rely
on having his life preserved ; that is, in fact, the old
argument for allowing slavery. (*b*) If a contract
framed in accordance with the law of equal freedom
implies that the contracting parties give what are
approximately equivalents, and if the judgment of
contracting parties as to equivalence is to be over-

---

[1] Cf. *Elements of Politics*, chap. iv. § 2, end.

ruled here, why not interfere further to secure
equivalence? (*c*) Why are the terms ' incommensurable'? Life is not infinite.

As regards what is said in § 316, on freedom of international exchange, I will only remark that even Mr.
Spencer can hardly believe that the present growth of
protectionism outside England is due to 'militancy.'
Consider, *e.g.*, the case of the United States. Again,
it is absurd to suppose (cf. § 317) that the ' recent
revival of militancy' has anything to do with the
English 'interdict on taking meals in match factories
except in certain parts '!

There are similar difficulties in the deduction
from the formula of justice, of the Rights of Free
Belief and Worship, of Free Speech and Printing.
But I have already discussed enough examples of one
kind of failure of the formula.

I pass to chapters xx. and xxi., where I find another
kind. These chapters relate to the Rights of Women
and Children. The former are first considered
independently of marriage. Here, in §§ 332, 333,
Mr. Spencer argues as though those who would
restrict the freedom of women wished to do this on
some principle of ' rights proportionate to faculties,'
and justly says that this would 'add an artificial
hardship to a natural hardship.' But I conceive that
no opponent means this : it is not merely artificial
limitation but artificial *protection* which is avowedly
designed by those who would restrict the free competition of women with men. At the same time I think
that there is a practical justification for Mr. Spencer's

296 ON MR. SPENCER'S ETHICS LECT.

attribution of this theory to the opponents. For, whatever eloquence they use about the surprising development of women that will result from keeping them to their 'natural sphere,' and guarding them from the debasing effects of competition, I have never observed that they make the smallest effort to supply women with an artificial livelihood in their natural sphere, to compensate for the restrictions by which they would prevent them from obtaining one competitively.

In passing to consider the case of married women, the first question, which Mr. Spencer passes over remarkably lightly, is : Why and how far freedom of contract is to be limited? This is a difficulty which a thorough-going Individualist—especially on the 'high priori road'—ought to face. If he means to allow perfect freedom of contract in determining the conjugal relations of men and women, he ought to say so, and frankly admit his opposition to the law and custom of all civilised societies. If not, he ought to make very clear how far and on what principle restriction is justified. From the individualistic point of view restraints on free contract in marriage can, I conceive, only be justified in the interests of children ; therefore the discussion in chapter xxi. ought to precede that in chapter xx. But when we come—in chapter xxi.— to consider the mutual rights and duties of children and parents, it becomes evident that we want a different formula of justice to settle the question.

Thus Mr. Spencer states broadly the claim of children, as follows :—

The members of each generation have not only to be supplied by parents with such food, clothing, and shelter as are requisite, but have also to receive from them such aids and opportunities as, by enabling them to exercise their faculties, shall produce in them fitness for adult life. . . . In estimating the relative claims of child and parent, it is inferable that parental sacrifices must not be such as will incapacitate for the full performance of parental duties. Undue sacrifices are eventually to the disadvantage of the offspring, and, by implication, to the disadvantage of the species. To which add that, since the wellbeing and happiness of parents is itself an end which forms part of the general end, there is a further ethical reason why the self-subordination of parents must be kept within moderate limits (§ 338).

And he goes on to recognise the counter-claim of parents :—

Though, as we have seen, the child has a rightful claim to food, clothing, shelter, and other aids to development, yet it has not a right to that self-direction which is the normal accompaniment of self-sustentation. There are two reasons for not admitting this right—the one that exercise of it would be mischievous to itself, and the other that it would imply an ignoring of the claim of parent on child which is the reciprocal of the claim of child on parent. The first is self-evident, and the second scarcely needs exposition. Though here there can be made no such measurement of relative claims as that which the law of equal freedom enables us to make between adults ; yet, if we guide ourselves by that law as well as may be, it results that for sustentation and other aids received there should be given whatever equivalent is possible in the form of obedience and the rendering of small services (§ 339).

All this is sound but vague ; what is surprising is that Mr. Spencer should suppose that we can 'guide ourselves by' the law of equal freedom in determining it. If either claim is put forward as just, we want a different formula of Justice. We have for the former to go to Utilitarianism. For limits for the latter what are we to go to? Some law of fair exchange, or what? And it is surprising that Mr.

Spencer does not recognise the need of such a formula
and the inadequacy of his own.   Who, for instance, is
to determine what 'aids and opportunities' are due to
children—the Parent or the State?   Not the State,
we should infer from § 343, and therefore I suppose
the rightful claim of children is not legal.   But why
not?   If the claim of the child is a right, why is it
not legal?   If it is legal, the State must determine
what education the child shall receive.   All this
wants more explanation.

Turning back to chapter xx. :—Apart from any
question of overriding free contract, let us assume as
regards the relations of husbands and wives that responsibility and power are to be equitably divided.
What is here the principle of equity?   'Nothing more,'
we are told, 'than a compromise varying according
to the circumstances seems here possible.   The dis-
charge of domestic and maternal duties by the wife
may ordinarily be held a fair equivalent for the
earning of an income by the husband' (§ 334).
'Justice appears to dictate' a certain kind of
compromise—but what is the principle of Justice
in this case?   All I can say is that it is certainly
not the Law of Equal Freedom, and this is the
more surprising because it is obvious that the
relative powers and duties of the married might be
settled by free contract; consequently Mr. Spencer's
discussion in §334 wanders quite loose, governed
by conceptions of equity and justice which are not
defined or analysed.   For instance we are told (§ 334,
p. 161) that 'since, speaking generally, man is more

judicially minded than woman, the balance of
authority should incline to the side of the husband.'
Whether this conclusion is sound or not, it seems
clear that it has nothing to do with the law of equal
freedom, and I may add that *prima facie* it is very
like the principle of Justice 'developed from the idea
of inequality' (cf. § 268, p. 39), which leads Aristotle
to conclude that the relation of master and slave is
advantageous and just.

Similarly as regards the brief anticipatory discussion
of the political rights of women and men, in § 336 :—
it is, I think, a sound principle that political rights
should be connected with political burdens ; though it
would, I submit, be hasty to conclude that even under
the present prevalence of militancy, political rights
should be confined to those who are prepared personally to fight, and this Mr. Spencer sees quite clearly
when he is comparing ancient and modern civilisation (§§ 381, 382). But in any case the principle
has nothing to do with the Law of Equal Freedom.
I refer to this point primarily as illustrating the
formal defect just mentioned ; but I may perhaps
add that in my view Mr. Spencer's argument is not so
much erroneous as misleading. If stress is laid on
equality of political rights and burdens, the force of
the argument seems to me undeniable. But his
statement of it would suggest to the reader that it
adequately supports the exclusion of women from the
franchise. Now, considering that on Mr. Spencer's
view the franchise and political rights generally are
means to the end of protecting civil rights, and

that he makes no attempt to show that the civil rights of women do not need protection as much as those of men, or that they can obtain adequate protection otherwise; considering, again, that the duty of compulsory service in the militia is one that no Englishman expects to see enforced in his own case; considering that, if it were enforced, men unfit for service from age or bodily infirmity would be relieved of the obligation (and Mr. Spencer does not suggest that they should be excluded from the franchise); considering that, while this burden remains for long periods purely hypothetical, the actual and palpable burden of paying taxes is performed by women no less than by men : the conclusion which Mr. Spencer does not expressly draw, but which his English readers will commonly understand him to draw—that the question of admitting women to any franchise but the municipal may equitably be adjourned till war has come to an end,—this conclusion, I submit, cannot be sustained by this argument. It would seem more reasonable to conclude that some special burden ought to be laid on women to balance the burden of compulsory service laid on men.

I have spoken of 'Political Rights,' but when we come to chapter xxii. we see that I should have added the qualification 'so-called.' For in chapter xxii. we find that, in Mr. Spencer's view, political rights are like snakes in Ireland—there really are none (§§ 343, 344). Political rights—improperly so-called—are only 'means to the preservation of rights properly so-called.' The structure of government seems to be

determined by a mere consideration of its relation
as means to the end above defined.   Still this is not
quite clear, for Mr. Spencer implies (§ 352) that there
is a 'constitution of the State . . . justified by absolute
ethics'; but he makes no attempt to determine what
it is except by the very vague phrase 'representation
of interests' (§ 351).   While in determining civil
rights, Absolute Ethics intrudes itself too much
into Relative Ethics, in considering constitutional
rights (or claims) the absolute method is almost
entirely abandoned.   For instance the further discussion of the political rights of women, § 353, is
conducted on a purely utilitarian method.

Though into the political discussion that follows I
propose hardly to enter, I may observe that when in
§ 354 we come to 'distribution of State - burdens,'
Equity is again referred to, but there is no attempt
to formulate a principle of Equity—all we can say is
that it must be quite different from the formula of
Justice previously laid down.   We are told that

    . . . nothing more than a rude approximation to a just incidence
of public burdens can be made.
    One conclusion, however, is clear.   State-burdens, however
proportioned among citizens, should be borne by all.   Every
one who receives the benefits which government gives should
pay some share of the costs of government, and should directly
and not indirectly pay it (§ 354.)

Yes, but this is not Equal Freedom, and how are
burdens estimated ?   In fact we may say that
throughout the latter portion of Part IV., both the
need and the absence of some principle of Distributive
Justice, other than any principle of Justice expressly
recognised by Mr. Spencer, are very marked.

The question of Just Distribution occurs again in considering, in chapter xxv., the Duties of the State. Mr. Spencer holds that the 'defence of citizens against one another' is not satisfactorily performed in modern societies, since it is ' the duty of the State to administer justice without cost.' The matter is more difficult than Mr. Spencer recognises. For instance, ought the State to pay for the advice and eloquence of experts in actions at law ? I do not, however, say that the difficulties here are insoluble, but I urge that the principle for distributing burdens cannot be the Law of Equal Freedom.

In respect of State Interference for making railways, etc. (referred to in § 360), Mr. Spencer's treatment is odd; he omits the whole question of compulsory purchase. He seems to assume that the property already belongs entirely to the State ! The ' equitable arrangement' of which he speaks is at any rate not according to the Law of Equal Freedom.

LECTURE X

To go further into Mr. Spencer's discussion of Politics would not be in accordance with my plan, but before proceeding to Part V. I will sum up my objections to Spencerian Justice :—

(a) The Biological basis underrates the effects of 'gregariousness' in the highly developed form in which it is manifested in human society, with the continually increasing implication of interest which industrial progress brings, and the development of natural sympathy.

(b) The definition of Justice is formally bad, because Common Sense—and Mr. Spencer—apply the notion in cases in which the Law of Equal Freedom is, by his treatment, inapplicable. Take, for instance, the case of (1) Compensation due for infringement of equal freedom (e.g. as between those who have private property in land, and the landless). (2) Rights and duties of husbands and wives; of parents and children. (3) Taxation.

(c) Even the fundamental institutions of the existing social order—a Socialistic Jurist might argue

—are not strictly defensible as deductions from the
Law of Equal Freedom ; *e.g.* (1) Marriage, permanent
and monogamic.   (2) Private property in land.   (3)
Bequest and inheritance.

As regards (*a*), Mr. Spencer admits in chapter i. of
Part V. (*Negative Beneficence*), to which I now pass,
that 'the highest form of life, individual and social,
is not achievable under a reign of justice only,' there
'must be joined to it a reign of beneficence' (compare the quotation from *The Data of Ethics* in § 389),
but he thinks that 'Justice and Beneficence are to be
discriminated,' as Justice is of public concern, Beneficence of private concern (§ 390).   For, he says :—

> Beneficence exercised by a society in its corporate capacity,
> must consist in taking away from some persons parts of the pro-
> ducts of their activities, to give to other persons, whose activities
> have not brought them a sufficiency.   If it does this by force it
> interferes with the normal relation between conduct and conse-
> quence, alike in those from whom property is taken and those to
> whom property is given.   Justice, as defined in the foregoing
> pages, is infringed upon.   The principle of harmonious social co-
> operation is disregarded ; and the disregard and infringement, if
> carried far, must bring disasters.

On this I should remark that I do not see how the
argument applies to Negative Beneficence.   Take, for
instance, Restraints on Competition and Free Contract in the next two chapters.   The imposition of
such restraints does not necessarily involve the taking
of A's products to give to B ; but only limitation of
A's activities in B's interest.

Mr. Spencer, taking the old distinction between
what is of public and what of private concern, adds a
second, maintaining that Justice is needful for social
equilibrium, and therefore is of public concern, while

Beneficence is not needful for social equilibrium, and therefore is of private concern. But it is difficult to trace this distinction clearly in the details that he brings forward : in fact, when he comes to discuss these details, his own language throws aside the distinction. This point is of such fundamental importance that I proceed to discuss it somewhat further. Such discussion will, I think, be more profitable than disputation on the numerous practical questions of varying importance on which Mr. Spencer expresses dogmatic opinions in the course of Parts V.-VI. (on *Negative Beneficence* and *Positive Beneficence*), as clearness and consistency of method are what we are specially concerned to aim at. When Berkeley said 'Few think, but all have opinions,' he was unduly depreciatory of the average intelligence. I should rather say that on practical questions most have opinions, and the frequent collisions of opinion lead many to think, but few think systematically, so as to bring their practical reasonings to clear consistency of method. Accordingly, it is this that should be the special aim of the academic student of Ethics and Politics.

Let us then, from this point of view, consider Mr. Spencer's reasoning in chapter ii. on *Restraints* (beneficent) *on Free Competition.*—Here it appears (§ 396) that while an artizan cannot go too far in appropriating by competition the advantage which superiority gives him over his fellow-artizan, and trades-unions are 'unprincipled' in acting against such free competition, an employer may go too far; for instance, he

may ruin competitors by unscrupulous underselling ;
he thus inflicts 'intense evils' which might 'not unfitly
be called commercial murder' ; also he employs ' the
forms of competition . . . to destroy competition ' and
achieve ' a practical monopoly.' And in § 397 we
read as follows :

> Anyone who, by command of great capital or superior
> business capacity, is enabled to beat others who carry on the
> same business, is enjoined by the principle of Negative Benefi-
> cence to restrain his business activities, when his own wants and
> those of his belongings have been abundantly fulfilled.

This conclusion, however, would seem to go beyond
what the premises justify, as what seems injurious is
not the extension of business through cheapness, so far
as cheapness is *bona fide* obtained by economies ; but
the adoption of underselling at unremunerative prices
(cf. § 397, p. 281) in order to injure competitors and
establish a monopoly.   Now, both in the case of
trades-unions establishing monopoly through combination, and employers establishing monopoly by
aggressive combination, industrial freedom, advocated
as leading to the advantages of free competition, in
fact leads to the opposite result.   Why is so important a result, if as bad as Mr. Spencer holds,
not to be prohibited by law ?   Why is it not a
disturbance of social equilibrium, and a breach of
Justice ?

Mr. Spencer's Political Economy seems a little
old-fashioned—*e.g.* he does not seem to see the
fundamental importance of the question as to the
legitimacy of monopoly due to free combination.
This is shown oddly enough in § 404, where he seems

not to disapprove of boycotting, though he dis-
approves of underselling. He says that from boycotting 'no appreciable evil would result if each person
remained not nominally but actually free to join or
not to join the combination.' But how can he know?
Boycotting is a more extreme form of commercial
warfare than underselling. Again, why is moral
coercion in the second degree—coercion to coerce[1]—a
breach of Justice in Mr. Spencer's view? It is only
an exercise of the same freedom of combination. If,
generally, there is no breach of the Law of Equal Freedom in workmen declining to work or trade with a
man they disapprove; why is there a wrong done by
refusing to work or trade with a man who is disapproved on the special ground that he declines to
enter into the combination?

But further: in this chapter (chapter iii. on *Restraints on Free Contract*), Mr. Spencer's inconsistency
becomes manifest in his own use of ethical terms.
As I said before, he seems to throw over his own
distinction. He says that Natural Justice as distinct
from Legal Justice should prevent a landlord from raising the rent on a tenant who has taken a stony and
boggy tract of land on a short lease and reclaimed it. I
do not myself see why Natural Justice does enjoin this,
supposing the terms of the contract understood by the
tenant. We must not complicate the abstract question
by surreptitiously assuming—what may no doubt have
been often the case in fact—that the tenant had a
reasonable expectation, arising from tacit understand-

---

[1] Cf. the Author's *Elements of Politics*, chap. xxviii. § 3.

ing or prevalent custom, that the rent would not be raised ; apart from this, I see no evidence of the failure of Natural Justice. But if we grant Mr. Spencer's view as to what Natural Justice enjoins, why should it not also be Legal Justice—since in chapter viii. of Part IV. we seemed to be told that Legal Justice derives its warrant from Natural Justice. If Justice is in some cases not to be enforced by law, how are we to distinguish the cases in which it ought to be so enforced ?

Mr. Spencer passes to cases such as those of Skye crofters 'in which the making of contracts though nominally free is not actually free,' and calls on the landlord in such cases 'to refrain from actions which the restraints of technically-formulated justice fail to prevent.' But surely this fundamentally important limitation of the notion of Freedom should have been introduced, if at all, in the previous discussion of the Right of Free Contract (§ 315, p. 129). Surely the 'Freedom' of the Law of Equal Freedom ought to be real and actual: if a contract is not in reality free when one of the parties is in extreme need, surely the whole previous deduction needs remodelling. In short, all this tends seriously to weaken the individualistic position taken up in Part IV. For the Rights of Property, Free Exchange, and Free Contract were there exhibited as necessary corollaries from the Law of Equal Freedom ; and as therefore embodying not merely 'legal' or 'technical' Justice, but Justice pure and simple. The absolute duty of Governments to enforce these rights rigidly, even when their enforce-

ment fails to realise Natural Justice, requires a kind
of proof which Mr. Spencer's line of reasoning does
not furnish.

Another, even more startling, qualification of the
notion of a contract is still more strangely illustrated
by the following case :—

a contractor . . . has undertaken an extensive work on terms
which, to all appearance, will leave him only a fair remuneration,
making due allowance for ordinary contingencies—say a heavy
railway cutting, or a tunnel a mile or two long.   No one sus-
pected when the contract was made, that in the hill to be
tunnelled there existed a vast intrusion of trap.   But now
where the contractor expected to meet with earth to be ex-
cavated he finds rock to be blasted.   What shall be done ?
Unless he is a man of large capital, strict enforcement of the
contract will ruin him ; and even if wealthy he will do the work
at a great loss instead of at a profit.   It may be said that even
justice, considered not as legally formulated but as reasonably
interpreted, implies that there should be a mitigation of the
terms, since the intention of the contract was to make an exchange of benefits ; and still more is mitigation of the terms
required by negative beneficence—by abstention from that course
which the law would allow.   But clearly it is only where a
disastrous contingency is of a kind greatly exceeding reasonable
anticipation, that negative beneficence may properly come into
play (§ 402).

Ought we then not to enforce any contracts that turn
out to be highly disadvantageous to one of the parties ?

Chapters iv.-vii. may be passed lightly over.   I
observe that, in the Preface to his second volume, Mr.
Spencer says with regard to Parts V. and VI. generally that they 'fall short of expectation.'   'The Doctrine of Evolution,' he explains, 'has not furnished
guidance to the extent I had hoped.   Most of the conclusions, drawn empirically, are such as right feelings,
enlightened by cultivated intelligence, have already
sufficed to establish.'   Certainly, the chapters in Part

V. on *Restraints on Undeserved Payments*—in which tips to guards and extra sixpences to cabmen are reproved at length—and on *Restraints on Displays of Ability*—in which we are warned not to beat a father at chess when his son is looking on, or convict an interlocutor of bad logic in the presence of his *fiancée*—might have been composed by the most empirical of Benthamites.   So in chapter vi.—*Restraints on Blame*—amid the sensible talk on the moderation with which even deserved blame should be applied to children, servants, etc., one misses such discussions of *media axiomata* as Mill's on social pressure in his *Liberty*.   It is almost as if Mr. Spencer had sought out the trivialities.   Similarly in chapter vii.—*Restraints on Praise*—where by the way he mixes up the question of insincere praise with that of praise injurious as tending to foster vanity and egotism. Surely the propriety of expressions of gratitude for bad music and of testimonials to persons who have only done their duty might be left to the daily paragraphist.

I pass now to Part VI. (*Positive Beneficence*), where again we have for the most part Utilitarianism empirical to triviality; for instance, in the chapters on Marital, Parental and Filial Beneficence, and in those which discuss the positive duties of 'aiding the sick and the injured,' and giving 'pecuniary aid to relatives and friends,' Mr. Spencer's counsels, judicious for the most part, are usually courageously commonplace.   He tells us that when a man in business thinks of asking a brother to lend him money, ' there may fitly be hesitation on both sides ' ; and suggests that the brother who hesitates to lend may feel that he is taking a 'wise forethought' for the welfare of a brother disposed to borrow, by sparing him the anxiety that the debt would cause. Perhaps it would be difficult for philosophy to illuminate further this delicate problem; but certainly one hardly required to have surveyed the process of the world from the nebula to the nineteenth century, in order to attain this degree of insight into fraternal duty.

The chapter on the *Relief of the Poor* is at any rate more original. It is undoubtedly true of Positive Beneficence—what Mr. Spencer affirms of Beneficence generally—that it, when 'exercised by a society in its corporate capacity, must consist in taking away from some persons . . . products of their activities, to give to' others. No doubt, as Mr. Spencer urges, if carried too far it will bring disaster; but it does not therefore follow that if carefully limited, it may not do more good than harm. Mr. Spencer's attack on Poor-Relief, whether State-paid or organised by charitable associations, and his proposal to substitute the old method of relief by individuals, seem to me wild, in the present state of mobility of labour. However, the point is that this is a detail of Utilitarian politics. He does indeed refer to the Evolutional Formula and the principle of the Survival of the Fittest, but he does not consider the organism struggling for existence to be a *Society; e.g.* in speaking in § 458 of the survival of the fittest he only considers the effect of the struggle on individual human beings. It is a defect in Mr. Spencer's argument that he does not more

distinctly recognise the difficulty and the complication
introduced into his reasonings by the double point of
view.   Perhaps he might say that a Society in which
the survival of the fittest individuals is most rigorously
effected, is also as a Society fittest to survive ; but it is
difficult for him to maintain this, after admitting (§ 389)
that a society under the reign of justice does not achieve
'the highest form of life.'   This once being admitted,
Evolution cannot afterwards be simply used as a con-
clusive argument against public or organised poor-
relief ; we have to fall back on empirical Utilitarianism.   As regards poor-relief practically, Mr.
Spencer is, I think, uninformed—he does not seem to
know anything of the Charity Organisation Society,
or of the need of it.   His great concern is that
paupers should not propagate ; but this certainly
would not be prevented if left to private almsgiving,
whereas the workhouse and the Charity Organisation
Society might do something to prevent it.

The other chapters in *Positive Beneficence* are
mostly trivial though sometimes entertaining—as in
the chapter on *Social Beneficence,* where the philosopher seriously enjoins resistance to absurd fashions
such as London evening parties, ' elaborately-orna-
mented coal-scuttles,' and ' silver butter-knives.'   Let
me here end in hearty sympathy with the distinguished
thinker whom I have so long been criticising, and
wish him all success in his crusade against the follies
of the fashionable world.   I fear, however, that he will
not persuade any large part of that world to follow him
through the two volumes of *The Principles of Ethics.*

ON MARTINEAU'S
TYPES OF ETHICAL THEORY, PART II.
(INTRODUCTION AND BOOK I.)

LECTURE I

INTRODUCTION

MARTINEAU'S arrangement and treatment of his subject has certain peculiarities, which I must briefly explain before I enter upon a discussion of his views. He includes in his two volumes a critical account of the doctrines of certain other writers on Ethics, along with an exposition and defence of his own. The plan is peculiar, but there is something to be said for it, as a method of enabling the reader to form a clear and precise view of ethical truth as Martineau sees it; since one understands more thoroughly what a man thinks and why he thinks it, when one understands clearly why he rejects the various opposed views which other minds have found acceptable. In fact, my present course of Lectures is framed on substantially the same principle : it appeared to me that having expounded my own system in my book, what I could further do in the way of making it clear would be best done in the form of criticism on the views of others.

It might, however, have been expected that, if this plan were adopted, Martineau's own system would have been given either at the beginning—so that the

reader, before proceeding to the critical exposition of
any other doctrines, might have clearly before his
mind the point of view from which the criticisms
were made ; or at the end—so that the reader might
be led through various forms of error to the truth.
For error in philosophy, or at least error that is or
has been widely accepted, is never error pure and
simple, but contains an element of the truth exaggerated and distorted by neglect of other elements ;
so that an examination of these one-sided and partial
views is a fitting preparation for the completer and
more balanced view which sums up the elements of
truth contained in errors that are or have been current.
But Martineau has adopted a different course from
either : he has placed in the first volume a critical
exposition of certain leading thinkers—chiefly Plato,
Spinoza, and Comte—which belong to European but
not to English thought.   Then the first half of his
second volume is occupied with his own system; and
lastly there follows a discussion of the leading English
modes of ethical thought, under three heads :—
Hedonist Ethics, Dianoetic Ethics, and *Æsthetic
Ethics*.

The explanation is that Martineau regards ethics
as properly psychological, based on the study of the
moral consciousness, as each individual finds it by introspection.   Now among erroneous methods or systems
of ethics some, in his view, are erroneous because
they are ' unpsychological ' — *i.e.* because instead
of beginning with the study of the human mind or
soul, as known to each thinker introspectively, they

begin with the study of Nature and God, and then carry the conceptions they derive from these into the study of the human mind—' explain the human mind by their analogy and expect in it a mere extension of their being.' One chief objection to this latter procedure is that it leads to a denial or imperfect recognition of freedom and of moral responsibility. Others again are erroneous because they are, in his phrase, 'heteropsychological,' instead of 'idiopsychological '—*i.e.* instead of accepting 'the story' that the moral consciousness 'tells of itself,' they try to 'evolve the moral from the unmoral phenomena of our nature,' and explain away 'moral differences' into 'sensational,' 'intellectual,' or 'æsthetic differences.' And he considers that while the 'unpsychological' systems are most properly treated before his own, the 'heteropsychological' are most properly treated after. The reasons for either order I will try briefly to make clear.

First, I should explain that among these unpsychological methods of ethics some are 'metaphysical,' others 'physical.' The metaphysical attempt to penetrate to the eternal ground and essence of the Universe, and then descending into the human world, treat human virtue as having a community of essence with this eternal reality, a 'blossoming in the consciousness of man of the real root of the eternal universe.' Such metaphysical methods exclude — no less than the physical — any proper notion of responsibility : moral evil becomes merely natural evil, in the form of ugliness and unreason.

And for the ethical notion of freedom is substituted
the notion of spontaneity—the spontaneous energy of
eternal thought manifesting itself in connexion with
the human organism.   Such metaphysical methods
may be further divided into those that regard the
eternal ground of the Universe as Transcendent of
the world of experience, and those that regard it as
Immanent in that world.   Of the former, the Transcendental, Martineau selects Plato as the best developed example ; of the latter, the Immanental, he
takes Spinoza as the type.

To both of these metaphysical doctrines of ethics
'stands opposed (still within the unpsychological circle)
the *physical*; which descends into human life from
the *phenomenal* instead of the *real* side of the world ';
and 'resolving everything' knowable 'into phenomena,
. . . recognises in man' nothing but a product of this
phenomenal world, absolutely subject to its laws
throughout his being ; and refers his seeming activity
back into prior conditions not inherent.   Of this
manner of thought Martineau takes Comte as a type.
You will see from this selection that so-called unpsychological theories are not things of the past : in
fact both the metaphysical and physical are power-
fully represented at the present time ; since the metaphysical, Martineau says, survives in the school of
Hegel.   At the same time Martineau regards the
development of psychological ethics as '*altogether
peculiar to Christendom*'; and probably this view of
the earlier stages of development as essentially unpsychological has led him to treat them first in his

book. I think myself that it is misleading to call the
Ethics of Plato 'unpsychological,' since—among other
things—his doctrine of the virtues is based on psychological analysis, though I should agree that the prominence of the notion of the Ego and the question of
Free Will is characteristic of modern thought. Comte
may be fairly called 'unpsychological' among modern
writers, since he discards the introspective method.
But it is to be observed that the general description
which Martineau gives of that division of his unpsychological group which he calls 'physical,' does
not necessarily exclude the fullest application of the
introspective method and of empirical psychology.
This general description is that it examines the
phenomena of the human mind as a part of the
whole aggregate of natural phenomena, and no less
subject to unvarying laws than any other part. But
this view is quite compatible with the full acceptance of the introspective method—as in the case of
Spencer.

This Martineau sees in the Introduction to the
second volume,[1] though he does not recognise it in
the Introduction to his first volume, and it is an
awkward fact for his classification. Even if we exclude
such 'dualistic' methods as that of Spencer, I think it

[1] 'As the process which they [Darwin and Spencer] describe is, in their
view, only the latest section of a development that indefinitely preceded all
conscious life, their theory would seem to fall, no less than Comte's, under
the category of *Physical* Systems, and so to demand our next attention. But
it differs from the unpsychological schemes in this : that, though it links the
moral phenomena to the physical in one unbroken chain of causality, it
allows that we have *internal* cognisance of the one, and external of the other ;
so that, while Nature is *monistic*, our knowledge of it is *dualistic* ' (*Types of
Ethical Theory*, 2nd edition, vol. ii. p. 3).

an exaggeration to put forward Spinoza and Comte as
good types of the metaphysical and physical methods
in current philosophy, as Martineau does. If, he
says, the Ego is determined into existence from God,
'we take the pantheistic track, never far from Spinoza ;
if from Nature, we take the pamphysical, within sight
of Comte' (*Types of Ethical Theory*, 2nd edition,
vol. ii. p. 3). It is a long way from Spinoza to Hegel,
and a long way from Comte to current Materialism.
The truth is that Martineau makes his distinction
turn too much on Free Will. Still I agree that the
clear recognition of Introspective Psychology as a distinct study, and the attempt to base ethics on it as so
recognised, does belong to modern thought, and so far
may justify his order, as regards the priority of the
Unpsychological systems.

The justification of the second point—the priority
of the Idiopsychological over the Heteropsychological systems—he gives on pp. 16, 17 [1] :—

Entering on this process, we might (he says) follow either
of two methods. We might first review the several attempts to
evolve the moral from the unmoral phenomena of our nature ;
prepared either to rest in any one of them that may really fulfil
its promise ; or, in case they should all fail, to invite the conscience itself to declare *its own psychology*. Or, we might invert
this order : having first defined the inner facts of conscience
itself, with the best precision we can attain, we might then compare with the *Idiopsychological Ethics*, so obtained, the several
attempts to find the phenomena under *other categories*, by advocates of this or that scheme of *Heteropsychological Ethics*. The
latter arrangement has the decisive advantage of compelling us,
at the outset, to visit the moral consciousness in its own home,
to look it full in the face, and take distinct notes of the story it
tells of itself. And not till we have thus gained a definite

[1] Unless otherwise stated, references are to *Types of Ethical Theory*, vol.
ii. 2nd edition, 1886.

intimacy with its real contents, can we have any just measure of aberration by which to try the claims of professed equivalents. I propose, therefore, to hear, in the first instance, what the Moral Sentiment has to say of its own experience ; and then, to let other faculties advance each its special pretensions to be the original patentee and source of supply.

I agree broadly with Martineau's view—indicated in his term 'idiopsychological'—that we must first have a clear and full view of the existing moral consciousness, before we can judge of the value and importance of any 'psychological' theory that professes to explain it. I also agree with what he says (p. 4) of the psychogony of evolutionists, which, as he observes,

usually begins with the psychological preconception that, in the individual, the ethical sentiments are derivative from other feelings and ideas, *e.g.* of sympathy, of beauty, of self-regard, so as to be resolvable into a generic term ; and is then extended, by help of some law of heredity, to the inward life of parents and ancestors, and turned out complete in the form of a hypothetical psychology for the race or a catena of races. How are we *to test* this imagined history ? One condition is at all events indispensable : we must be sure of the ultimate phenomena, viz. the existing moral consciousness, of which this story undertakes to render account ; to pronounce upon the adequacy of the cause, we must accurately estimate the effect. Else the causality, however truly put on record, may give account of the wrong thing. Since, therefore, we must carry with us a clear and correct insight into the contents of our present moral affections and beliefs, I shall not take up the consideration of the evolution doctrine till we have scrutinised the phenomena to be evolved.

But at the very outset I have to notice that what appears to me an unwarranted assumption underlies Martineau's whole procedure. He professes to give first the 'story' that the moral consciousness 'tells of itself,' or 'what the Moral Sentiment has to say of its own experience.' And he appears gener-

ally to entertain no doubt that there is one and the
same 'story' to be told in all cases; that if the
same question be definitely put to the moral consciousness of any number of different individuals,
they will definitely return the same answer as his
own.   I think this an unwarranted assumption; and
I find it necessary to note this at the outset as
regards the first postulate which he lays down.
' Nothing (he. says) can be *binding* to us that
is not higher than we; and to speak of *one part of
self imposing obligation on another part*,—of one
impulse or affection playing, as it were, *the god* to
another,—is to trifle with the real significance of the
sentiments that speak within us' (p. 5).   As regards
this, the 'stories' that the consciousnesses of different
persons tell appear to me to be fundamentally different.
To make this clear I will begin by stating the
amount of my own agreement with Martineau.   I
agree that 'the broad fact' of the moral consciousness
is that 'we have an irresistible tendency . . . to pass
judgments of right and wrong'; and that when I
pass such judgments on my own conduct 'I speak of
my Duty'—a word which 'expresses the sense we have
of a *debt* which . . . we are *bound* or *obliged* [to pay].'
This sense of obligation implies, in my view, a conflict between the moral judgment and some impulse
prompting us to conduct disapproved by our moral
judgment.   I also agree that a moral judgment
affirms objective truth, valid not merely for the
individual that affirms it, but for all similar persons
in similar circumstances; *e.g.* the axiom of prudence

if true at all, is true not only for me.   In this sense
I agree with Martineau when he says :—

Conscience does not *frame* the law, it simply *reveals* the law,
that holds us; and to make everything of the *disclosure*, and
nothing of the *thing disclosed*, is to affirm and to deny the revelation in the same breath.   It is an inversion of moral truth to
say, for instance, that honour is higher than appetite, *because* we
feel it so; we feel it to be so, because it *is* so.   This '*is*' we
know to be not contingent on our apprehension, not to arise
from our constitution of faculty, but to be a reality irrespective
of us, in adaptation to which our nature is constituted, and for
recognition of which the faculty is given (p. 5).

But Martineau affirms more than this.   In his
view the idea of Duty necessarily implies the recognition of ' another Person ' who has authority over
us.   This he means to imply in a passage on p. 5,
which must be interpreted by pp. 104, 105.   He
says on p. 5 :—

It is further necessary that our psychology should be dualistic
in its results, recognising, as in its doctrine of perception, so in
its doctrine of conscience, both a *Self* and an *other than Self.*   In
perception, it is *Self and Nature;* in morals, it is *Self and God,*
that stand face to face.

And on pp. 104, 105, we read :—

Suppose the case of one lone man in an atheistic world ; could
there really exist any 'authority' of higher over lower within
the enclosure of his detached personality?   I cannot conceive
it; and did he, under such conditions, feel such a thing, he
would then, I should say, feel a delusion, and have his consciousness adjusted to the wrong universe.   For surely, if the sense
of authority means anything, it means the discernment of something *higher than we,* having claims on our *self,*—therefore no
mere part of it ; . . . the predicate 'higher than I' takes me yet a
step beyond ; for what am I ?   A *person:* 'higher' than whom
no '*thing*' assuredly,—no mere *phenomenon,*—can be ; but only
another Person, greater and higher and of deeper insight. . . .
over a free and living person nothing short of a free and living
person can have higher authority.

The dictates of conscience, Martineau holds, are unmeaning unless we give them a Theistic interpretation. Now I quite admit that a Christian Theist must necessarily conceive of the dictates of conscience as Divine commands ; but I think it rash and unwarrantable in him to affirm that they cannot be regarded as authoritative unless they are so conceived. To me, indeed, it is inconceivable that the authoritativeness or bindingness of moral rules should depend essentially on the fact that they emanate from 'another Person.' Martineau himself admits — or I should rather say emphatically declares — that it is not a Person regarded apart from moral attributes that can be conceived as the source of the authority of which we are speaking; it is, he says, 'an inward rule of Right which directs the action of His [God's] power . . . which first elevates into 'Authority' what else would only operate as a necessity or a bribe' (p. 113). If then moral rules, when conceived as Divine commands, are thought to have authority not because they emanate from an Omnipotent Person, but only because they emanate from a person who wills in accordance with a rule of right, I cannot conceive how they should lose this authority even if the 'other person' is eliminated altogether, provided that the 'rule of right' is left. I am not now arguing whether a true philosophical conception of the rule of right would not recognise that the cognition of such a rule as a thought valid for all minds, involves the recognition of a Thinker —an eternal and universal subject of this and all

other thought. That is a question of Rational
Theology rather than Ethics. It is not denied that
there are many minds for whom this implication is
necessary. And what I am now arguing is that the
'authoritativeness' or 'obligatoriness' of the rule
is not necessarily connected with this implication in
Truth of a Thinker who thinks what is true.

I may perhaps make this clearer by referring to
an analogy which Martineau draws between mathematical and moral truth.

There is (he says) as much ground, or as little, for trusting to
the report of our moral faculty as for believing our intellect
respecting the relations of number and dimension. Whatever
be the 'authority' of Reason respecting the true, the same is
the 'authority' of Conscience respecting the right and good
(p. 114).

Now I presume that Martineau does not maintain that
the authority of Reason respecting the relations of
number and dimension cannot 'really exist' for an
atheistic mathematician. And he would not deny
that there have been atheistic mathematicians: whether
or not it is true that Laplace answered Napoleon's
question by saying that he had no 'besoin de l'hypo-
thèse de Dieu' in his system of the physical universe, at any rate the utterance would have probably
expressed his conviction. But if Martineau does
not deny that the 'authority of Reason' respecting
relations of quantity may exist for the atheistic
mathematician, I think he is bound, in consistency,
to admit that the 'authority of Conscience respecting
the right' may similarly exist for the atheistic
moralist.

I have accepted, for the sake of argument, Martineau's distinction between 'Reason' and 'Conscience.' But, to prevent misunderstanding, I ought to explain that, in my view, the 'authority of Conscience' is the authority of Reason in its application to practice : 'authority' or 'obligation,' in my view, expresses the relation that we recognise on reflection between a judgment as to what ought to be willed by us and a non-rational impulse prompting in a direction opposed to this judgment. I can imagine no other kind of ultimate authority than this. If rules are binding as Divine it is, in my view, because Reason is an essential attribute of Divinity. With this important difference, I accept Martineau's view of psychological assumptions, understanding objectivity here to import the universal validity of all truth, but not necessarily the existence of another person. I do not wish to exclude the theological conception of Ethics, but I do not think it ought to be imposed as necessary.

Martineau proceeds to argue the possibility of introspection disclosing facts and laws, and, in Hamilton's manner, lays down the axiom that 'we must accept as veracious the immediate depositions of our own faculties, and that the postulates, without which the mind cannot exert its activity at all, possess the highest certainty.' What we have to do is to 'state accurately the essence of the moral sentiments and find the propositions they assume.' My view is somewhat different.[1] I accept in-

---

[1] Compare chap. xi. of Book III. of *Methods of Ethics*.

tuitions (self-evident propositions) as veracious so far as they can be freed from inconsistency and conflict; also propositions logically implied in these —but not as quite equally certain, as the process of educing the implication is one liable to error. Martineau goes on (p. 9) to raise a difficulty. He says :—

Suppose that the postulates of one faculty should turn out contradictory to those of another ; what becomes of the reliance due to both ? If, *e.g.*, external observation should imply or exhibit *succession without causality ;* and if the inner exercise of will should enforce belief in causality with or without succession ; or, if the one should teach universal necessity, and the other human freedom ; which has claim to our assent ? I reply, each is to be dictator *in its own sphere*, and no further ;—perception, among the objects of sense, — conscience, as to the conditions of duty ; and for this plain reason, that neither has any jurisdiction or insight with regard to the realm of the other. Moral objects cannot be tasted, seen, or heard ; nor are sapid, visible, audible objects appreciated by the moral sense. And hence it will turn out that the contradictions alleged between two separate faculties are only apparent: the postulates will really be distinct and never meet ; the opposition will be merely negative, amounting not to a confutation, but to simple absence of evidence.

I agree with Martineau that so far as the spheres of different faculties really are distinct, the postulates of one need not harmonise with those of another ; but the case is different where two lines of thought lead to conclusions that contradict each other, and this seems the case with Free Will as understood by Martineau ; universal necessity does leave no room for human freedom. So far as this is so, I can only accept the division of spheres as a provisional practical solution.

In speaking of 'faculties' Martineau, as he

explains, does not mean 'separate agents.' He says (p. 13) :—

Faculties (if the word be widened so as to cover the suscepti-bilities too) are distinct *functions* of one and the same organised *Self* or *Person :* active, if modes of the undivided personality ; *passive*, if modes of the divided sensory organisation : giving us in the latter case, what I have called *susceptibility ;* in the former, *faculty* in the narrower and exacter meaning. But in all instances, the proper *subject*, that which acts or is acted on, is not the faculty or the organ, but the *Unitary Ego*. This Ego *knows ;* the Ego *wills ;* the Ego *feels ;* three functions, of which the last alone is passive. For the distinction of these functions it is not necessary that they should never go together ; and they are in fact usually, though not inflexibly, concomitant.

With this I agree, except that I hold that 'feeling' must be attributed to the mind and not merely to the body, as 'sensory organisation' seems to imply. But in my view the division between Conscience and Perception does not correspond to the divisions between Knowing, Feeling, Willing ; if there is moral truth it belongs to the intellect to know it, as much as to know physical truth. Hence pp. 15, 16 seem to me misleading. I do not say that the intellect which knows moral truth is 'only the scientific Understanding,' and that the 'right and the wrong' are 'simply the true and the false, and should be regarded with no dissimilar affection.' To know ethical truth and not to desire and will to act in accordance with it, implies defect in the mind that thus knows ; but this is quite consistent with the view that Conscience is essentially Intellect or Reason applied to Practice, which Martineau's language ignores and obscures.

LECTURE II

FUNDAMENTAL ETHICAL FACT

I now pass to the 'Fundamental Ethical Fact' (omitting the theological implications which I have already dealt with). This is :

that, distinctively as men, we have an irresistible tendency to *approve and disapprove*, to pass judgments of right and wrong. Wherever approbation falls, there we cannot help recognising *merit ;* wherever disapprobation, *demerit.* To the former we are impelled to assign honour and such external good as may express our sympathy, and to feel that no less than this is due : to the latter we award disgrace and such external ill as may mark our antipathy, with the consciousness that we are not only entitled but constrained to this infliction (p. 18).

He goes on to explain that the objects on which our moral judgment directs itself are '*persons* exclusively, and not *things*' (p. 21).

The approbation or disapprobation which we feel towards human actions is directed upon them as *personal phenomena ;* and if this condition failed, would disappear, though they might still as natural causes be instrumental in producing much good or ill (p. 23). . . . It follows that what we judge is always the *inner spring* of an action as distinguished from its outward operation (p. 24).

Hence he infers that the principle of moral judgment is directly opposed to the maxim, that the only value of good affections is for the production of good actions :—a maxim which is a just rebuke to idle and barren good affections as compared with the healthy and fruitful, but which becomes monstrously false when it demands not only inward creative

329

energy, but outward opportunity and success, and treats with
slight even an intense fidelity and love, because its field of life is
small, and its harvest for the world is scanty. Instead of
measuring the worth of goodness by the scale of its external
benefits, our rule requires that we attach no *moral value* to these
benefits, except as signs and exponents of the goodness whence
they spring; and graduate our approval by the purity of the
source, not by the magnitude of the result. Here, therefore, we
touch upon an essential distinction between the Christian and
the Utilitarian ethics; and confidently claim for the former the
verdict of our moral consciousness (p. 26).

And there does appear at first sight to be a
fundamental difference between Utilitarianism and
Martineau. And perhaps we may ultimately conclude
that there is such a difference ; but on examination it
will, I think, be found to be at any rate less than
appears at first sight. I proceed now to note that
there are, in my view, two distinguishable forms of
moral judgments on conduct with corresponding
sentiments :—those in which Ought, Right, or Duty
are used, and those in which Goodness or Badness are
predicated. The former are what I call Jural, the
latter Æsthetic. The notions of Right and Wrong,
and the corresponding sentiments, in the strictly
ethical sense seem to me peculiar to actions viewed on
their psychical side—to volitions. Good and Bad are
wider : as to these I think that we apply the notions,
with corresponding or at least cognate sentiments, to
other things besides volitions or persons willing. Still
here, too, I think we can distinguish what I should call
'strictly moral' approbation, and specific accompanying sentiments, as appropriate to volitions, and to
volitions only ; so far I agree with Martineau. And
we find that he, like all other writers on questions

of practice, has to use the two pairs of terms—as in the passages above quoted from pp. 18, 23, and 26.

But he seems (p. 23) to regard the judgment of good and ill as non-ethical.   I cannot agree with this view, and it does not seem to me in harmony with Common Sense.   Good, in my view, is what it is reasonable to seek to keep, or aim at getting ; and Evil is what it is reasonable to seek to get rid of and avoid.   Or if it be said that Good is pleasure or the pleasant, the same relation to volition and practice comes in when we define pleasure. [1]   There is of course much good—e.g. the advantages of external nature unlaboured by man —which comes without our having done anything to gain it ; often without its having been in our power to do anything.   And similarly with evil — e.g. influenza.   Still, in calling such things good and evil it is none the less implied that they are the kind of things which we ought as rational and sentient beings to desire and aim at, or try to avoid, for ourselves or for others.   The Stoic view, that reason is its own sole good, would be true if this were not so.   The judgment of good and ill is therefore either directly or indirectly ethical.   And this is admitted by Common Sense.   In the recognition of the virtues of Prudence and Benevolence it is allowed to be (1) right and reasonable (and even virtuous if under strong temptation) that a man should prefer greater to lesser good in his own case, and (2) virtuous to promote good generally for others—for men, for the living universe.   And the only difference between

---

[1] Cf. *Methods of Ethics*, Book I. chap. iv., and Book II. chap. ii.

Common Sense and Utilitarianism as regards the outward act is, that in the view of Common Sense these
rules are but rules among others, while in the view
of Utilitarianism, the rule of promoting the greatest
good is supreme, and the highest good is interpreted
as happiness.   I conceive therefore, that there is
nothing inconsistent with Utilitarianism in holding
that the specific moral judgment of approbation, and
the accompanying sentiment, are properly directed to
human volitions only, while still holding that the
ultimate criterion of right volitions is that they
should be such as tend to produce in the greatest
degree consequences of a certain kind — namely,
general happiness.

But it may be said :—Suppose a worse intention
would produce a better result, would you then
approve it more ?   If I were convinced that this was
the case, I certainly should.   Probably there is
here a real disagreement between Martineau's view
and mine.   But it is only very rarely that the
question can practically arise.[1]   It cannot be directly
a question for me, whether I should intend to do what
is right or intend to do what would produce the best
result.   But in the case of another man I may judge
that—owing to intellectual defect—if he intends to
do what is right he will do more harm than if he has
what is subjectively a worse intention.   Whately
declared that it would be a ' consolation to him on his
death-bed that he never gave a halfpenny to a beggar
in the street.'   The intention to do this would be

---

[1] Cf. *Methods of Ethics*, Book III. chap. i. § 3, p. 207.

wrong in Whately or in me, but is doubtless subjectively right in most of those who give the half-
pence.

How deal then with the problem ?   I would first
break up the simple notion of approbation by means
of the distinction between Subjective and Objective.
The intention of the indiscriminating almsgiver is
subjectively right but objectively wrong.   Suppose,
however, that Martineau or my reader should press
me with the question : Which do you prefer, subjective or objective rightness, in another ?   I answer :
So far as this is a practical question, it depends
for a Utilitarian upon the magnitude of the evil that
may be produced by an act that is subjectively right.
As I have said, it is only rarely that it becomes a
practical question ; never in a man's own case ; and
usually what one has to do in dealing with the case
of another whose intention is subjectively right and
objectively wrong, is to convert him to a better view
of his duty.   If this fails, it may become a question whether appeal should not be made to lower
motives.[1]

It may be said :—Why do you as a Utilitarian,
in this case value rectitude of intention at all, its
effects being admittedly bad ?   The answer (which Martineau certainly overlooks) is that not *all* the effect is
bad here, from the Utilitarian point of view—the effect
on the agent's character is not so ; it is ordinarily
conducive to the general happiness that he should
have a habit of intending to do what he thinks right.

---

[1] Cf. *Methods of Ethics*, note 1, p. 208.

On this distinction of Subjective and Objective
Martineau remarks :—

Professor Sidgwick well says that a man who makes no
failure *here* is 'right' '*in another sense*' from that in which the
epithet was allowed to the simply conscientious man; but seems
to me hardly to appreciate the whole difference.   Are right and
wrong '*judgments*' no less ethical acts than right and wrong intentions?   Or are they not, when initiated by the same intention,
intellectual instead of *moral*?   If guilt is incurred by an erroneous
computation of conduct, why not by a faulty column of statistics
or a mistaken prophecy of market prices?   Surely the word
right has an obvious ambiguity, and denotes now the ethically
good, and now the intellectually *true*.   In the phrase 'Subjective
right' it has the former meaning; in the phrase 'Objective
right' the latter.   To treat it as covering the same quality in
both is to make it a fruitful source of illusions.   To guard
against these, the *whole moral essence* of voluntary conduct must
be planted in its inner spring, while its outward history must be
judged by the canons of *rationality* (pp. 55, 56).

My answer is (1) that I am not aware of having
in any way slurred over the fundamental importance
of the difference between subjective and objective
rightness; (2) that Martineau's language certainly
overlooks the fact that our common moral sentiments towards, say, a fanatic who commits crimes
are very different from our sentiments towards, say,
a paradoxer who squares the circle.   Our sentiment
towards the former is, in fact, a sentiment of moral
aversion ; and though people whose intellectual
development is such that they can direct this sentiment exclusively on the act, while combining with
it a respectful recognition of the agent's rectitude of
purpose—though these ought, I admit, to make this
distinction, I do not think that a plain man does do
this or can do it.   It is still more clear to common
sense that bad acts may be done from the best con-

ceivable motives; indeed we are all familiar with historical examples of men prompted by religion, patriotism, or philanthropy to acts that have excited most general and intense moral disapprobation. When we contemplate Torquemada torturing a heretic for the eternal good of souls, Ravaillac assassinating a monarch in the cause of God and his Church, a Nihilist murdering a number of innocent persons in order to benefit his country by the destruction of an emperor, a pastor poisoning his congregation in the sacramental wine in the hope of securing their eternal happiness,—we recognise that such acts are (so far as we know) not only subjectively right, but done from the very highest motives; still common sense does not therefore hesitate to pronounce them profoundly bad. Does Martineau wish that these acts should cease to be regarded with moral aversion?

In this discussion, in speaking of the object of approbation, I have said 'volition' and 'intention,' not 'spring' or 'affection,' and Martineau also says :—

We only judge our volitions. This distinction is one of the greatest importance in many relations; but for the present we have to do with it in only one. We need not decide whether Socrates is right in rating the self-possessed and open-eyed faculties of Reason and Conscience as the crowning glory of our nature; or whether Carlyle is justified in setting above them the workings of 'unconscious' genius. Whatever be their relative place, the fact remains, that the *moral life* dwells exclusively in the *voluntary sphere*' (pp. 34, 35).

At the same time (pp. 25, 26) he speaks of 'affections' as the object of approbation.—The explanation is that while Martineau holds that what we approve is always voluntary choice, he also holds that it is always choice between motives.

I do not, however, think that in this part of his discussion it has always been present to Martineau's mind what the exact issue is between him and such opponents as myself. I find that in discussing this question he, on the one hand, labours needlessly a point not likely to be disputed; and, on the other hand, confuses or slurs over the distinction which I regard as fundamentally important. We shall all, I conceive, agree that moral approbation, strictly taken,[1] relates to what Martineau loosely calls the 'inner spring' or 'principle' of an action — *i.e.* that it relates to the mental or psychical element of the complex fact which we call action; as distinct from the muscular movement that follows the psychical volition, or any external consequences of this movement considered as external and not as foreseen by the agent. Further, I agree with Martineau in defining the object of the common moral judgment as volition or choice of some kind. Our difference begins when we ask what the object is which is willed or chosen. In Martineau's view the choice is always between particular impulses to action—whether 'propensions,' 'passions,' 'affections,' or 'sentiments'; in my view it is, in the largest and most important class of cases, among different sets of foreseen external effects, all of which are con-

---

[1] I say 'strictly taken,' because in a wider sense of the terms we 'approve' or 'disapprove' of a human being and his actions without distinguishing between their voluntary and involuntary elements; just as, in Martineau's words, we 'approve a house' or 'condemn a ship,' from a consideration of its fitness or unfitness for some accepted end.

ceived to be within the power of the agent. That
Martineau has not clearly seen the point at issue
may, I think, be inferred from the language (compare
pages 129, 130) in which he criticises my own procedure. He says that I, among others, 'by no
means call in question the general principle that
moral worth or defect is to be estimated by the
inward *affection or intention* whence actions flow';
and implies that I have thereby 'admitted the necessity' of 'enumerating' and 'classifying' motives or
impulses to action, though I afterwards 'run away
from the work as unmanageable and superfluous.'
But it is plain that if I am right in regarding the
choice of right outward effect as being, in the most
important cases, the primary object of ordinary moral
judgment, my primary business is to enumerate and
classify, not the propensions or passions that prompt
to choice, but the outward effects that ought to be
chosen and intended. It is always the choice or
intention, and not its actual result, that is approved
or disapproved; but the differences of choice or intention, on which the moral judgment turns, can only
be conceived as differences in the objects chosen;
and can therefore, on my view, only be sought in
that 'field of external effects of action' which Martineau would relegate to a separate and subsequent investigation.

This is an important point that Martineau has
not dealt with, and, in fact, his ethico-psychological
theory precludes his dealing with it; because, as we
saw, he holds that if the same question be definitely

put to the moral consciousness of any number of different individuals, they will return definitely the same answer as his own.   He holds that all impulses and incentives to action are capable of being arranged in a series in order of merit, and are so arranged potentially in all minds, so that when there is any conflict of motives, every man can tell which motive is highest.[1]

[1] Cf. *e.g.* pp. 48, 49, 53, 61.

LECTURE III

AT the beginning of chapter ii. (*Theory of Prudence*)
Martineau points out that 'while the objects of
moral preference are the *springs of action within us,*
the objects of *prudential* preference are the *effects of
action upon us.*' I agree with him in accepting the
distinction between Moral and Prudential, since, however we ultimately deal with it, we must recognise it as
a fundamental distinction of our common moral consciousness (taking 'moral' in a wide sense). But I
cannot accept as important Martineau's antithesis
between 'springs' and 'effects'; since, as I said in
the last Lecture, I hold that we judge of 'springs'
by the effects to which they are directed. Hence I
cannot agree with his extrusion of End from moral
judgment. It is not merely, as might be thought,
that in his view 'not End but choice of End' is
the object of moral judgment : even on the Utilitarian view, what is approved as morally 'right'
for the agent is the intention to produce certain
results, not their actual production. Martineau has
cut himself off from this explanation of his view by

the assertion that it is the 'characteristic of impulse
to send us *blindly* forward' (p. 74).

I agree with him, indeed, in holding that as
impulses are not necessarily directed to pleasures and
pains, moral judgment on volition is conceivable apart
from susceptibility to non-moral pleasure and pain,
and that even granting consciously wrong volition to
be normally followed by some degree of *moral* pain—
which, however, seems to me an exaggeration—it is
not the avoidance of that pain which is the end of a
right volition.   But Martineau's distinction among
the effects of action in foreseeing which Prudence consists (pp. 73, 74) leads him to a most paradoxical
definition of Prudence as 'self-surrender to the
strongest impulse.'   This seems to me a wilful
paradox, because the definition is only reached by
suppressing 'ulterior considerations.'

Till we are corrected by ulterior considerations (he says), we
must pronounce it the law of prudence to gratify the tendencies
in the order of their eagerness, and live chiefly in the indulgence
of the ruling passion, whatever it be (p. 74).

But it is the very essence of prudence to control
impulse in view of these ulterior considerations.   Of
course I should admit that if yielding to the impulse
felt as strongest was followed by no consequences
except gratification of impulse, Rational Self-love
would *prima facie* dictate yielding to impulse;
though I do not think it ought to be assumed
that intensity of immediate gratification is always
in proportion to intensity of pre-existent desire.
Even when in pp. 75-79, Martineau takes ulterior
consequences into account, he still retains the

conclusion that the 'prudential scale' of motives, arranges motives in 'order of strength' (p. 77). I conceive that if prudence arranges motives in any scale, it must be in accordance with an estimate of the whole foreseen consequences to the agent's happiness of the acts to which they prompt.

In pp. 75-77 Martineau maintains his peculiar view by what seems to me extraordinarily perverse reasoning, in which the 'external and ulterior effects' that he admits as 'corrective consequences of precipitate action' are treated as 'creations, direct or indirect, of our *moral constitution*' (p. 75). He therefore conceives them not to belong to the 'Prudential scale,' as it would exist independently of the 'Moral scale,' but only to Prudence as modified by co-existing moral judgments. No doubt such consequences of our moral constitution are part of what Prudence takes into account. There is, as Martineau says, (1) 'compunction' proceeding from conscious neglect of higher principle, or, as I say, 'consciousness of having chosen against judgment of right.' (But we may note that a milder form of compunction arises if we did not know that we were doing wrong, though we think we should have known if we had made the most of our opportunities.) There is also (2) 'indignation of our fellow-men' proceeding from their moral nature. (I hold, however, that this is actually directed primarily against acts presumed intentional, though motives doubtless come into consideration.) So far, I admit that the prudential judgment as to which motive is to prevail is partly dependent on the co-existence of moral judgments in

342   ON MARTINEAU'S ETHICS   LECT.

self and others. But so far as an individual has to
consider prudentially the moral judgments of others,
what he has to take into account is something quite
different from his own scale. He has to consider
not what sentiments his choice ought to arouse in
others, nor even what it would arouse if they knew
the inner choice as he knows it; but rather what
sentiments the volition that is only externally and
partially known will produce on certain minds,
which are under the influence of a generally imperfect morality to some extent, but also under
other influences. When, however, Martineau goes
on (3) to consider 'suffering in fortune and health'
as 'modifications by co-existing moral judgments,' his
argument is surely perverse. He says that 'only in
a morally constituted world could such sad consequences arise.' Does this mean that we never
suffer 'in fortune and health' except when the act
which entails the suffering was due to consciously
wrong choice? This is a hardy statement: I do not
think experience bears it out. Surely we suffer
bitterly for mere rashness and inexperience. At
any rate these consequences would remain objects of
prudential judgment, whether recognised as penalties
or not. The 'headache next morning' may be explained by purely physiological laws, its existence in
no way depends on a moral order of the world; but
it is none the less a consequence that prudence must
take into account.

As regards the relation of Prudential to Moral
preference, Martineau's view seems to be that Interest

and Duty coincide in the sense that 'a good man would be a fool if he were other than good,' but that this is because Prudence in his case has to take into account moral sensibility ; ' a bad man without conscience is not a fool for not acting as if he had one.' Still, this does not quite meet the case; for the bad man — unless he is from a moral point of view so bad as to be hopeless—may still be called a fool for not trying to develop his conscience. Is this Martineau's view ? I do not think that he clearly answers the question.[1]

On chapter iii.—*Merit and Demerit*—I have not much to say. My view of ethical notions is practical, therefore according to me in asking what Merit means as an ethical term, what we really ask is : How will a judgment of merit affect actions? So far as actions towards others are concerned, the question is of requiting desert. Of this I myself ultimately take the utilitarian view.[2] So far as the question is whether the agent should regard Worth or Merit in himself, as a result to be aimed at, the answer is that it is rather Worth. It is only another form of the question whether Virtue, Excellence, or Perfection is an Ultimate Rational End.[3] What Martineau gives is a theory of *demerit* rather than of *merit*. Thus he says (p. 80) :—

Where the order of strength among the springs of action is at variance with the order of their excellence (as, more or less, it is in all of us), inclination will often stand in the way of duty.

[1] Cf. *Methods of Ethics*, Book II. chap. v., and concluding chapter.
[2] Cf. *op. cit.* Book III. chap. v., and Book IV. chap. iii.
[3] Cf. *op. cit.* Book III. chap. xiv.

It is evident that, in such cases, the vehemence of the temptation will be proportioned to the extent of discrepancy between
the two scales. In the choice between competing impulses, the
agent suffers no violent wrench from the right course, unless the
lower passion is by far the intenser of the two ; if its importunity
is faint, its conquest involves no fierce struggle. . . . The
demerit and disgrace of wrong-doing become greater, as the
temptation is less.

'Between the two scales' means between the moral
and prudential scales—or let us say, between Duty
and Inclination or Interest, since Martineau's use of
prudential is paradoxical. Again we find him saying
(p. 83) :—

Where the discrepancy is greatest between the moral and
prudential order of principles, the guilt [demerit] is least ; and
where the discrepancy is least, the sin is greatest.

I agree that the common judgment of demerit does
not depend on the external badness of an act, and
that it is severer if the inducement is faint, but do
we 'assume as the ground of that opinion that a faint
inducement of pleasure was allowed to set aside an
intense shrinking of the moral sense' (p. 81)? I do
not think we make any such assumption. I should
rather say that we judge a bad act to be worse when
the inducement was comparatively faint, because we
infer a more alarmingly immoral tendency,—that is,
a greater tendency to cause mischief in the future.
For, we argue, if a man has committed a crime under
a slight inducement, what will he not do under a
strong one ? Martineau seems to assume quite arbitrarily that the man in question has so wicked a
contempt for his own moral nature that he prefers
inclination to conscience, though the voice of conscience is loud and inclination is weak. But 'bad' men

are often altogether free from these pains of conscience, and certainly I think Martineau goes beyond Common Sense in supposing that we commonly attribute an ' intense shrinking of the moral sense' to the man, for instance, who murders a boy for his boots : we have to suppose knowledge in order to attribute demerit, but not, I think, 'intense shrinking.'

Into Martineau's criticism of Mr. Leslie Stephen I will not enter, but I may say I agree with Martineau in thinking that we commonly apply the notions expressed by the terms *merit, meritorious,* to conduct rather than to character : but not *worth,* which rather belongs to character ; I distinguish worth from merit. I think, however, that our notion of degrees of worth is very vague. Further, I agree with Martineau that we do not attribute merit to God, and that in the view of Common Sense, merit implies free will and conflict ; but, as I have said, I think it easy to introduce a utilitarian interpretation of Merit and Worth — meaning by them the quality of action and character that it is right (that is, conducive to the general happiness) to praise.

On the question of authority dealt with in chapter iv. (*Nature of Moral Authority*) I have already said something. I will now briefly try to make clear my relation to Martineau's view, with which I largely agree. Let us take separately (*a*) Moral judgments (in the narrower sense of moral), and (*b*) Prudential judgments. As to (*a*) I hold : — (1) That the 'authority' attaches not to the mere sentiment as such, but to a judgment of rightness at least implicit

in it. (Compare the difference between Moral and
Quasi-moral sentiments.[1]) (2) That the judgment
implied is—like all judgments—valid for all minds
unless erroneous. (3) That though it may be passed
on one particular case, it is by implication valid for
all similar cases. In this sense I agree that the
'authority' is not merely subjective, and that it
essentially claims to be 'independent of the individual's idiosyncrasies' just as the truths of
mathematics are. But—as before argued—I do
not think that it necessarily implies 'another
person,' except so far as, like the truths of mathematics, it implies a universal reason which the
judging individual shares so far as he judges truly.
The 'authority' would not exist for me—except so
far as the prudential obligation of obeying superior
power goes—unless this reason was *mine*, though not
merely mine. Martineau in his comment on Green
(p. 106) seems to come near this view. Further, I
think the conception of myself as a part of a larger
whole inevitably comes in when I take the point
of view of Universal Reason. But I agree with
Martineau (p. 117) that the notion of 'authority' in
the fundamental ethical prescription 'seek the good
of the larger whole,' cannot be extracted from the
conception of the 'relative bulk' of the larger whole.
I arrive at it by the conception of the similarity of
the other parts of the whole to myself. Apprehending
their similarity in other ways, I cannot avoid concluding that each of them has an Ultimate Good

---

[1] Cf. *Methods of Ethics*, Book I. chap. iii. § 1, pp. 27, 28.

similar to mine, and as valuable from the point of view of Universal Reason. Martineau prefers to conceive Reason as imposing not the obligation of aiming at the general good, but the obligation of conforming to the type of perfect humanity. My argument against this is given in *The Methods of Ethics*, Book III. chapter xiv. I find myself led to futile tautology if Perfection is interpreted as Moral Perfection, and regarded as Ultimate End. As to the question 'whether obligation can be transcended,' there is no material difference between Martineau and myself. I agree that 'what I ought to do' includes more than 'what others may reasonably censure me for not doing,' though I should apply a different standard from Martineau's in determining how the line is to be drawn.[1]

I pass to consider the authority of Prudence. Martineau admits that we commonly condemn imprudence. He says (p. 126) :—

The fact, I suppose, can hardly be called in question, that we look with positive *disapproval* on rashness and recklessness as not simply foolish and hurtful, but as *wrong*, even where no interests are visibly affected except the offender's own.

Observe that he states the issue unlike what one would have expected from a writer whose 'moral scale' was framed on non-utilitarian principles. My disagreement from Martineau here simply lies in my recognising the validity of the fundamental axiom : That Hereafter is to be regarded as much as Now, apart from any relation to others. As to the 'moralised prudence' which Martineau speaks of at

---

[1] Cf. *Methods of Ethics*, Book III. chap. ii.

the close of the chapter, it seems to me to be merely
a confusing mixture of Morality in the narrower
sense, and Prudence.

In what is said in chapter v. of the absence of
any conscious foresight of effects in the case of the
springs of action distinguished as primary, Martineau
seems to me to mix up two distinctions; namely
(1) the distinction between impulses which are instinctive or blind, and those which are directed to a
pre-conceived end; and (2) that between impulses
which are extra-regarding, and those aimed at
pleasure. In drawing the line (p. 135) between
primary and secondary springs of action, he charac-
terises the primary impulses of a man as

those which urge him, in the way of unreflecting instinct, to
appropriate objects or natural expression, . . . [while the
secondary are those] which supervene upon self-knowledge and
experience, and in which the preconception is present of an end
gratifying to some recognised feeling.

And again, on p. 137, he speaks of the primary
principles as

impelling us to certain objects without prevision or self-consciousness on our part . . . tendencies towards ends which we
seek blindly, without preconception of their character.

I quite agree with him, and I have argued at length
in Book I. chapter iv. of my *Methods of Ethics*, that
we have 'primary impulses' prompting to actions for
results distinct from the individual's pleasure—disinterested impulses; and that these extend throughout
the whole range of our appetitive nature, and are
throughout distinguishable from the desires directed
towards the pleasures that attend the satisfaction of
the primary impulses—for instance, appetites for food

and drink, and 'thirst you wouldn't sell for ten dollars.' In this sense the distinction of primary and secondary propensions, etc., seems to me true and important, and Martineau's illustrations of it throughout chapter v. are interesting and impressive. But these primary impulses are not normally 'blind,' in the mature human being, nor do they cease to be 'extra-regarding' when a clear foresight of their immediate end is added to them. I do not say that we have no blind impulses : I quite admit that they have a recognised place in experience—though a smaller place than Martineau gives them. Also blindness is a matter of degree ; the immediate end, of which there is clear foresight, may not be the ultimate end in relation to which the impulse is developed. For instance, the impulse to drink may continue 'blind,' in the sense that a boy who drinks may not be definitely aware of the need of fluid for health ; or in the case of resentment, the man who retaliates an injury may not be conscious of the utility of such retaliation in repressing future injury. But in a certain sense, as Professor William James says,

It is obvious that *every instinctive act in an animal with a memory must cease to be 'blind' after being once repeated*, and must be accompanied with foresight of its 'end' just so far as that end may have fallen under the animal's cognisance.[1]

Hence it is difficult to see how these impulses in the adult can have remained 'blind' for the most part. And in the primary impulses which Martineau classifies, he clearly has in view the adult man : for

---

[1] Cf. James, *Principles of Psychology*, vol. ii. p. 390 (1st edit.).

instance, he says nothing of the instinctive impulses which children have to suck, bite, grasp objects, utter sounds, move the limbs. I observe, too, that among the impulses which remain in adult man, imitativeness—which in some of its manifestations remains blind longer than most—is not mentioned.

But in any case I do not think that such impulses are morally judged as blind; I conceive that the effects of the action to which such unreflecting impulses prompt, however absent or faintly represented when the impulse operates, are necessarily represented when it becomes the object of a moral judgment. This will appear, I think, if we reflect on any example included in Martineau's exposition of the 'scale of springs of action'—for instance in comparing the appetite for food with the desire of the pleasure of eating, he says, 'it is surely meaner to eat for the palate's sake than to appease the simple hunger' (p. 193): well, it seems to me clear that, so far as I pass this judgment, it is not on hunger, *qua* blind impulse, but on hunger conceived as an impulse directed towards the removal of an organic want.

LECTURE IV

THE details of Martineau's *Classification of the Springs of Action* are given from the psychological point of view in chapter v., and from the ethical point of view in chapter vi. Before I proceed to examine this in detail I must again recall that Martineau and I approach the examination of Common Sense from essentially different points of view. I do not regard the verdict of Common Sense, even when it is clearly pronounced, as final : if I find it conflicting with what appear to me clear deductions from self-evident principles—such as those which according to me lie at the basis of Utilitarianism—I venture after full consideration to dissent from it, though even so I may not think it right to proclaim my dissent.

This attitude, which in my mind is primarily arrived at independently of a study of the history of morality, is yet confirmed by such a study ; which leads me to regard the current civilised morality of the present age as merely a stage in a long process of development, in which the human mind has, I hope, been gradually moving towards a truer apprehension of what ought to be. We do not find merely change, when we trace the history of morality ; we see progress through wider experience, fuller knowledge, more extended and refined sympathies. Thus reflection shows us in the morality of earlier stages an element of what we now agree to regard as confusion and error. Therefore it seems to me reasonable to suppose that similar defects are likely to lurk in our own current and accepted morality ; even if observation and analysis of this morality had not led us— as they have in fact led me—to see such defects in it. How to eliminate, if possible, these elements of error, confusion, and uncertainty is, in my view, the fundamental question of ethics, which can only be answered by the construction of an ethical system. For this we have two things to do : we have to arrive at a clear conception of the Ultimate End or Good, and we have to penetrate to fundamental universal intuitions determining the individual's duty of promoting general good. In any case, I do not expect to find this true moral system where Martineau looks for it ; that is, by introspection directed to the moral sentiments and apparently immediate moral judgments caused in my mind by the contemplation of particular acts, apart from systematic consideration of these acts and their consequences in relation to what I adopt as the ultimate end of action. That I should have such spontaneous sentiments, and, where prompt action is needed, should act on such immediate judgments, is at once natural and, in my opinion, conducive to the ultimate end ; but I continually find that these immediate pronouncements have to be corrected and restrained by a careful consideration of consequences; and I do not regard them as having ultimate validity if they conflict with such calculations.

But again : before I discuss the Scale of Motives in which Martineau expresses the results of his reflection on the moral consciousness which we share, I must repeat that this, from my point of view, is only a part of the whole, and not the most important part.   My view is that, according to Common Sense Morality it is intentions directed to outward effects, and not motives as distinguished from intentions, which are primarily of consequence in the moral judgments or intuitions that relate to the most important branches of duty.   Thus (as I say in my *Methods of Ethics*, Book III. chapter ii.) we call a man veracious if his speech exhibits, in a noteworthy degree, a settled endeavour to produce in the minds of others impressions exactly correspondent to the facts, whatever his motive may be for so doing. The details with which Ethics is primarily concerned in my view of Common Sense Morality are to be sought in the region of external effects, and not among the ' propensions, passions, affections, and sentiments ' felt to impel the agent's volition.   This I hold to be the Common Sense view, and I also hold it to be the right view, since I regard actions as right or wrong according to their conduciveness to external results; and propensions, passions, etc., as right or wrong because of their conduciveness through actions to such results : the latter therefore, being more

2 A

remote from the end, are naturally and properly judged as secondary.

To sum up, then : I cannot regard the construction of a scale of motives in harmony with Common Sense as having the fundamental importance that Martineau attributes to it, because (1) I cannot regard the judgments of Common Sense on particular volitions as having the final decisiveness which Martineau appears to credit them with ; and because (2) the judgment on motives seems to me secondary to the judgment on intentions. At the same time, I quite agree that the distinction of 'good' and 'bad' 'higher' and 'lower' motives is found by reflection on Common Sense, and that it is the duty of the moralist to make this distinction as precise as possible in its application to different classes of motives. With these preliminary limitations, I pass to examine Martineau's attempt to work out his distinction in detail.

I have pointed out that there are two classifications: that in chapter v. which is Psychological, and that in chapter vi. which is Ethical. I do not propose to criticise in detail the psychological chapter, though I may just note, among other things, that I think the term 'passion' is oddly restricted to Antipathy, Fear, and Resentment; that Sympathy should be treated earlier and with more breadth; and that Emulation and Rivalry are inadequately treated as dependent on Love of Power. Again, I do not see why Conjugal Affection is omitted from the primary affections. And in my opinion Censoriousness is not a proper term for the desire of malevolent pleasure; nor can Suspiciousness be regarded as a taste for indulging fear.   Nor, again, do I think that Wonder can properly be regarded as a definite motive; and the impulse to seek knowledge seems to me more complex than Martineau makes it.   And I consider that Constructiveness should be recognised along with tendency to (unselective) Spontaneous Activity as a more primary impulse, before we come to Love of Power.

I pass then to the Ethical scale in chapter vi., but before I begin to criticise it in detail, I wish to make clear my general and fundamental disagreement with the plan on which it is composed.   Here I must repeat with some expansion what I have said in Book III. chapter xii. of *The Methods of Ethics*.   According to Martineau the springs of human action may be arranged in an ethical scale,[1] so constituted that whenever any of the 'propensions,' 'passions,' 'affections' and 'sentiments' thus classified comes into

[1] For the reader's convenience, I give the *Table of the Springs of Action* in which Dr. Martineau has collected the results of his survey (p. 266) :—

LOWEST.

1. Secondary Passions—Censoriousness, Vindictiveness, Suspiciousness.
2. Secondary Organic Propensions—Love of Ease and Sensual Pleasure.
3. Primary Organic Propensions—Appetites.
4. Primary Animal Propension—Spontaneous Activity (unselectiye).
5. Love of Gain (reflective derivation from Appetite).
6. Secondary Affections (sentimental indulgence of sympathetic feelings).
7. Primary Passions—Antipathy, Fear, Resentment.
8. Causal Energy—Love of Power, or Ambition ; Love of Liberty.
9. Secondary Sentiments—Love of Culture.
10. Primary Sentiments of Wonder and Admiration.
11. Primary Affections, Parental and Social — with (approximately) Generosity and Gratitude.
12. Primary Affection of Compassion.
13. Primary Sentiment of Reverence.

HIGHEST.

conflict with one higher in the scale, right volition
consists in choosing the 'higher' in preference to the
'lower.' Now I might criticise this scale minutely
and propose a different order of merit. But to do
this would not indicate the extent of my disagreement. My point is that no such *universal* relation of
higher or lower subsists between any pair of impulses as is here affirmed. The higher and lower are
only so *generally* not *always*. The view of Common Sense appears to me rather that, in all or most
cases, a natural impulse has its proper sphere, within
which it should be normally operative, and that the
question whether a motive commonly judged higher
should yield to a lower, is one that cannot be
answered decisively in the general way in which
Martineau answers it : the answer must depend on
the particular conditions and circumstances of the
conflict. For we recognise that a higher motive may
and sometimes does intrude unseasonably into the
proper sphere of the lower, just as the lower is liable
to encroach on the higher ; only since there is very
much less danger of the former intrusion, it naturally
falls into the background in ethical discussions and
exhortations that have a practical aim. Thus—not
to take the highest motives—a regard for health is
higher than an appetite for pleasant food ; but it is
not desirable that a normally healthy man should
select his food and drink from sanitary calculations.
Within limits, he is more likely to be healthy if he
follows appetite.

The matter is complicated by this further con-

sideration : we recognise that as the character of a
moral agent becomes better, the motives that we
rank as ' higher ' tend to be developed, so that their
normal sphere of operation continually enlarges at
the expense of the lower, though not so far as to
supersede the lower.   Hence there are two distinct
aims in moral regulation and culture, so far as they
relate to motives : (1) to keep the 'lower' motive
within the limits within which its operation is
considered to be legitimate and good on the whole,
so long as we cannot substitute for it the equally
effective operation of a higher motive : and at the
same time (2) to effect this substitution of ' higher '
for ' lower ' gradually, so far as can be done without
danger, up to a limit which we cannot definitely fix,
but which we certainly conceive, for the most part,
as falling short of complete exclusion of the lower
motive.   Such complete exclusion we commonly
regard as undesirable, from a general assumption
that it would be unfavourable to moral health and
balance.

I may illustrate by reference to the passion of
personal resentment of which I before spoke.   The
view of reflective Common Sense is, I think, that the
malevolent impulse so designated is of a kind highly
dangerous, *i.e.* of a kind that prompts to wrong
actions much more frequently than to right ones ;
and which, therefore, on a broad view of consequences
we unhesitatingly judge to be bad or low.   Still, I
think we agree with Butler that as long as it is
strictly limited to resentment against wrong and

operates in aid of justice, this malevolent impulse
has a legitimate sphere of action in the social life of
human beings as actually constituted : that, indeed,
its suppression would be gravely mischievous, unless
we could at the same time so intensify the ordinary
man's regard for justice or for social wellbeing that
the total strength of motives prompting to the punishment of crime should not be diminished. It is no
doubt to be wished, as Butler says, that men would
repress wrong from these higher motives rather than
from passionate resentment ; but we cannot hope to
effect this change in human beings generally except
by a slow and gradual process of elevation of character : so that within its sphere it would be often
undesirable to overrule resentment by a motive commonly judged to be higher. Therefore supposing a
conflict between ' Compassion,' which is highest but
one in Martineau's scale, and ' Resentment,' which
he places about the middle, it is by no means to
be laid down as a universal rule that compassion
ought to prevail. We ought rather, with Butler, to
regard resentment as a salutary ' balance to the
weakness of pity,' which would be liable to prevent
the execution of justice if resentment were excluded,
although common sense would agree with Martineau
as to the general relative rank of the two.

Or we might similarly take the impulse which
comes lowest (among those not condemned altogether) in Martineau's scale—the Love of Ease and
Sensual Pleasure. No doubt this impulse, or group
of impulses, is continually leading men to shirk or

scamp their strict duty, or to fall in some less definite
way below their own ideal of conduct; hence the
attitude habitually maintained towards it by preachers
and practical moralists is that of repression. Still,
Common Sense surely recognises that there are
cases in which even this impulse ought to prevail
over impulses ranked much above it in Martineau's
scale : we often find men prompted—say by Love
of Gain or Love of Culture—to shorten unduly
their hours of recreation ; and in the case of a conflict of motives under such circumstances we should
judge it best that victory should remain on the side
of the 'love of ease and pleasure,' and that the un-
seasonable intrusion of the higher motive should be
repelled. Hence we look on not only with indulgence
but with satisfaction when we see a man, who is in
danger of 'overdoing it' in either business or study,
seduced by a friend into idleness or amusement.

Perhaps it may be said that in neither of these
instances would the conflict of motives remain such as I
have described ; that though the struggle might begin,
so to say, as a duel between resentment and compassion, or between love of ease and love of gain, it would
not be fought to a finish in the lists so marked out,
since in each case still higher motives would come in
—regard for justice and social wellbeing on the side
of resentment, regard for health and ultimate efficiency
for work on the side of love of ease ; and that it
would be the intervention of these higher motives
that would decide the struggle so far as it was decided
rightly and as we should approve. It seems to me that

this is certainly what would happen if the supposed
conflict were at all serious and its decision deliberate.
Suppose a man has injured me from some ill temper
or selfishness, and I have an opportunity of making
him uncomfortable in return ; resentment prompts me
directly to make him feel pain, then compassion
comes in and I am moved to let him off.   Probably
this conflict of motives concentrates attention on the
point.   If so, I certainly should not rest in the consideration whether resentment or pity is higher : I
should certainly go on to the consideration whether
the immediate evil of the pain I was proposing to
inflict is or is not outweighed by its ulterior good
effect in teaching him not to offend again.

It is for this reason that such a scale as Martineau
has drawn up, of motives arranged according to their
moral rank, can never, in my view, have more than a
very subordinate ethical importance.   I admit that
it may serve to indicate in a rough and general way
the kinds of desires which it is usually best to
encourage and indulge, in comparison with other
kinds which are ordinarily likely to compete and
collide with them ; and we might thus settle by
means of it some of the comparatively trifling conflicts of motive which the varying and complex play
of needs, habits, and interests, with their accompanying emotions, continually brings forth in our daily life.
When a lower motive—commonly so judged—conflicts with what is commonly judged as higher, it
would be usually right to follow the latter ; and if it
is not worth while thinking much about the matter,

this criterion may suffice.   But if a serious question
of conduct is raised, I cannot conceive myself deciding
it morally by any comparison of motives below the
highest: the case must, as I have elsewhere said,
be carried up for decision into the court of the
motive which I regard as supreme, *i.e.* the desire to
promote universal good, understood as the happiness
of sentient beings generally.   Thus the comparison
ultimately decisive on the particular question raised
would inevitably be not a comparison between the
motives primarily conflicting, but between the effects
of the different lines of conduct to which they respectively prompt, considered in relation to whatever
we regard as the ultimate end of reasonable action.
And this, I conceive, is the course which moral reflection tends to take in the case not only of Utilitarians, but of all who follow Butler in regarding
our passions and propensions as forming naturally a
" system or constitution," in which the ends of lower
impulses are subordinate as means to the ends of
certain governing motives, or are comprehended as
parts in these larger ends.[1]   So far as any view of
this kind is taken, any tabulation of the moral rank
of motives other than the governing ones can, at best,
have only a quite subordinate interest: it cannot
possibly furnish a method of dealing with the fundamental problems of ethical construction.

I would now notice that Martineau's general
answer in *Types of Ethical Theory* to my argument
—in the form in which it was originally stated in

---

[1] *Methods of Ethics*, Book III. chap. xii. § 3.

Methods of Ethics—will be found in chapter vii. pp.
299, 300.   He quotes the passage[1] in which I expound my argument, and then says that the reasoning
there set forth

addresses itself to some doctrine wholly unlike any which I can
undertake to defend.   It assumes that in the scale of springs of
action will be found a special class distinguished from the rest
by being '*virtuous motives*,' possibly all fused *into one* in the shape
of 'Rational Benevolence,' or desire for 'universal happiness.'
. . . It is also assumed that there can never be a conflict of incentives without one of these 'virtuous motives' (*i.e.* love of
this, that, or all virtues) being present, so that not only is one
inferior motive higher than another, but both are eclipsed by a
superlative third, and dispensed from further attendance.   With
the removal of the class of 'virtuous motives,' this assumption
also disappears: there is no absolute and constant 'highest,'
appearing over the heads of all conflicting incentives; but the
'highest' which claims us is simply the relatively superior of the
contending two, and the duty, the moral quality, the call to
virtue, consist simply in that felt superiority; so that our rule,
'Go with the highest,' is just as applicable to the humbler as to
the loftier steps of the scale, and involves no leap up to the
summit before it can be obeyed (p. 299).

The same misuse of the word 'highest' in an absolute sense,
instead of relatively to the other incitements in each act of
choice, leads to Professor Sidgwick's final argument: viz. that
it is against common sense to affirm that the higher motive
ought always to prevail over the lower: inasmuch as this would
require us to banish 'all natural impulse in favour of reason,'
and fetch in the supreme spring of action to work the most insignificant problems: in other words, never to descend from the
top of the scale. . . . As I do not admit 'Reason' to be a spring
of action at all, it would indeed be strange in me to 'suppress
the natural impulses in its favour': the only effect would be to
stop the clock altogether (p. 300).

This furnishes a striking illustration of the differences in the moral experiences of different minds.

I am surprised that Martineau should deny what
I argue—that if a serious question of conduct is

[1] *Methods of Ethics*, pp. 370, 371 in the 3rd edition.

raised, I cannot conceive myself deciding it morally
by any comparison of motives below the highest :
the case must be carried up into the court of the
motive which I regard as supreme—and his denial
surprises me the more when I consider what he says
of altruistic affections :—

Consequences to the general happiness can carry no obligation, *unless the altruistic affections are in their nature invested with
authority over impulses that conflict with them.* . . . There are
cases in which one and the same principle has the choice of
several possible actions ; and among these the election must
be made by the balance of pleasurable and painful effects
(pp. 300, 301).

I am even more surprised when I turn to examine
the particulars of chapter vi.   Let us begin with
Love of Gain (p. 195).   Common Sense does not
separate 'judgment of principles' from 'canon of consequences,' as Martineau here tries to do, nor estimate
consequences only prudentially, *i.e.* egoistically ; it
considers both in relation to rational wellbeing, and it
is artificial to leave this consideration out of account
in estimating the moral rank of motives.   So
when love of gain is measured against antipathy,
by a would-be butcher, Martineau admits (p. 196)
that moral comparison of motives is ' in practice '
influenced by 'special intensity' and 'external relations.'   The question, therefore, is : Is it *rightly*
so influenced ?   If not—Martineau loses the support
of Common Sense ; if it is — then his ' canon of
consequences' gets mixed up with his scale of motives
in a hopelessly confusing way.

Similarly with Fear (pp. 197, 198).   Martineau in
fact admits ultimately that ' fears cannot be appraised

without reference to the worth of the objects feared,'
and 'cannot claim a definite and invariable place'
in the 'moral hierarchy' of springs of action. Very
well, let us go on then to Resentment (p. 199). The
Resentment considered here is really Resentment
moralised—it is 'just anger' that is explained to
be higher than 'mere interest.' I am surprised that,
after this, Martineau should not see my point about
the 'higher motive' coming in. For at any rate,
in judging the choice, regard for Justice has a place.
Why not, then, in the choice itself? And again,
'well-grounded resentment' (p. 201) is not simple
resentment, but resentment moralised by a view of
ulterior consequences—here it is quite evident that
the 'virtuous motive,' regard for Justice, is supposed to enter. And in treating of the Love of
Power we find that judgment is given in view of
results, as also in comparing Secondary Affections
and Primary Passions.

When we come (p. 216) to the Primary Affections as compared with Wonder and Admiration,
where Martineau says *affection* I should say *duty*—
for we condemn neglect of children equally whether
the parent feels affection or not. And similarly of
the Primary Affections *inter se*. Surely it is the fact
that a man has brought children into the world, and
not the fact that he is fond of them, which constitutes the basis of their claim upon him. It is on this
ground that the claim of children is preferred to
Friendship (p. 220). And in the case of conflict
between Friendship and Pity, it is always the con-

sequences—or claims grounded on objective fact—
not the mere impulses, which are compared.

Passing over Reverence, I come, in § 10, to the
question 'how to estimate Mixed Incentives.' I have
drawn attention to the difficulty arising out of these,
in *Methods of Ethics*, pointing out that the more we
contemplate the actual promptings that precede any
volition, the more we seem to find complexity of
motive the rule rather than the exception, at least in
the case of educated persons : and from this composition of impulses there results a fundamental perplexity
as to the principles on which our decision is to be
made, even supposing that we have a clear view of
the relative worth of the elementary impulses. For
the compound will generally contain nobler and baser
elements, and we can hardly get rid of the latter.
Suppose then that we are impelled in one direction
by a combination of high and low motives, and in
another by an impulse that ranks between the two in
the scale, how shall we decide which course to follow?
Such a case is by no means uncommon : *e.g.* an
injured man may be moved by an impulse of pity to
spare his injurer, while a regard for justice and a
desire of revenge combined impel him to inflict
punishment. How are we to deal with such a case
as this?[1] Martineau's answer is very simple and
confident; it can be done, he thinks, by synthetic
intuition (p. 236). But it does not follow, because
we may feel that incentives are mixed, that it is easy
to estimate their rank as mixed. In answer to me in

[1] Cf. *Methods of Ethics*, Book III. chap. xii. § 3, p. 368.

the next chapter, he is still more contemptuous about the difficulty.

All the difficulties charged upon the composition of motives appear to me (he says) a mere nightmare of unreal psychology. Practically, every one knows at first hand his own incentive, and, unless he has learned the tricks of a cheat, need be at no loss about its relative worth (p. 297).

Let us see, then, whether it is so easy to estimate mixed motives. On p. 296 Martineau considers my argument to show that even if we put out of sight the Moral Sentiment and Self-love, it is still scarcely possible to frame a scale of motives arranged in order of merit, for which we could claim anything like a clear consent, even of cultivated and thoughtful persons. He represents me as putting the question asked just above :—

What am I to do . . . if I am driven in one direction by a chain-shot of high and low motives, and in the opposite by a single impulse of intermediate worth ? *e.g.* to punish my injurer by love of justice plus vindictiveness, and to spare him by compassion. It has been agreed on both sides to treat vindictiveness as not only relatively but absolutely bad, and to place it, as purely malevolent, altogether outside the admissible parts of the graduated scale. The active presence of such a feeling implies much more, I should say, than the mere lowering of a coexisting superior impulse ; it so conflicts with it that any blending of the two in a common function is no less impossible than the co-operation of aliment that feeds the life and poison that destroys it.

This seems to me to mean that the presence of the lower motive destroys the higher, or renders it valueless. If so, there is no difficulty. But is this the meaning? In the discussion of Resentment on p. 199 we read :—

Whenever resentment is *bought off* by mere interest, whenever a man with just anger in his heart remains placid only because *he cannot afford* to let his indignation appear, we cannot help despising such self-control as sordid.

There would seem to be mixture here.

Among 'mixed incentives' I may notice Martineau's treatment of Generosity. In my *Methods of Ethics* (Book III. chapter viii. p. 326) I have regarded Generosity as a Virtue, *i.e.* as a quality of character exhibited in conduct that we approve. But no doubt some acts in which generosity is exhibited are not approved; hence it is quite legitimate to treat it as Martineau does, merely as a 'mixed incentive.' I think, however, that he takes too limited a view of the motives with which the generous impulse may collide. It is no doubt prominently manifest, as he says, in conflict with the love of money and with resentment; but it is also—as I say —manifested in competition for other objects of desire as well as money: a man may be generous to a rival for fame or power, in cases where no resentment comes in. However, the important point to notice is, that here again Martineau recognises implicitly that for determining the decision between generosity and a conflicting impulse in any particular case, we have to appeal to the 'canon of consequences.'

In § 11 of chapter vi. (*Relations of Merit, Gratitude, Generosity, Justice*) and § 12 (*Veracity*) Martineau goes on to consider certain moral sentiments as 'derivative springs of action.' I pass over what he says, with apt eloquence, of Gratitude—remarking, however, that it seems to me somewhat oddly described as a 'variety' or 'modified example of generosity,'

since, according to Martineau himself, Generosity
'has its field in the play of social affection beyond
the limits of what could be demanded as a right,'
and this cannot be similarly said of Gratitude.   Gratitude, we think, is due to a benefactor, and it is the
characteristic of Generosity that it is not 'due.'
There is, however, this resemblance, that a certain
indefiniteness is held to be normal and proper in the
outward manifestation of Gratitude and Generosity,
as contrasted with the exactness characteristic of the
external realisation of Justice : it is this that has led
Martineau to a too complete identification of the two.

Of Justice Martineau gives the following account :—

Justice, therefore, let us say, is *the treatment of persons
according to their deserts*.   And in this two things are involved :
viz. (1) that there is *somebody to treat them ;* (2) that in treating
them he has the disposal of something which they care for, in
quantities divisible and proportionable, so as to correspond with
the ratios of their deserts.   These conditions at once bring
before us the image of a *Judge*, presiding over the trial of some
charged offence or some disputable claim between two applicants
for his decision ; on him their treatment depends ; and it
consists in his award of penalty or of partition, in conformity
with their estimated wrongs and rights ; these consequences, as
well as his own graduated words of condemnation or acquittal,
are the common matter which he can distribute, in measures
accurately representing the relative values he has determined.
If we start from this point, it is plain that, to constitute justice,
there must be a triad of persons at the least, viz. A and B,
whose shares in some common matter of good and ill are in
doubt, and a dikast who solves the doubt ; and that it is of the
dikast, in his award, that we predicate justice or injustice, and
not of A or B in their relation to each other (pp. 249, 250).

If you will compare here what I have said in
Methods of Ethics (Book III. chapter v. § 1), you
will see that I agree with Martineau in considering

Justice as essentially *distributive*, involving allotment of something 'divisible and proportionable'
among a number of persons.   But as regards Martineau's formula, I should observe (a) that Desert is
used in a wider and narrower sense : in the narrower
sense in which I use it in the passage referred to
'treatment according to desert' implies previous
conduct on the part of the person treated for
which requital is held to be due.   But surely the
'disputable claim' which Martineau's judge has to
settle need not be a claim arising out of desert
in this narrower sense : justice and injustice may
equally be shown by a judge in dividing an inheritance according to the wishes of a testator ; and if in
such a case the legatees may be said to be treated
according to their deserts, we are obviously using
the word in an unusually wide sense : to treat a man
according to his deserts seems to mean no more
than treating him as he ought to be treated in a
question of distribution or allotment.   (b) Secondly,
in Martineau's original statement what the judge
distributes is conceived as something that men
care for—some 'divisible stock of recompense.'   But
this does not sufficiently recognise—what, however,
Martineau in other phrases does recognise — that
pains and penalties have to be justly allotted in
judicial decisions, as well as advantages.

On p. 251 Martineau imagines that I differ from
him more than I do, that I 'consider the meaning of the word [justice] satisfied by any conduct
which fulfils the warranted expectations of another.'

But I never intended to omit the notion of 'distribution' or 'allotment'—compare the passage above referred to, in my book.   I agree with Martineau that when we apply the term 'justice' there is always a comparison, and usually some comparison of cases, implied.   I think, however, that 'injustice' is used more widely than justice.   Probably Martineau is right in saying that we should never think of quoting the simple observance of contract as an example of justice; yet we should certainly regard the breach of contract, causing serious damage, as an example of injustice.   But I think that the comparison, though normally, is not always between persons; for instance, in the case of 'just punishment,' it seems to be a comparison between the gravity of the crime and the gravity of its punishment.   This Martineau half sees in one of the examples which he gives on p. 251.

He goes on to describe (pp. 252, 253) how 'the idea of justice undergoes another extension into cases not originally embraced in it'; 'in spite of the strict limits of the realm of Justice, its central idea spreads widely over the indefinite life beyond, and carries its controlling presence into generosity and love themselves.'   With this I agree.   But I think that Martineau in expressing this wider notion of Justice—'we ought to treat others according to their *merits*, etc.' (p. 253)—has again been misled by a confusion between the wider and narrower meanings of desert.   For the more indefinite claims, beyond the sphere of legal rights, which the spirit of

justice moves us to satisfy, are by no means limited
to claims based on the *moral* worth of others : they
may arise out of friendship, consanguinity, economic
relations, previous services, special needs, or other
causes independent of the moral character of the
claimants. Hence the 'love of Justice,' which on
p. 254 he recognises as a 'new spring of action,'
cannot be interpreted as merely a 'love of *proportionate treatment* of men and their character according to their worth,' without narrowing the sphere of
justice in a manner altogether opposed to Common
Sense. Thus we cannot say :

the love of justice . . . is only a higher figure of the original
sense of right: it is the *preference for worth*. Or it might be
called the *enthusiasm of conscience for its own estimation of character ;*
and, so far as it assumes a missionary energy, for a conformable
adjustment of social life.

This point is important in considering the issue
between Martineau and myself as regards the 'loves
of the virtues.'

In § 12 Martineau goes on to speak of another
moral quality, Veracity. His discussion here is a
good example of his treatment, in the combined
vigour and delicacy of its rhetorical expression.
What primarily impresses him in unveracity is the
treachery of 'wielding the instrument of speech and
all the simple trust which leaves an open path before
it, to gain' secret ends. But, while recognising that
the social union rests on mutual confidence which
unveracity tends to weaken, he argues further that
the liar in 'declining to accept the consequences of
truth' really 'quarrels with the realised order of the

world'; so that 'veracity . . . wields the authority not
of social affection only, but of *Reverence* also'—the
highest among Martineau's tabulated springs of
action. It does not follow that there are no cases
to which the rule of truth-speaking does not apply;
for there are persons, such as 'assassins, robbers,
enemies with arms in their hands,' who are really
beyond the pale of the 'common understanding' on
which the social factor in the obligation of veracity
is based. Nor does 'reverence for the Divine order
of reality' require me to disclose it to a 'false
brother' who 'seeks access to the truth in order to
desecrate it'; 'on the contrary, I uphold the inmost
spirit of that order by preventing it from being
turned into an accomplice of crime.' Even the
question whether falsehoods may be told to persons
who put unwarrantable questions to find out secrets,
Martineau is prepared to treat neutrally as a difficult
case to be determined by 'careful attention to the
canon of consequences.' Still, after all, Martineau's
love of truth remains unconquered by the arguments
which commend themselves to his intellect, as he
avows impressively in the concluding paragraph :
'Yet, when I place myself . . . at one of the crises
demanding a deliberate lie, an unutterable repugnance
returns upon me, and makes the theory seem shame-
ful, etc' (p. 265).

It is impossible for a reader of the sections which
I have briefly summarised to doubt that Martineau
has the sentiments known as Love of Justice and
Love of Truth in an eminent degree. Why he

considers that there are no other moral sentiments which need to be discussed in relation to his scale of springs of action, I do not quite know; but, at any rate, I should have thought that his discussion of them makes these two important moral sentiments stand out clearly as distinct though derivative impulses. I am therefore surprised at the way in which he meets my argument[1] in favour of including in our list of motives the Moral Sentiments, or impulses towards particular kinds of virtuous conduct as such, *e.g.* Candour, Veracity, Fortitude. His answer (pp. 284, 285) to my argument is as follows :—

I cannot admit either the *loves of virtues*—of 'candour, veracity, fortitude'—or the virtues themselves, as so many additional impulses over and above those from the conflict of which they are formed. I do not confess my fault *in order to be candid*, or encounter danger *in order to be brave*, or resist temptation *in order to be virtuous*, and give a sample of what virtue is. Unless I am a prig, I never think of candour, or virtue, as predicable or going to be predicable of me at all, etc.

Compare, however, what he says on pp. 254 and 265, quoted above.

I now go on to the question discussed in § 14 (pp. 266 *seqq.*) : How far a life must be chosen among the springs of action enumerated in the table which Martineau gives. He states the question of § 14 fairly on pp. 267, 268, and seems to hold that a moral agent is morally bound to choose his sphere in life in view of the superior opportunities it offers for developing higher moral motives. This would seem to imply that higher motives should be substituted for lower as far as possible. And this he appears to

[1] *Methods of Ethics*, Book III. chap. xii. § 2.

hold theoretically but not practically—for reasons, however, which are somewhat obscurely and rhetorically explained (p. 269). What is Martineau's view as to the extent to which an individual ought to try to cultivate higher motives? What is supposed to be the motive prompting to such cultivation? He says (at the conclusion of § 14, p. 270) :—

> It suffices, then, for us to admit to our questioner, that a man ought not to become so absorbed in his business or his studies as to leave no scope for the free movement of his higher affections and no time for the duties they enjoin. But this very obligation I would rather rest on the objective claims of the relations, human and Divine, which he is in danger of guiltily setting aside, than on the subjective need, in his self-formation, of being less a stranger to the upper storeys of his spiritual experience.

How is this consistent with making the judgments between particular motives final, if the sentiment of Reverence is thus the motive for setting them aside?

Finally, in one sentence (p. 275) Martineau concedes more than I should have expected, stating as one way in which computation of pleasurable and painful consequences may be admitted in morals, that ' the computation is already more or less involved in the preference of this or that spring of action; for in proportion as the springs of action are self-conscious, they contemplate their own effects, and judgment upon them [the effects] is included in our judgment on the disposition.'

Printed by R. & R. Clark, Limited, *Edinburgh*

WORKS ON ETHICS AND METAPHYSICS.

Works by Professor HENRY SIDGWICK.

PHILOSOPHY : Its Scope and Relations. 8vo. 6s. 6d. net.

THE METHODS OF ETHICS. Sixth Edition, revised. 8vo. 14s. net.

OUTLINES OF THE HISTORY OF ETHICS FOR ENGLISH READERS. Crown 8vo. 3s. 6d.

A HANDBOOK OF MORAL PHILOSOPHY. By Rev. HENRY CALDERWOOD, LL.D. Third Edition. Crown 8vo. 6s.

A SHORT STUDY OF ETHICS. By CHARLES F. D'ARCY, B.D. Crown 8vo. 5s. net.

ELEMENTS OF METAPHYSICS. Being a Guide for Lectures and Private Use. By Dr. PAUL DEUSSEN. Third Edition. Crown 8vo. 6s.

DICTIONARY OF PHILOSOPHY AND PSYCHOLOGY. Edited by Dr. JAMES MARK BALDWIN. With Illustrations and Extensive Bibliographies. In 3 vols. Large 8vo. Vol. I. A to Law. 21s. net.

OUTLINES OF COSMIC PHILOSOPHY, BASED ON THE DOCTRINE OF EVOLUTION. By JOHN FISKE. 2 vols. 8vo. 25s.

THE IDEA OF GOD AS AFFECTED BY MODERN KNOW-LEDGE. By JOHN FISKE. Globe 8vo. 3s. 6d.

PROGRESSIVE MORALITY : An Essay in Ethics. By THOMAS FOWLER, D.D., LL.D., F.S.A. Second Edition. Crown 8vo. 3s. net.

GENETIC PHILOSOPHY. By President DAVID J. HILL. Crown 8vo. 7s. net.

A HISTORY OF MODERN PHILOSOPHY : A Sketch of the History of Philosophy from the Close of the Renaissance to our own Day. By Dr. HARALD HÖFFDING. Translated from the German by B. E. MEYER. 2 vols. 8vo. 15s. net each.

THE LIMITS OF EVOLUTION, and other Essays illustrating the Metaphysical Theory of Personal Idealism. By Prof. G. H. HOWISON. Crown 8vo. 7s. 6d. net.

PRACTICAL IDEALISM. By W. DE WITT HYDE, President of Bowdoin College. Crown 8vo. 5s. net.

KANT'S CRITICAL PHILOSOPHY FOR ENGLISH READERS. By J. P. MAHAFFY, D.D., and J. H. BERNARD, B.D. 2 vols. Crown 8vo.—Vol. I. The Kritik of Pure Reason Explained and Defended. 7s. 6d.—Vol. II. Prolegomena. Translated, with Notes and Appendices. 6s.

KANT'S KRITIK OF JUDGMENT. Translated by J. H. BERNARD, D.D. 8vo. 10s. net.

THE CRITIQUE OF PURE REASON. By IMMANUEL KANT. Translated by F. MAX MÜLLER. With Introduction by LUDWIG NOIRÉ. 2 vols. 8vo. Vol. I. Historical Introduction, by LUDWIG NOIRÉ, etc. 16s. Vol. II. Critique of Pure Reason. 15s. net.

MACMILLAN AND CO., LTD., LONDON.

WORKS ON ETHICS AND METAPHYSICS.

ASPECTS OF THEISM. By WILLIAM A. KNIGHT, LL.D. 8vo. 8s. 6d.

NEW ESSAYS CONCERNING HUMAN UNDERSTANDING. By GOTTFRIED WILHELM LEIBNITZ. Translated by G. A. LANGLEY. Extra Crown 8vo. 14s. net.

FROM COMTE TO BENJAMIN KIDD. The Appeal to Biology or Evolution for Human Guidance. By the Rev. ROBERT MACKINTOSH, B.D., M.A. 8vo. 8s. 6d. net.

PAIN, PLEASURE, AND ÆSTHETICS. An Essay concerning the Psychology of Pain and Pleasure, with special reference to Æsthetics. By HENRY RUTGERS MARSHALL, M.A. 8vo. 8s. 6d. net.

ÆSTHETIC PRINCIPLES. By the same Author. Crown 8vo. 5s. net.

INSTINCT AND REASON. An Essay concerning the Relation of Instinct to Reason, with some special study of the Nature of Religion. By the same Author. 8vo. 12s. 6d. net.

RECENT BRITISH PHILOSOPHY. A Review, with Criticisms, including some Comments on Mr. Mill's Answer to Sir William Hamilton. By DAVID MASSON, M.A., LL.D. Third Edition. Crown 8vo. 6s.

PHILOSOPHICAL REMAINS OF R. L. NETTLESHIP. Edited, with Biographical Sketch, by Prof. A. C. BRADLEY. Second Edition. 8vo. 8s. 6d. net.

LECTURES ON THE REPUBLIC OF PLATO. By R. L. NETTLESHIP. Edited by G. R. BENSON. 8vo. 8s. 6d. net.

A SKETCH OF THE DEVELOPMENT OF PHILOSOPHIC THOUGHT FROM THALES TO KANT. By LUDWIG NOIRÉ. 8vo. 7s. 6d. net.

A BRIEF INTRODUCTION TO MODERN PHILOSOPHY. By ARTHUR KENYON ROGERS, Ph.D. Fcap. 8vo. 5s. net.

STUDENTS' HISTORY OF PHILOSOPHY. By Dr. A. K. ROGERS. Extra Crown 8vo. 8s. 6d. net.

THE WORLD AND THE INDIVIDUAL. *Gifford Lectures.* By JOSIAH ROYCE, Ph.D. Extra Crown 8vo. First Series. 12s. 6d. net. Second Series. 12s. 6d. net.

THE PROBLEM OF CONDUCT. A Study in the Phenomenology of Ethics. By A. E. TAYLOR. 8vo. 10s. net.

ANCIENT IDEALS. A Study of Intellectual and Spiritual Growth from Early Times to the Establishment of Christianity. By HENRY OSBORN TAYLOR. 2 vols. 8vo. 21s. net.

A REVIEW OF THE SYSTEMS OF ETHICS FOUNDED ON THE THEORY OF EVOLUTION. By C. M. WILLIAMS. Crown 8vo. 12s. net.

HISTORY OF PHILOSOPHY. With especial reference to the Formation and Development of its Problems and Conceptions. By Dr. W. WINDELBAND. Translated by J. H. TUFTS. 8vo. 21s. net.

MACMILLAN AND CO., LTD., LONDON.